The DU PONT DYNASTY

by

JOHN K. WINKLER

REYNAL & HITCHCOCK: NEW YORK

PRINTED IN THE UNITED STATES OF AMERICA
BY WAVERLY PRESS, INC.
BALTIMORE, MD.

E I du Pont de Nemours discussing the location of the first du Pont powder mill with Thomas Jefferson, President of the United States, his friend and customer   *From a painting by S M Arthurs*

TO

THEODORE SANDERS

C. CHARLES BURLINGAME

*Two Gentlemen of Science
and Understanding*

Acknowledgment

TO

ADELE BAKER NORTON

for her research and hearty cooperation
in the preparation of this biography

AUTHOR

Contents

CONTENTS

WHO ARE THE DU PONTS?

HIDDEN in one of the smallest states of the Union, living in feudal splendor, is a singular family—proud, aloof, prolific—, which today controls a greater slice of American wealth than has ever before fallen into private hands.

They are the Du Ponts of Delaware.

Unlike the Morgans, the Mellons, the Rockefellers and other financial giants of yesterday, now visibly contracting and retrenching, these Du Ponts are not only the outstanding Money Kings of the day, but still in ascendancy. Nor is their supremacy threatened by any rival.

In 1800, following the French Revolution, a turbulent old Huguenot, who had been a noble, and his two sons came to America to retrieve their fortune. One son did, by establishing himself modestly near Wilmington, Delaware, as a maker of gunpowder. Successive wars and successive generations added to the family coffer, until today the fifth generation controls vast industries valued at approximately five billions of dollars.

Following the World War, in which their profits were fantastic, the Du Ponts plunged boldly into new fields. Some of the war gains went into the gigantic General

Motors Corporation, over which they now hold absolute sway. They also became pioneers of the Synthetic. Rayon, cellophane, fabrikoid, pyralin, shatterproof glass, paints, dyes, photographic film, artificial rubber, camphor and ammonia, and even pharmaceuticals and cutlery are some of their numerous ventures; not to mention large investments in U. S. Rubber and other lucrative enterprises.

The family, which now numbers several hundred members, has always been ruled by one overlord—the clan chieftain. Seldom has his authority been challenged, but when it is the Du Ponts can wage as royal a battle among themselves as any nation that purchases their powder. Intermarriages became so prevalent during one period that successive clan chieftains were forced to forbid them—though, paradoxically, one of these chieftains was himself wed to his mother's niece.

Chemists, engineers, inventors, plodders, traders, aviators, bankers, politicians, with now and then an artist, poet or knife thrower, are some of the numerous progeny this family has produced and is still producing. Each new generation outnumbers the last, and is carefully culled for promising talent.

The Du Ponts, who have long dominated Delaware, have only recently emerged into the larger arena of national affairs. In 1932, several prominent members of the clan, ardent wets, supported Franklin D. Roosevelt. This they consider their biggest blunder and are now vigorously fighting the New Deal through the American Liberty League.

The present volume is the first full length portrait of this extraordinary family.

Part One

SOURCE

The early chapters of this book, dealing with family history, are largely based upon the extensive writings of Mrs. B. G. du Pont.

Chapter One

ANNE DE MONTCHANIN SAYS NO

IN THE boudoir of her Paris mansion, warm and soft with rich furnishings of damask, silk and velvet, Madame le Marquise de Jaucourt-Epenilles pulled a cord and summoned her fifteen-year-old ward, Anne de Montchanin.

The year was 1735, well along in the reign of that accomplished petticoat pursuer, Louis XV.

Anne Alexandrine de Montchanin herself was the daughter of an ancient and noble French house, now desperately impoverished because of long and stubborn adherence to the Huguenot faith. Her father, a widower with six children, was custodian of the Jaucourt-Epenilles estates in Burgundy. It was there, twelve years earlier, that Madame d'Epenilles, attracted by the beauty and bearing of the child, had carried her off to Paris as a playmate for her own little girl.

Anne entered the boudoir on this particular morning with a light and happy step. She was straight and slim and glowing with the first hints of young womanhood. She curtsied and stood with perfect composure before Madame d'Epenilles, whose manner seemed strained.

"Anne," began the Marquise, "many years have

passed since Monsieur d'Epenilles and I took you into
our home. You have always been as one of the family.
We have grown to love you and it has been a pleasure to
give you the same advantages as we have our own
daughter. There has, as you know, been no distinction."

"Oh, Madame, do not think that I am not grateful!"
interrupted the girl. "You have indeed been my only
mother!"

"And you have been a true daughter to me," added
the Marquise quickly, patting the child with a cool,
tapering hand. "But the time has come, my dear, to cast
your future. You are now becoming a young lady. My
husband and I have talked it over and we have decided
that it is impractical for you as well as for ourselves to
maintain you longer as a member of the family."

Slowly the roses drained from Anne de Montchanin's
cheeks.

"Does that mean," she faltered, "that I must leave?"

"No, no, my dear," the Marquise reassured hurriedly,
"not if you agree to a plan we have made for you. As a
young lady you must have a dot. That is most essential,
my dear. M. d'Epenilles is not rich. We are not in a position to do for you in this respect as we shall for our own
daughter. But we thought if you would care to under-
take certain duties here in the household we could manage to pay you a small salary which you could save
toward your dot. Now these duties—"

The girl stood as though stunned. The Marquise's
assurances made no sense to her save that her words, one
by one, were cataclysmically destroying a world. Each
"duty," like some huge diminishing lens, took this
woman, whom but a moment before she had called

her only mother, further and further away. Slowly, it seemed, though in reality but a moment, it crashed upon her that she was being offered, here in the only home she had ever known, a position as a domestic!

Then the color flowed back into her face. She thrust out a firm little chin, so determinedly that the deep dimple embedded in its center sunk even deeper. She spoke, a daughter of the fine old house of de Montchanin.

"Madame," she said proudly, "it is quite out of the question for me to remain under such circumstances. I shall leave at once. You have been kindness itself. I shall always remember that. But it is impossible for me to become a servant."

Though the parting was managed without bitterness, Anne de Montchanin and Madame d'Epenilles never saw each other again.

That decision of a fifteen-year-old girl was to have far-reaching results.

It not only dropped her from an environment to which she was accustomed and where no doubt she would have eventually mated with one of her own breeding, but brought about instead a fusion of blood that for seven generations has been stamped with her characteristics, even to that defiant dimple in her chin. Anne de Montchanin's descendants, in their turn, were to leave their home land and to seek, too, to make their way in a new world, where they have become mighty.

They are the Du Ponts of Delaware.

Anne de Montchanin took refuge with her brothers in the rue de Harlay. In 1735 the rue de Harlay was a nar-

row little street in Paris housing a group of clever crafts-
men engaged in the fashionable art of watchmaking.
These men considered themselves the aristocrats of labor, called themselves artists, as indeed some of them
were, and looked with scorn upon the grosser trades.

The Montchanin brothers, Pierre and Alexandre, had
joined this skilled brotherhood. They taught their sister
to fashion and gild hands for watches and soon she became expert at the work. Nevertheless, she was far from
happy. Though she would not admit it, she missed the
Epenilles atmosphere, terribly.

One afternoon, as she sat in her small room, applying
just so much paint to the minutest of minute hands, she
gazed out of the window to behold an apparition.

The window across the street, facing her own, revealed a young man some six feet in height, brown-
haired, scantily clad, plunging this way and that, foil
in hand. He was fencing. Anne forgot her minute hands
and time itself as she stared transfixed at this athletic
figure in action. The gyrations continued for some time
until finally the fencer, with something of a flourish,
threw himself into a chair. Then, to Mlle. de Montchanin's amazement, he picked up a flute and began
tooting, execrably it must be confessed.

The girl laughed until the tears ran down her cheeks.
It was the first time she had laughed in months.

Before long the master of the flute and foil, in turn,
spied Mademoiselle from his window. He, too, was a
watchmaker. Introductions were arranged and a court-
ship began. His name was Samuel Dupont.

Dupont was a name common in various regions of
France. It originally designated one living near or "of
the bridge." Samuel Dupont's ancestors, from the earli-

[6]

est record, about 1500, lived in Rouen. Whatever bridges may have been back of them, these Rouen Duponts certainly crossed another during the Reformation of 1555–1560 when they abandoned Catholicism to follow the bold and dangerous Protestant trail blazed by John Calvin. With other Calvinists, these religious dissenters gradually became known in France as Huguenots. The origin of the term is still an historical mystery.

As Huguenots the Duponts were drawn into the vortex of the persecutions that followed their faith. They survived the general massacre which began in Paris on St. Bartholomew's Day, 1572, and quickly spread to Rouen and other parts of France. Their tidy properties were confiscated in 1591 and they were expelled from Rouen. Seven years later, after the Edict of Nantes, they returned and one stands out as a successful dealer in brass and copper. With bulldog tenacity they clung to their faith, meeting in guarded and out of the way places, baptizing their numerous children secretly, burying their dead, graves unmarked, in fields, gardens, even cellars and courtyards.

Under Louis XIV, the persecution reached the zenith of malignity. The Edict of 1656 barred all Protestants from public office, the practices of law, medicine, surgery and even midwifery. Nor could they employ a Catholic servant. The Grand Monarque's most effective weapon, however, was the so-called "*dragonnade.*" Soldiers, rude, bearded louts most of them, were quartered in the homes of the Huguenots, invading at whim wine cellars and bedrooms. More than one Dupont joined the jostling thousands of Huguenots who fled to England, Holland and elsewhere.

Most of the clan, however, remained in Rouen, ac-

[7]

quiring property little by little and avoiding what pitfalls they could. The struggle seems to have weakened a
bit at the beginning of the eighteenth century, for
Samuel Dupont, born April 19, 1708, was christened a
Catholic. This, however, was probably a concession to
the latest subversive royal decree. Samuel, one may be
sure, privately went through his "real" Huguenot
baptism.

Except for the fortitude of their religious convictions,
there is nothing outstanding about the Rouen Duponts.
They were for the most part merchants, small traders,
burghers. They were thrifty, long-lived and prolific.
Samuel Dupont was one of eleven children and his
mother was to die at the age of eighty-five of a fall while
riding horseback. Samuel, however, was the first Dupont
to tempt his fortune in Paris.

He was a good craftsman, thorough and tenacious in
getting what he wanted. And, from the moment he met
her, he most assuredly wanted Anne de Montchanin,
even though she could bring him no dot. His kinsmen in
Rouen were rather noted for picking wives with fat dots.

Under other circumstances, it is doubtful if this son
of the bourgeois could have won Anne de Montchanin.
But he *was* handsome. She accepted him.

In 1737, Anne de Montchanin and Samuel Dupont
were married by civil ceremony in Paris. She was seventeen, he twenty-nine. They went at once to Tournay for
a second ceremony in the rites of the Huguenot faith.
Upon their return they took rooms in Paris. Here their
first child, a boy, died in infancy.

On December 14th, 1739, a few weeks before her twentieth birthday, Anne Dupont gave birth to a second son.
He was named Pierre Samuel. This child had the blue

eyes of his father, the deep dimple in the chin of his mother.

From the very beginning Pierre Samuel's life was turbulent.

As was the custom with city babies, he was "boarded out" with peasant farmers. His first foster mother starved him. He was quickly changed to another, but this one had a bibulous husband who "aired" the baby in the village tavern and kept him quiet with sips of brandy. When Madame Dupont rescued her son at the age of three, he was pale, anemic and walked with a limp. The lameness gradually disappeared but the joints of his 'arms and legs remained swollen and he never attained his natural growth.

At five he fell and broke his nose, an injury that marred his appearance thereafter.

Samuel Dupont had meanwhile established himself in a business of his own, taken on weight and was thoroughly satisfied with his progress. Anne Dupont was not. Gradually she realized she could never make the gentleman she wanted out of her bourgeois husband. She found him obstinate and opinionated. She loved to read, while he detested books. They found less and less in common. Even his spelling was atrocious. So the young wife turned her attention toward her child. She taught him to read and write and to spell and little Pierre Samuel's imagination became filled with great heroes who rose from humble beginnings like his own.

Concerning Pierre's education, the parents clashed from the outset. The mother insisted the child's natural talents should have an opportunity to determine and develop themselves. Samuel, who was suspicious that his wife's ideas were "fancy," contended a successful

watchmaker's son could do no better than to learn
watchmaking.

Anne prevailed. "But remember," Samuel Dupont
sternly warned M. Viard, the boy's first schoolmaster,
"my son is not to write verses. I won't have a poet in
the family."

Though the father did not know it, he not only had a
young poet on his hands but he nearly had a seer.

About this time Anne Dupont had become friendly
with the Marquise d'Urfé, whose fad was spiritualism.
Madame d'Urfé thought the sensitive, pale little Pierre
would make a splendid medium. In a darkened room she
placed a cross under a glass of water, mumbled magic
incantations and assured him that if he looked into the
glass with faith in his heart, he would see and hear the
archangel Uriel, who would tell him great truths. At
several séances, attended by a fashionable coterie, Pierre
went into a trance and repeated, as from the archangel,
advice to his awed audience on politics, business affairs
and personal problems. He was a great success—until his
conscience began to twinge. Then he broke down and
confessed he hadn't really seen or heard Uriel at all.
Appreciative neither of the boy's imagination nor newly
awakened honesty, Madame d'Urfé became thoroughly
indignant and banished Pierre and his mother from her
drawing room.

M. Viard, the schoolmaster, was more understanding,
however, of the boy's talents. It did not take him long
to realize that he had corralled a very unusual pupil. Not
only did Pierre read everything he could lay his hands
on, but he remembered with an amazing accuracy what
he read.

Finally, when the lad was twelve, the schoolmaster

could no longer restrain himself from displaying his prodigy. The honor and glory of the school demanded a public exhibition, no less. Forthwith came an announcement: "Pierre Samuel Dupont, aged twelve, will translate at sight passages from the best Latin authors, answer questions on French and Latin grammar, on logic, rhetoric, fables, poetry, literary style and civil law." On the designated night several hundred spectators gathered. Young Dupont came through with flying colors. M. Viard strutted about like a peacock. Madame Dupont was in a transport of delight. Even Samuel Dupont was impressed. But he still insisted the sooner the boy became a watchmaker the better.

Anne Dupont now had to fight desperately to keep this versatile fledgling of hers out of the workroom. Playing upon her husband's piety she announced one evening, having failed on other tacks, that Pierre wanted to become a Huguenot minister. She won another round. So the boy was tutored in "religious knowledge" which included great draughts of Tacitus, Horace, Cicero, as well as some physics and metaphysics.

Pierre, though, soon decided that he preferred philosophy. "An intelligent man," concluded this precocious youth, son of generations of fighting Huguenots, "can be neither a Protestant nor a Catholic. He should respect the morality of every form of religion and worship according to the laws of his country." The decision was indicative both of his independence and moderate trend of mind.

Reluctantly, Samuel Dupont next agreed that a knowledge of mathematics might be useful to a future watchmaker. So a year's study of geometry, algebra, conic sections and some more physics was slipped in.

These excursions were terminated abruptly by a severe attack of smallpox. One night the attending physician, detecting no beat of heart or pulse, pronounced the patient dead. Dazed with grief, Anne Dupont prepared her son's body for burial. A woman, as was usual, sat beside the body to keep "watch" and the family retired. A few hours later came crashing sounds. To the horror of the attendant, who knocked over a chair and a table in her fright, the corpse not only moved but spoke. Pierre recovered.

This sickness left a peculiar effect upon his vision. Though the left eye remained normal, the right eye became very nearsighted with an acute vision for almost microscopic detail. He wrote of this condition forty years later as proving "extremely useful."

As he grew stronger, his father saw his opportunity at last to make of him the man he wanted. He got out his foils and taught his son to fence. No sooner did the boy look at the foils than he began reading everything he could find on military tactics and engineering. He dreamed of joining the army and winning a marshal's baton. But Samuel Dupont had had enough nonsense. He ordered Pierre to report at once to the Dupont workroom and don the apron of an apprentice watchmaker.

This time Anne Dupont realized the battle was lost. She could fight no longer. Her vitality and health had been sapped by the birth in quick succession, and almost immediate death, of two little girls. At thirty-six she gave up the struggle.

On her death bed she joined the hands of father and son and begged them to love and try to understand each other.

Chapter Two

THE RISE OF PIERRE SAMUEL

WHEN his mother died Pierre Samuel Dupont was sixteen, an engaging youth of quick intelligence, warm manner and unusual facility of expression. When his eyes lighted with the glow of an idea, words came in a veritable cascade and one forgot his undersized frame and flattened nose. He made friends easily, and held them.

Though he progressed as a watchmaker, he made no headway with his father. The latter was a stern taskmaster, determined to fit the boy into the only pattern he knew. He flogged Pierre unmercifully for a mild flirtation and the lad left home. He was never to return.

After he had starved for some months in an attic room, a partial reconciliation was arranged by his mother's brother, Pierre de Montchanin, but the boy went to work for another watchmaker. Here he shared quarters with a youth who died after a lingering illness. Pierre and the attending physician, Dr. du Bourg, became friendly. Wholeheartedly, as was his habit, he plunged into medicine. Du Bourg answered showers of questions and gained admission for him into lectures and clinics. He crowded every spare minute with medical books and watched operations.

Within a few months young Dupont knew as much about medicine as the average practitioner. An article by him was published in a medical journal. Though a degree was never obtained, he always spoke proudly of himself, thereafter, as a physician.

Nor were lighter pursuits neglected. Pierre joined a group of amateur players and wrote two tragedies, in which were provided fat and heroic parts for himself. He attended artists' balls, often dancing with a merry young model, Mademoiselle Rançon, *la petite* Rançon, they called her. Neither then dreamed they would meet again some day when she would dominate the prodigal pleasures of Louis XV as Madame du Barry.

For five years or more young Dupont toiled at the trade he detested. By night he read and studied and played. He passed his precious furloughs in the picturesque little Seine-et-Marne town of Nemours. Here he visited M. Doré and his wife, friends who had formerly lived in Paris. Madame Doré was a sentimental soul who insisted upon Pierre calling her "*Maman*." She loved to listen to his talk and especially his verse. She herself often relieved the tedium of country life by composing sonnets.

Pierre usually trudged the fifty miles to Nemours and the walk was far from wearisome, in fact an adventure, enlivened as it was by meetings with other wayfarers and chats with farmers, innkeepers, merchants, and village characters. He always arrived with a welcome fresh budget of gossip and anecdotes. The Doré household included a vivacious young person with laughing eyes and a funny little retroussé nose. This was Madame Doré's cousin, Marie Le Dée, daughter of a minor government official. She was three years younger than Pierre and he accordingly treated her as a little sister.

However chance, perhaps fate, altered the relationship. On one of his visits, the young man from Paris discovered Marie in tears. She confided that Madame Doré was arranging to marry her to an "old ogre" of a widower. "He is fifty-five," she sighed, "and looks even older."

Much perturbed, Pierre marched into the garden, where he found Madame Doré, and asked her what in thunderation she meant by trying to ruin her cousin's pure young life. "Ah, my friend," replied Madame Doré, "it is time Marie became affianced. She is nineteen. M. des Naudières is a good catch. He may be grouchy and he may be fifty-five but, after all, he has property."

Then, and no one was more surprised than Pierre himself, he blurted out: "But I, too, will have property! I shall earn a fortune with my pen. Give me two years to prove it and I will marry Marie!"

Madame Doré looked at him agape and then, also much to his astonishment, accepted his proposal. Mademoiselle Le Dée was summoned. Gratefully, she threw herself into Pierre's arms. The youth felt himself a hero. His chest expanded as he dried his fiancée's tears of relief and joy. That night wine flowed as never before in the *maison* Doré.

It was a sober young man who returned to Paris. Pierre concentrated now in deadly earnest upon a career. The new responsibility gave him courage. Straight off he set about fashioning the finest watch he could conceive. It was of gold and of rare and delicate design. When completed, this beautiful piece of workmanship demonstrated conclusively his mastery over the art he hated.

On New Year's Day, 1763, he presented this master-
piece to his father and announced that he was forever
finished with watchmaking. Samuel Dupont held the
exquisite timepiece in his hand and thoughtfully regarded the engraving—*Dupont filius composit, fecit, dedi-
cavit Patri Suo.* He had both won and lost. He shook
hands with his son and bade him Godspeed.

Pierre wondered, as he walked back to his room, what
the future held for a scholar whose savings amounted to
a meager six hundred francs.

At that time new currents were stirring in France.

The Seven Years' War was drawing to a close. This
conflict, as well as the limitless extravagances of Louis
XIV and Louis XV, had strained the public treasury
beyond endurance. The King's ministers grew gray
seeking to effect economies and devise new methods of
taxation, the burdens of which fell upon the common
people; the nobles and the clergy being, for the most
part, exempt. There came forward in this crisis young
and intelligent men to deal with the problem and social
conditions generally. They were the brain-trusters of
their day. One, Denis Diderot, whose father, a cutter,
had sacrificed to give him a classical education, headed
a group of rebel writers who had broken away from the
school of the Jesuits and called themselves *Encyclopaed-
ists.* They denounced the slave trade, unfair taxation,
the corruption of justice, the wastefulness of wars and
were in sympathy "with the rising empire of industry
which was beginning to transform the world."

Young Dupont met and talked with Diderot and his
head buzzed with these new ideas. He resorted to his
pen, hoping to win a government post.

Each week the Duc de Choiseul, the King's minister of finance, held a public audience at Versailles. Dupont drew up a paper on free trade, the abolition of subsidies, the possibility of employing soldiers to build roads in times of peace and other matters, and tramped out to Versailles where he boldly presented the memorandum to de Choiseul. It was Dupont's first intimate view of the great seat of Bourbon monarchy.

With its parks and gorgeous gardens, terraces and twinkling fountains, Versailles was a veritable symbol of royal splendor. Here moved, like people out of a picture book, a race of gentlemen in powdered wigs, ruffled coats and high red heels; and ladies, under tiers of powdered hair, wafted about in voluminous skirts of silk and satin. Dupont was impressed. Surely, he thought, it should be possible for a young man to find a patron among this brilliant throng. He succeeded but by a circuitous route. And the manner of it illustrates the part chance plays in the affairs of men.

On one of his hikes to see Marie Le Dée, he fell in with one Bosquillon, who related a long tale of abuse by a government official in a matter of compulsory labor. Dupont listened patiently and, returning to Paris, managed to meet M. Méliand, administrator for the province of Brie, through which Dupont had passed. M. Méliand was interested in the story, even more so in his young visitor's apparent grasp of conditions in the province, and asked for a written report.

Dupont rushed to his room, concentrated for a while, as was his custom, with his hands over his eyes and his elbows on the table, then began to write. He wrote of the simple things he had learned along the roadside: the cost of raising farm products, the difficulties of marketing, the condition of the highways, the various taxes and what the people thought of them. He peppered the report with philosophy and bits of description.

A few days later, M. Méliand looked up from the manuscript and exclaimed: "Splendid! You are a worthy pupil of Mirabeau." The name of the noted political economist was new to Dupont. Méliand slipped into the young man's hand two of Mirabeau's treatises, *L'ami des hommes* and the *Theorie de l'impot*.

Dupont read them avidly. He learned for the first time that the measure of population is largely determined by the food supply. Quivering with enthusiasm, he wrote to Mirabeau at the latter's estate, Bignon, near Nemours. It was the beginning of a life-long association.

A power at court was Francois Quesnay, physician to the King and adviser to Madame de Pompadour who, although no longer the King's mistress, retained much influence. Quesnay was a brilliant economist as well as an eminent physician. He was particularly interested in measures for the relief of agriculture.

Quesnay and his friend Mirabeau were leaders of a group, *les économistes*, who later were known as Physiocrats—from the Greek "let nature rule." The Physiocrats extolled nature as the sole source of wealth: real wealth consists only of land and unmanufactured products. Government must not interfere with natural laws. The school stood also for a broad social program, including freedom of person, trade, speech and opinions.

There came to Quesnay's desk now, at frequent intervals, pamphlets signed "D. P." They were so thoughtful and so well phrased that Quesnay asked Mirabeau if he knew the author, remarking: "Either you or I must have taught him." "No," replied Mirabeau, "nature

[18]

and intelligence teach as well as we. Here is your correspondent's address."

Then came the turning point in young Dupont's career.

"Quesnay invited me to go to him at Versailles," Dupont wrote later. "He became my master, my teacher, my father. He accepted me, treated me for eleven years as the son, the disciple whom he loved. His great soul and his profound genius did not often show tender feeling, but it has been my good fortune to know that he had much for me. I was only a child when he held out his arms to me; it is he who made me a man."

Quesnay made Dupont his secretary, procuring a study for him in the palace. The young man's first task was an inquiry into the importation and exportation of grain. Quesnay suggested dedicating the treatise to Madame de Pompadour, who received Dupont in her apartment and completely charmed him.

He went to the country to complete the manuscript and, before his return, visited the Marquis de Mirabeau at Bignon. Here he met the extraordinary son of the household, the young Comte Gabriel Honoré Riquetti de Mirabeau. Although not yet sixteen, this impulsive, willful youngster was already launched in the unbridled dissipation that was to kill him at forty-two, when he might have averted the Reign of Terror and saved the head of Louis XVI.

Dupont's ambitious essay on grains was ready for the press in April, 1764. Then Madame de Pompadour died. However, the brochure sold well and attracted a new patron who was to have an even greater influence upon Dupont's life than Quesnay.

This was the young Baron de L'Aulne, Anne Robert

Jacques Turgot, the ablest financier in France, who rushed to congratulate the young author upon his work. The two became inseparable. For three years Turgot had been administrator for the province of Limoges. A dozen years Dupont's senior, he had studied theology and law before entering the service of the government.

The next year was a busy one for Dupont. Although not regularly employed he made several surveys for the government, wrote pamphlets, continued to meet men of influence and gained entrée to noted salons. About this time he began a correspondence with Voltaire. His fiancée, Marie Le Dée, spurred him on, though Papa Le Dée was not so encouraging. He considered Dupont an insubstantial gadabout, a Protestant to boot, and forbade his daughter to see the young man. Dupont formally denied that he was a Protestant and pledged in writing that Marie could rear any issue of their union as Catholics if she wished. Still Papa Le Dée was stony.

In the summer of 1765, the government established the *Journal de l'agriculture, du commerce et des finances* and Dupont was made editor. Now, at last, he enjoyed a regular salary. He and Marie resumed the bombardment of Papa Le Dée, who finally melted. On January 28, 1766, the young journalist took to wife "Demoiselle Nicole Charlotte Marie Louise Le Dée" in the Church of St. Sulpice, Paris. The bridegroom definitely broke the long Huguenot tradition of his family.

In the fall of that year Dupont lost his editorship when he rebelled against a government order to censure the Parlement of Brittany in a controversy over an unpopular tax measure. However, he was promptly employed by another branch of the government to assemble statistics for the provinces of Limoges and Soissons. The fees enabled the Duponts to take comfortable rooms, with garden attached, in the rue et Faubourg St. Jacques.

Here, October 1, 1767, was born their first child. They christened him Victor Marie.

Dupont had contributed often to a review called the *Ephémérides du Citoyen*, edited by the Abbé Nicolas Baudeau. In the spring of 1768 the Abbé was offered a position in Poland and turned over the paper to Dupont who, with his usual optimism, saw a fortune in the offing. He pitched in and wrote with vast enthusiasm, advocating freedom of the press and religious conscience, abolition of slavery in the French colonies, wider educational opportunities, land taxes, etc.

Widening fame and personal prestige emboldened him and soon he was entangled with the censors. Then he ran into financial difficulties, was plagued by the gout and, to cap his troubles, baby Victor came down with smallpox. Madame Dupont had hardly nursed the child back to health when a second son, Paul Francois, was born. This baby lived only a few days.

Though the *Ephémérides* continued to lose money, Dupont wrote Turgot the following year that another child was expected and asked his patron to act as Godfather. "Yes, certainly, my dear Dupont," responded Turgot. "I accept the gift you offer me. If it is a boy will you not call him Eleuthère Irénée, in honor of liberty and peace? If a girl the names Eleuthérie and Irène would be equally as good."

The newcomer, a boy, arrived June 24, 1771. He was named Eleuthère Irénée.

Dupont did not mourn when the government sup-

pressed the *Ephémérides* in November, 1772. For a while
he eked out a living supplying monthly letters—fore-
runners of the present market and economic forecasts—
to Gustavus III of Sweden, the Margrave of Baden and
other rulers. He visited the Margrave in Carlsruhe and
was given the title of Aulic Councillor.

When he returned to Paris, Abbé Baudeau, back from
Poland, greeted him with an offer that seemed at once
to solve all his problems. The elective King of Poland,
Stanislas Poniatowski, and his brother-in-law, Prince
Czartoriski, wanted a French scholar to supervise the
education of little Prince Adam Czartoriski, aged four,
and to act as secretary of the Council of Public Education. The tutor would have a suite in the palace, carriages, liberal salary and living allowances and, at the
end of ten years, a bonus of 100,000 francs. Best of all,
one-third of the bonus would be paid in advance.

Dupont snapped up the offer. The cash advance would
gratify a growing desire to own land. A land deed was
proof of citizenship and carried the right to unrestricted
suffrage and other privileges. The Duponts combed the
country about their beloved Nemours and came upon a
small estate near the village of Chevannes, upon which
they promptly made a first payment of 33,000 francs and
named it Bois-des-Fossés. Then the family started for
Warsaw, traveling in carriages over rutty roads.

The Duponts were scarcely settled in the Polish palace
when word came from Paris that Louis XVI, who had
succeeded to the throne upon the death of his grandfather the preceding May, had appointed Turgot Minister of Finance. Turgot wanted Dupont to serve as Inspector General of Commerce and the King, exercising

[22]

his royal prerogative, ordered the latter's immediate return. Prince Czartoriski was reimbursed. Dupont, assured that he could hold on to his land, once more piled his family into carriages and made posthaste for Paris. Early in January, 1775, he was again at Versailles, an important cog in the new ministry.

The atmosphere in the palace was not markedly different from the intrigue-drenched days of Louis XV. The new ruler was a mentally sluggish though well-meaning individual, proud of his marksmanship and his ingenuity as an amateur locksmith. He bored his giddy and extravagant wife, Marie Antoinette, sister of the Emperor of Austria. Although not yet nineteen, Marie Antoinette had been married for three years. Her features were somewhat heavy but she was sufficiently comely to assume the rôle of a romantic, haughty Queen. Her diversions were gambling, collecting jewels, flirting.

All might have been well if she had halted at these comparatively harmless pursuits. But she loved to toy with affairs of state. Soon Turgot and his deputy, Dupont, found her petulantly thwarting all their efforts at real economy. Turgot abolished trade monopolies, prepared a budget, wiped out many court sinecures, even proposed a constitution for the Kingdom. The dose was a bitter one, too, for Maurepas, the King's chief minister. So a very ingenious plot was concocted. Letters purporting to pass between Turgot and a friend in Vienna, and containing uncomplimentary references to the King, were forged and placed before the King.

The plot succeeded. After twenty months in office, during which he had accomplished much, despite ill health, Turgot was dismissed. Dupont left with him.

[23]

He retired to the Bois-des-Fossés and for a time reveled in the freedom of country life. Although the estate was not owned outright, Madame Dupont had made it self-supporting. This intensely practical woman personally supervised the harvest and the vintage and sold hay and wine, eggs and produce, chickens and ducks.

Dupont resumed his correspondence with Gustavus III of Sweden, and other princes, and proudly wore the green ribbon of the Order of Vasa, a decoration conferred by Gustavus. He might be only a commoner in France but he was a Chevalier in Sweden. Occasionally he went to Paris for long talks with Turgot and a group of intellectuals who gathered in the library of a wealthy young cleric, the Abbé de Perigord, destined to become the famous Talleyrand. One of the group was Vergennes, Minister of Foreign Affairs.

The war in America was an exciting subject. This war was exhausting the exchequer, and Necker, the finance minister, reluctantly considered resurrecting some of Turgot's measures to find new revenue. With equal reluctance Necker accepted the suggestion of Vergennes that Dupont, Turgot's former right hand man, should be drafted for his old post of Inspector General of Commerce. Again Dupont went back to Versailles.

Moving through the artificial glitter of the court, with his long hair, plain raiment and pawky manners, was the American Ambassador, Benjamin Franklin. Dupont had known Franklin years before as colonial agent for Pennsylvania. Franklin wrote him as early as 1768 expressing sympathy with the broad social philosophy of the Physiocrats.

Turgot, Dupont and their associates eagerly aided Franklin's successful efforts to bring France into the Revolutionary War on the side of the Colonies, not because they loved America particularly but because they saw a chance to weaken England. Toward the close of the war, Dupont's letter-writing proclivities were found to be very useful to the French foreign office. He was able to sound out sentiment and peace possibilities through Franklin in America, James Hutton in England, and others. Dupont was entrusted with the preliminary negotiations with England upon which was founded the Peace Treaty of 1783, acknowledging the independence of the United States. The Treaty of Paris was signed September 3, 1783.

Three months later Dupont received his reward. The King raised him to the ranks of the nobility. Although no title or material benefit was attached, the award bestowed certain coveted privileges: he could bear crested arms, become a *seigneur* of a fief or estate and his sons could enter professions barred to the bourgeois.

Just twenty years had passed since the sanguine little watchmaker had trudged out to Versailles and presented his paper on taxation to the Duc de Choiseul.

Dupont promptly selected a coat of arms, showing a crest of ostrich plumes with a lion and eagle as supporters and the motto: *Rectitudine Sto* (Be Upright).

To obtain his *lettre de noblesse*, Dupont had to swear that he was a "Catholic apostolic and Roman." In reality he was of no formal religious persuasion, yet the fiction was necessary even in a time when those in high place professed belief in the church publicly and flouted it privately. However, Marie Le Dée Dupont and her sons were exceptions. They attended their parish church regularly.

In addition to handling every detail at the Bois-des-Fossés, Madame Dupont mothered the tutors whom her husband selected for the boys. She found time, also, to enjoy neighborhood activities—dinner parties, amateur theatricals, country fairs. In 1783 she was able to write an exultant little note to her husband: "We are out of debt, let it be for always!" That fall the family took an apartment in Paris and Marie Dupont splurged a bit, as became the wife of a nobleman. She bought frocks and furniture and drove about in her own carriage. It was her first, and last, fling of luxury.

The following summer she was back in the country, looking after the chickens and the ducks, the haying and the grapes. She entered each item in her neat little account books.

In late August, the weather turned blustery and she took to her bed with symptoms of typhoid fever. Her head ached and she was tired, she wrote her husband, but she would be all right "tomorrow." She grew weaker and died September 3, 1784, in her forty-second year.

Dupont and the boys were heartbroken. Irénée, the youngest, was thirteen. His nature was very much like his mother's, the same practicality and unemotional control. On the other hand, the traits of Victor, now a strapping youth of seventeen, more than six feet tall, were those of his father. He was volatile, visionary, easily roused to enthusiasm.

Three days after the funeral, Dupont invested Irénée

with his first sword in a ceremony at once dramatic and significant. The scene was planned and written by himself. Seated in a huge armchair, with the bust of his dead wife at his left, he had the boys, who stood before him, repeat pledges of honor and respect to France and to their parents. He struck Irénée on the left shoulder, saying: "The blow that I am giving you, my son, is to teach you that you must bear any blow when it is honorable and right to accept it."

Then he directed the boys to draw their swords, salute and embrace. "Promise each other," he said solemnly, "to be always firmly united, to comfort each other in every sorrow, to help each other in all efforts, to stand by each other in all difficulty and danger."

Each son in turn replied: "I promise it, my father; I promise it to you and to the memory and the portrait of my mother."

Whereupon Dupont delivered this invocation:

"I bless you, my children, may Heaven bless you! May your works and your children be blessed! May your families be perpetuated by wives who are good, reasonable, brave, economical, generous, simple and modest like the mother you have lost. May each generation of your descendants strive unceasingly to make the next generation better than his own. I shall try to do my best for you, oh my friends; try to do still better for your children."

With these words ringing in their ears, the motherless boys, now approaching manhood, returned to Paris with their father.

THE BROTHERS DUPONT

W HEN Pierre Samuel Dupont and his sons took up life together in Paris, they had no prevision of the impending revolution, which was to shape and change their destinies.

As well as crowded hours permitted, the father sought to mold and train the boys. His interests for years had centered in education and he outlined elaborate courses of study for them. However, neither Victor nor Irénée was particularly responsive. In fact books for the most part frankly bored them.

Victor was one of those pleasing barks that like to float lightly upon the surface of life. He was witty, gay, charming and a rover. The verb "work" he never learned to conjugate. Dupont tried him out as a junior secretary in his own Department of Commerce, with little or no success. So next he bundled him off on a long horseback tour of the provinces with instructions to send back commercial reports. The reports were excellent, when Victor found time to write any, and won from his exasperated sire reluctant admission that Victor could think—if and when he did any thinking. More often the brown-haired young giant described dances, fêtes, dinner parties.

Finally, in October, 1787, Dupont shipped Victor to

America as secretary without salary in the suite of the Comte de Moustier, first Minister of France to the United States. He carried letters of introduction from La Fayette and Jefferson to many prominent men: Generals Washington and Knox, Jay, Hamilton and Chancellor Livingston among others.

Jefferson was at that time Franklin's successor as American Minister to France. He and the elder Dupont had become friendly, a friendship that was to prove a valuable asset later. Jefferson's political philosophy coincided largely with that of the Physiocrats. Indeed some historians trace to Jefferson's extended stay in France his entire democratic creed, as well as that fondness for French wines and cookery which led Patrick Henry to accuse the Virginian of having "adjured his native victuals."

However that may be, Victor Dupont found the letters of introduction exceedingly useful. Soon all doors in New York were open to him and he was enjoying himself immensely.

His letters now were filled with contrasting scenes of early America. With the Comte de Moustier he sailed up the Hudson to Albany, and from there they made their way inland on horseback through a veritable wilderness to Lake Oneida to meet the Indians, known as the Five Nations, and arrange a treaty. However, only two of the nations, the Oneidas and the Onondagas, showed up and they promptly made merry on the white party's rum, tobacco and food, which was just as far as the treaty got.

Again, en route with de Moustier for a three-day visit to Mount Vernon, Victor stopped off in Philadelphia for a chat with his father's wise and kind old philosopher friend, Benjamin Franklin. At Mount Vernon he first met General Washington, whose dignity and naturalness impressed him. When next he saw Washington, in April, 1789, the master of Mount Vernon had become first president of the United States. New York was then the capital.

Soon after the inauguration Washington came to the French Minister's house for a tea party and Victor, in honor of the occasion, arranged a quadrille. Four French officers in white coats with red facings danced with four ladies in white with garlands of roses; and four American officers in blue with four ladies in blue and white. There were several figures in which all sixteen danced, as well as the quadrilles. The affair went off famously.

Irénée, on the other hand, was as serious as his brother Victor was jovial. Always aloof, few were able to penetrate his inner reaches. His studies held little interest for him unless they related to practical subjects, then he was tenacious. Dupont decided that this son's mind was scientific. Accordingly, when Irénée was sixteen, his father's friend, Antoine Laurent Lavoisier, made a place for the lad in his laboratory.

Lavoisier was the most eminent scientist of the day. His discovery of the principle of combustion had revolutionized chemical thought and research. For many years he had been director of the government powder mills. Pleased with Irénée's aptitude and industry, he soon took the boy with him to the arsenal at Essonne and taught him to make gunpowder. Irénée, who always had to work hard for what knowledge he gained, gradually mastered the complicated processes by which saltpeter, charcoal and sulphur were purified, pressed, polished and grained into black powder.

"Leave your boy with me and I will make him my successor," Lavoisier told Dupont senior. But that day never came in France.

The direst of events occurred—the court at Versailles ran out of spending money. Marie Antoinette could scarcely believe her ears when Calonne, Minister of Finance, and until that moment one of her favorites, confessed that the Grand Monarchy was bankrupt. His frankness was his downfall. The Archbishop of Sens, who was promptly put in Calonne's place, decided to raise funds by royal edict. Rioting began.

In October, 1788, Dupont wrote his son Victor in America of a sudden change in the temper of the people and their ominous defiance of the King's ministers:

Blackguards and brigands who gathered from everywhere within forty leagues set off fireworks on the Place Dauphine and broke the windows of those who did not illuminate or did not continue their illuminations until one o'clock in the morning, when their lamps had burned out and they could get no others. Then they hanged in effigy both the Archbishop and the Keeper of the Seals; then they stopped the passersby and demanded money to buy more fireworks; then they threw stones at the Guard; then they raised an uproar because the Guard defended themselves; then they broke down and burned three guard houses and drove out the sergeants and soldiers of the Guard who were there—in their shirts and without breeches.

For a few days this dangerous playfulness was checked by the French and Swiss troops. Then orders were issued that were so mild—so very mild that the mob and the scoundrels who were constantly joining it dared even to defy the Garde du Roi! to insult them; to fire gunpowder in their faces; to throw tiles at their heads; to attempt to burn houses in their presence. At last many men had to be killed to enforce peace; cruelty was the result of weakness. There is now no safety in Paris except that which is enforced by the courage, the coolness and the swords of the citizens. . . . . Altogether, for the last six months, we have had a helpless Government and no administration. 1 am writing you all this because my patriotism is so deeply hurt. However, we will have the States-General at the end of January and 1 will do all 1 can to be a member.

The States-General was a body made up of representatives of the nobles, clergy and the people, roughly comparable to the British Parliament. It had not met since 1614 and was therefore without any immediate tradition of procedure. The first meeting took place in Versailles on May 4th in the fateful year of 1789.

Irénée got a day off and watched the imposing parade. Each marcher carried a lighted taper. There were 285 nobles, 308 of the clergy and 621 deputies, among whom he spotted his father. Dupont, though of the *noblesse* for the past five years, had managed to have himself elected as a representative of the people in Nemours.

The three delegations convened separately. The deputies, who outnumbered the nobles and clergy, demanded a joint assembly. Weeks of wrangling ensued. Finally the deputies, the Third Estate they were called, declared that they alone represented the people, whereupon the King ordered the hall in which they were meeting closed. Undismayed and staunchly, they adjourned to a nearby tennis court and individually took oath not to separate until they had established a constitution in France. They formed themselves into the National Assembly.

Louis XVI sought to use force to break them up but the soldiers refused to act. Then, seemingly, the King gave in but in reality was playing for time. At Marie Antoinette's instigation, foreign regiments were brought up from the provinces. At once Paris and most of France revolted. Provisional governments were set up in the large cities. A new armed force, the National Guard, was established, with La Fayette as commander. Dupont and his son promptly enlisted. It swung into action too late to prevent rioting and pillaging of homes and shops in Paris.

On July 14th, the people of Paris stormed and destroyed the grim prison of the Bastille, murdered the garrison and released its seven prosaic prisoners. The insurrection spread to the provinces, where infuriated peasants burned many chateaus, destroyed title deeds and killed or forced into hiding their former masters.

A few breath-taking weeks marked the crumbling of the old and decayed aristocratic system. In this atmosphere of chaos and hysteria, the National Assembly took command. Amid the turmoil, Dupont was ubiquitous.

The National Assembly's attempt to build a new order faced enormous difficulties. Some headway, however, was made. In August a series of resolutions were passed, abolishing serfdom, tax exemptions and other privileges. Titles were abolished, too.

Although Dupont never had a title, he found it expedient about this time to enlarge his name. There were two other Duponts in the National Assembly, one from Lille, the other from Bigorre. To distinguish himself from them, our Dupont took to signing his name "Dupont de Nemours." Later he further embellished his cognomen by separating the two syllables, Du and Pont, but this flourish he saved for another country.

Meanwhile, food became scarce. Rumors of sumptuous banquets at court inflamed the hungry. Bread riots broke out in Paris. Finally, on October 5th, a huge and frenzied mob poured out from the city to Versailles. The National Guard, under La Fayette, reached the palace in the nick of time to prevent the royal family from being massacred. Louis XVI and Marie Antoinette were "escorted" to the Palace of the Tuileries in Paris, where they lived quietly and unmolested for two years and where they might have died had they not betrayed their people.

In a riding academy adjoining the garden of the Tuileries, the National Assembly resumed its hectic sessions. Dupont, who enjoyed speech-making, lost no opportunity now. Usually the galleries applauded him. On one occasion, however, the mob went for him. A detachment of the National Guard arrived just in time to prevent him from being ducked in the Seine. He had opposed, in his usual dramatic and eloquent fashion, the further issuance of *assignats* or paper money.

One June night, in 1791, the King and Queen, disguised, tried to escape France. They were discovered and returned to the Tuileries. Their attempt unleashed a fresh distrust of royalty and attracted new recruits to the Jacobin party. The Jacobins, most outspoken of extremists, formerly had been considered too radical in their zeal for freedom and equality. Their fearsome leaders were Robespierre, Marat and Danton.

The National Assembly completed the constitution in September, 1791, saw it signed by the King, turned over the administration of affairs to the new Legislative Assembly and disbanded. The country drifted steadily toward the radicalism of the Jacobins. There were no openings here for moderate constitutional monarchists, such as Dupont.

Dupont had been gradually shorn of his liberal government salaries and allowances which, at the beginning of the Revolution, totaled thirty thousand francs a year. At fifty-two he realized that he must earn his living outside the government service. He turned to the profession of printing and publishing. His sole asset was his place, Bois-des-Fossés, in Nemours. This he mortgaged to Lavoisier and opened a printing establishment in the Isle Saint Louis, Paris.

A flowery prospectus offered expensive work to those who "wish typographic perfection," lower prices for those who "want from a book only the truths and thoughts that it contains," and added: "I shall be glad to end where Franklin began and am in no way humiliated that there is between him and me the distance of a whole lifetime."

Irénée Dupont, now a young man of twenty, had for some time been courting comely young Mlle. Dalmas, daughter of a tradesman in Paris. Usually so retiring, he became most insistent where Mlle. Dalmas was concerned. Both fathers had considered them too young to be taken seriously. But now that Irénée had become a capable powder chemist and his position under Lavoisier seemed assured, the fathers gave their consent. Eleuthère Irénée Dupont and Sophie Madeleine Dalmas were married in November, 1791. Sophie was only sixteen.

Shortly after the marriage Lavoisier, renowned as he was, lost favor and was transferred from Essonne. Irénée found himself without a job. His father took him into the printing office.

France temporarily had been more or less tranquil, but a new phase of the Revolution was brewing. On the 10th of August, 1792, the Jacobins, grown strong, attacked the Tuileries. The vacillating King left his Swiss guard to face the fight and fled to the nearby Legislative Assembly for protection. As members of the National Guard, both Duponts were on hand. "Ah, M. Dupont," called the King, catching sight of his former Commissioner of Commerce as he crossed the garden, "you are always ready when one needs you!"

Though father and son escaped the massacre of the Swiss guards, the elder Dupont was definitely recognized as a defender of the King and, as such, he was forced into hiding. Concealed in a nearby garret room, he heard the mob attack his printing house, stoning windows and damaging the presses.

That very month, Irénée's and Sophie's first child, Victorine, was born. Irénée took the infant and her mother to Bois-des-Fossés and returned to Paris to brave the fury of the Jacobins. He repaired the presses and continued business. It was a heavy and dangerous responsibility for one so young.

Meanwhile, Dupont senior had been smuggled out of Paris to a farmhouse near Rouen. In November he joined Sophie and the baby at Bois-des-Fossés and for almost two years kept under cover while radical factions—each as dangerous to his safety as the other—wrangled and fought for control of the Republic.

Irénée carried on in a Paris swept by famine, disease and bloodshed. He was the sole support of the family. In addition to the printing office, he managed a saltpeter refinery for the government. For the time being, this assured his own immunity. Often he worked twenty hours out of the twenty-four, occasionally riding all night to snatch a few moments with his wife and child in the country.

At the height of the Reign of Terror, Victor Dupont returned from America. He entered blithely into the spirit of the day by becoming a gendarme. However, about the time Marie Antoinette was guillotined, Victor became noticeably pale. Though he later attributed his pallor to spinach juice, externally applied, the young man spent some sleepless nights. His constabulary duties included, among others, the arresting of Royalists. The possibility of having to arrest his own father was bad enough, but what worried Victor most was the fate of a younger Royalist. She had eyes of deep, dark blue and her name was Josephine de Pelleport.

Victor became so pale his resignation was accepted. Whereupon, in April, 1794, he and Josephine de Pelleport were quietly married. He brought his wife and her sister to live at Bois-des-Fossés. The addition of these two Royalists by no means added to the safety of the household.

The tension of the little group in Nemours became almost insupportable as, one by one, the elder Dupont's friends were condemned and executed. The shadow fell

[37]

heaviest when Lavoisier, on the eve of a visit to Bois-des-Fossés, was arrested. Popular feeling against him was bitter. He had grown rich as one of the royal agents to whom the tax-gathering privileges were farmed. His unparalleled achievements in chemical research were brushed aside by Robespierre's thunderous and devastating assertion that "the Republic has no need of scientists." The great chemist mounted the scaffold in May, 1794.

Dupont knew then his turn would soon come, and it did. On July 13th, the Committee of General Safety ordered the arrest and incarceration in the prison of La Force, Paris, of "Pierre Samuel Dupont, exconstituent," further described as "hair and eyebrows gray, forehead high and bald, eyes blue, nose flat, mouth large, chin cleft, face oval and full." It took the gendarmes nine days to find Dupont and execute the process. Those nine days saved his life. For the grotesque and fanatical Robespierre and the bloody Commune were nearing their end.

When apprehended it was Sophie, Irénée's young wife, who begged the government agents to let her accompany her father-in-law to Paris. They refused. Alone, she traveled to the ominously quiet city by coach and notified Irénée. There was nothing the latter, or anyone, could do except wait and pray.

However, the fates were kind. On the night of July 27th, Robespierre's forces deserted to the National Convention. Shot in the lower jaw, Robespierre lived in silent agony until the 29th, when he was guillotined —one of the last of four thousand to die under the knife.

In prison Dupont, as usual, was irrepressible. On the

last night of the Terror, when the tocsin sounded and heavy firing was heard, the prisoners feared a general massacre. "Dupont addressed us about the danger with which we were threatened," relates a fellow prisoner, Comte Jacques Claude Beugnot, in his *Memoirs*. "As for him he intends to sell his life dearly. He exhorts us to do the same and tells us his plan of defense. There are twelve of us who can arm ourselves more or less well with the fire-irons, which fortunately had not been removed, the two daggers that we possessed among us, our knives and the legs of the chairs. We must adopt the ancient order of battle—that is to say, the strongest one shall be the front rank, two more the second, three in the third and four in the last. That disposes of ten men; the two remaining, chosen from the youngest, shall flank the army on right and left to help wherever reinforcement is necessary. Then we must arrange for our retreat and we will make of our beds a strong barricade behind which we can collect our forces and where we can wait for help from outside. However alarming the situation, it was impossible not to laugh at the seriousness with which this good Dupont arranged his line of battle."

Fortunately, the "good Dupont" had no occasion to test his plan in action. He was back at Bois-des-Fossés for the vintage.

As the wine fermented, new sap flowed in his veins. With both sons married he felt lonely. Sentiments more intimate than friendship began to warm his letters to, the young and beautiful widow of Lavoisier. But she, still living in her tragedy, posted off to Switzerland. Dupont promptly began to court the widow of another old friend, Madame Francoise Robin Poivre, whose husband had been governor of the islands of Ile-de-France and Bourbon. They were married by the Mayor of Chevannes in September, 1795.

Irénée was a witness. Victor had returned with his wife to America as secretary of legation and was stationed at Charleston, South Carolina, where his first children, Amélie and Charles Irénée, were born.

With the end of the bloody Jacobin régime, the Legislative Assembly resumed its sway. Executive power was vested in the Directory, which consisted of five members and which was to last just five years. Dupont was elected a member of the Council of Ancients, the Directory's new law-making body.

With Irénée's assistance, Dupont got out a paper called L'Historien, about this time, in which he expressed his views quite freely. The five Directors, who were more anxious to hold on to the glories of their positions than promote the welfare of France, were exceedingly resentful of criticism. They feared, too, the growing popularity of that youthful military meteor, Napoleon Bonaparte, whose inspired armies were rolling back the enemies that had tried to engulf France. In September, 1797, L'Historien was suppressed, the office ransacked, some of the machinery broken, and the two Duponts lodged in La Force. Although their imprisonment lasted only a day, the espionage continued.

The Duponts began to cast longing eyes toward new pastures. Europe was filled with tales of fabulous fortunes to be made in America, particularly in land development. Dupont senior became entranced with the idea of founding a colony in Virginia or some other fertile region of the United States. He sent Irénée to see

Robert Fulton, the American inventor, who was experimenting on the Seine with a submarine boat.

Fulton assured Irénée that good farming land could be bought along the Ohio or the Mississippi for ten or twelve francs an acre. "Every year you could take a boatload of flax, tobacco, wool, skins, hams, salt pork and produce to New Orleans," explained Fulton. "You could dispose of these products at a profit of a hundred per cent. Then you could go up the coast to Baltimore or Alexandria, Virginia, load up with manufactured goods and sell this cargo on your way home, again doubling your money. The entire trip would require only three months."

Fulton's advice concerned a single sizeable stock farm. No such modest project for Dupont *père*. He talked with Jacques Bidermann, a Swiss banker operating in Paris, who owned several thousand acres of virgin land in Kentucky which he wished to have cleared and colonized. Dupont's imagination soared. Using Bidermann's tract as a base, he would found a veritable state of his own—Pontiania would be an ideal name—a vast development upon which he would build houses, schools, roads and waterways, lay out great farms and cultivate all manners of crops, perhaps even start manufactories. Both of his sons, of course, would be assets, especially Victor who had intimate knowledge of and connections in America.

There was now, also, another member of the family who would prove a valuable addition to the project. This was his new wife's son-in-law, Bureau de Pusy. De Pusy, an able army engineer, had served under La Fayette in America as well as in Europe.

[41]

THE DU PONT DYNASTY

Although Dupont found no time to consult or even inform Victor of the plan, Irénée and de Pusy readily enlisted their services. Soon the rosy-visioned scheme was in full swing, on paper. Dupont wrote flamboyant circulars outlining, in minutest detail, plans for what he called his Rural Society.

These were signed "Du Pont de Nemours." Requiescat forever Pierre Samuel Dupont, ex-watchmaker!

His sons were given a small "d"—du Pont. They later adopted this style of the name, which continues today.[1]

The circulars invited subscriptions, at ten thousand francs each, in a stock association called *Du Pont de Nemours Père, Fils & Cie*. Each shareholder's liability was to be limited strictly to the amount of his individual investment. The literature prophesied golden dividends.

The newly-christened Du Pont de Nemours canvassed bankers and business men, political and social acquaintances, and obtained some twenty subscriptions, with promises of as many more. His chief backers were Banker Bidermann and the latter's partner, J. J. Johannot, also a Swiss. At the end of the campaign, the energetic promoter was still some 3,800,000 francs short of his 4,000,000 franc goal. He decided then, as the first step in the grandiose plan, to establish *Du Pont de Nemours Père, Fils & Cie* as a commercial firm in New York.

Victor Dupont's name had been prominently displayed in the Rural Society's advertising matter, his consular connections floridly emphasized. Yet the only member of the family acquainted with current American

---

[1] The name used collectively, or standing alone, is usually spelled with a capital "D" as—Du Pont family, the Du Ponts.

conditions remained in complete ignorance, as the scheme developed and flowered. Victor could have told his father that the French, at the moment, were highly unpopular in the United States because of the Directory's seizure of many American ships. Further, that President Adams disliked the elder Dupont whom he had met years before in France.

In fact Adams had just refused an exequatur to Victor as Consul General of France to the United States. Victor, with his wife and two children, promptly sailed for home, arriving in July, 1798. He found that his father's stock-selling campaign and arrangements for the migration to America had gone too far to be halted. Accordingly, he enlisted in the scheme.

Du Pont de Nemours planned the pilgrimage to the last detail. De Pusy, his wife Julienne, and their small daughter, Sara, would go first and find living quarters in New York for the entire family, also offices for the mercantile house. The rest would follow as soon as possible. Madame de Pusy then confided that she was soon expecting a baby. Du Pont promptly substituted his wife in the first contingent.

De Pusy, Madame Du Pont and little Sara de Pusy sailed from Rotterdam in May, 1799. Du Pont's final word to de Pusy was assurance that he would soon have a million francs for his enterprise. Before his own departure in the fall, he had actually collected 241,347 francs, of which sum 27,000 francs was obtained by Irénée in the sale of the printing house and its equipment.

Weeks went in packing great crates of furniture, including pianos, books and other belongings; other weeks in arranging transportation. Victor finally obtained a low passage rate from the grateful master of an impounded American schooner, which Victor was able to have released by the French authorities. The *American Eagle* (never such a misnomer!), out of Rhode Island, had lain for two years at La Rochelle. She was barnacled and thoroughly unseaworthy.

Nevertheless, she cleared for America October 2, 1799, carrying thirteen souls under the banner of Du Pont de Nemours, including six small children. The Du Pont roster included:

Du Pont de Nemours; Victor du Pont, wife and two children; Madame de Pusy and infant; Eleuthère Irénée du Pont, wife and three children; and Charles Dalmas, twenty-two-year-old brother of Madame Irénée du Pont.

The trip was a nightmare. The voyagers were on the water for ninety-three days, almost a month longer than the time required by Columbus, three centuries before, to cross from Spain to the Bahamas. The *Eagle* whined and sighed and seemed to beg the battering elements to send her to her final rest. She leaked and she lost her course. Half the time a flag of distress hung from the mast head. Twice passing vessels had to be hailed for food and water. The sailors were in a mutinous mood and some sought to loot the passengers' belongings.

Only one individual aboard the miserable craft preserved his spirits: the master of the Pontiania that was never to be, who celebrated his sixtieth birthday at sea. Throughout the terrible voyage, Du Pont de Nemours joked, composed verses, sang to the children, cheered their parents, flouted discomfort and hardship.

However, even he sighed with relief when the *American Eagle* lurched into the harbor of Newport, Rhode Island, on January 1, 1800.

Part Two

THE AMERICAN ADVENTURE

THE DU PONTS WHO CAME TO AMERICA

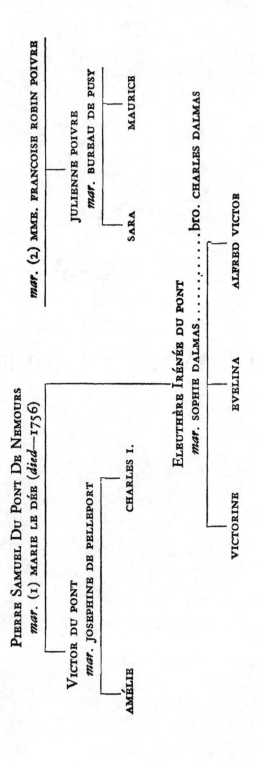

Chapter One

A FOOTHOLD

IN A rambling house on wind-swept Bergen Point, New Jersey, nine miles from New York, were reunited the four families who, for better or worse, had enlisted under the banner of Pierre Samuel Du Pont de Nemours.

The place, named Good Stay by the weary travelers, could be reached from the city in two or three hours by sailboat if the winds were favorable. Otherwise, one rowed across the North River and completed the journey in a horse-drawn vehicle over roads filled with fissures, ice, mud and stones.

Annexes had been hurriedly constructed by Bureau de Pusy, the engineer son-in-law, yet the new homestead was far too small to accommodate sixteen men, women and children in addition to a negro woman and her child whom Madame Du Pont had purchased. Accordingly, the Victor du Ponts found lodgings in New York City, on Pearl street. Later they rented a house at 91 Liberty street, near the North River, the first floor of which was given over to the family's business venture, *Du Pont de Nemours Père, Fils et Cie*, of New York and Paris.

From this headquarters the head of the house issued

an imposing prospectus (it reads like a manifesto)
introducing himself and his associates to press and
public:

We have the honor to inform you that a company has been
organized consisting of Swiss, Batavian, French and Han-
seatic merchants who have engaged us to be their correspondents in the United States of America.

We will do business on commission with the different
states of Europe, the Antilles and other parts of America, and
between them, in every branch of commerce; arrange for paying or receiving accounts, storing merchandise, exchange and
proper economy. . . . We will take charge of the dividends or
payments due from Congress on its various loans and forward
the remittances to Europe in whatever way may be most economical and convenient to our clients. . . . We will also enforce the payments of sums due to Europeans, either by the
State or by individuals.

We are willing to direct the administration of estates owned
in this country by Europeans—especially those of large extent. We possess some of our own that have been assigned to
us by our shareholders. Many of us have given careful study
to this industry, and we are in a position to offer useful service
to large investments for the purchase, improvement and sale
of land.

Commerce and all business between Europe and America
require, in view of present conditions and great distances, absolute confidence between the merchants and capitalists of
Europe and their correspondents in the United States. We believe that it is because of that confidence that we have been
entrusted with this enterprise. We will always try to observe
the trust with which we are honored.

The head of our firm is Du Pont de Nemours. He is perhaps
sufficiently known as the pupil and the most intimate friend of
the illustrious and worthy minister, Turgot, and as having

long and successfully held the position of Administrator-general of Commerce in France, before the Revolution. Living in America as a result of the persecutions that have at different times been suffered by all friends of justice, order, peace, industry, morality and honest liberty, he will change neither his principles nor his conduct.

The pronouncement went on to describe the distinguished attainments of Bureau de Pusy and of Victor du Pont and gave a brief line to the fourth member of the firm—"Eleuthère Irénée du Pont has had much experience of business methods in France, in agriculture, manufactures and the useful arts."

At once Du Pont de Nemours ran into difficulties that would have daunted a less doughty promoter. His friend, Thomas Jefferson, then Vice-President, wrote warningly against the purchase of land. Prices were high; unscrupulous speculators active. Jefferson also pointed out that there was a discriminating Customs duty of ten per cent on cargoes or merchandise consigned to aliens. Furthermore, under American law, each stockholder in a company such as Du Pont's was responsible for the entire indebtedness, not merely for the amount subscribed, as in France.

Du Pont's exuberant imagination had, of course, soared far above such concerns. His partners thought the matter of the Customs discrimination, at least, should be straightened out at once. Victor bundled his father into a chaise and they drove posthaste to Philadelphia, the capital, to consult Jefferson. It was a happy reunion for the two philosophers. They had many years to bridge. Business was quite forgotten in their long discussions of men and events. Victor tried not to appear impatient. Then Du Pont became utterly fascinated with Quaker meetings. Victor finally got his father around to the mission on which they had come.

Upon Jefferson's advice, it was decided that one member of the Du Pont firm should qualify immediately for citizenship. In Virginia the ownership of property was the only requirement. Victor bought a small house in Alexandria, which he promptly leased out, and was naturalized.

For months the firm of Du Pont waited for commissions and cargoes that did not come. Apparently, most of those in Europe, who had been lavish in promises of subscriptions, had forgotten all about *Du Pont de Nemours Père, Fils et Cie*. While their capital dwindled, the senior Du Pont was too busy to worry. Jefferson, with the University of Virginia in mind, had asked him for some brief suggestions on national education. Brevity, on such a subject, was impossible for Du Pont. He buried himself in an exhaustive treatise, proposing that the new Federal City (Washington) be made the ultimate educational as well as political center of the country, with a series of great special schools covering the physical sciences as well as the social and political, and including medicine and other professional subjects. The bulky document can still be examined, and sometimes is, by curious students.

This treatise was written in French. After much wrestling with torturous verbs and nouns of double meaning, Du Pont confessed that English was one accomplishment he would never attain. He never did. Irénée also found the new language difficult, while Madame Du Pont and her daughter, Julienne de Pusy,

ere homesick—they wanted to speak only French, but
France. With their husbands at home only on week-
nds, Bergen Point was lonely.

Irénée, too, was restless. Although unwavering in
yalty, he realized by the fall of 1800 that his father's
rm offered very poor prospects, at least immediately,
r the support of his own wife and children. He was in
his mood, one crisp day, when invited to go hunting
y his brother's friend, Colonel Toussard, who had
rved under La Fayette, and remained in America.

The hunters exhausted their supply of powder and
ought more at a country store. The quality was infi-
itely inferior to and the price higher than the British-
mported powder they had been using. The incident
aused Irénée to ponder. Aided by Toussard, he began a
uiet investigation. To his surprise he learned that there
ere scarcely any powder plants worthy of the name in
he United States. The largest, at Frankford, Pennsyl-
ania, owned by William Lane and Stephen Decatur,
hiladelphia merchants, employed sixteen men and sold
o the Government.

Irénée visited this Frankford plant and was astonished
t the incompetence and waste. The methods of manufac-
ure were half a century behind those in which he had
een trained at Essonne. The principal ingredient, salt-
eter, was poorly refined and mixed with charcoal and
ulphur while still damp, thus losing half of its power.
The powder was crushed, or grained, in such a crude
wooden sieve that much of it was reduced to dust and
ost. The buildings were badly arranged, too, in case
f an explosion.

Irénée got out his pencil and began figuring. He figured

[51]

that a well-constructed plant, consisting of but one stamping mill and one wheel mill, would produce 160,000 pounds of powder in a year of 200 working days. At the current government price, 47 cents a pound, this would yield $75,000. He calculated the cost of manufacture as: 120,000 pounds of saltpeter at 20 cents a pound, $24,000; sulphur and charcoal, $600; labor, $9,216.25; director's salary, $2,000; losses in manufacture, $7,183.75; annual repairs, $2,000—total $45,000, leaving a profit of $30,000.

Additional units, which could be built later without proportionate increase of overhead, would enlarge the percentage of profits. The chief customers, the young man estimated, would be the naval and military forces of the country, the forts, sportsmen, hunters, Indians. The West Indies would be a possible export market.

It was characteristic of Irénée to work out his plan in detail before taking it to his father. His capital requirements he placed at $36,000—$24,000 for the initial cost of land, buildings and machinery; the remainder for raw materials, additional payments on the land and reserves.

If even a pseudo-Uriel had been whispering prophecies, Pierre Samuel Du Pont de Nemours would have leaped to supply all the necessary capital, for he still had sufficient funds. But the old gentleman just then was head over heels in a project to establish a line of fast packet boats between America and France, and was grooming Victor for a trip abroad in the interests of this scheme, as well as to spur those tardy subscribers. Nevertheless, he saw possibilities in the powder plan and arranged that Irénée should sail with Victor in order that he might try to raise money for his project in France.

A FOOTHOLD

The brothers left New York January 5, 1801, on the peedy, copper-bottomed, 280-ton *Benjamin Franklin*. The passage on the trim *Franklin*, with its fine cuisine and comfortable sleeping quarters, was a delightful contrast to the former crossing on the *American Eagle*. They landed in Havre on February 2nd.

Moving in different circles, the brothers saw very little of each other in France. Victor plunged into gay social doings. With General La Fayette he attended a gorgeous fête given by Talleyrand for Bonaparte, then First Consul, at which the ladies appeared with their arms, shoulders and breasts bared. The frowning Napoleon accepted as a matter of course the adulation and flattery heaped upon him. Talleyrand, dandling about on his lame feet, took Victor under his wing and soon the stout, jolly Victor knew his way among the fops and fashionables of Paris.

Meanwhile Irénée, in duller surroundings, quietly and efficiently attended to his task. He obtained financial backing for the powder mills from Jacques Bidermann, the Swiss banker, from General Adrien Cyprien Duquesnoy and from Louis Necker, father of Madame de Staël and brother of the former Minister of Finance.

Better still, the French Government saw in Irénée's plan an opportunity to hurt the trade of its traditional enemy, England, who largely monopolized the American powder market. Accordingly, it offered Irénée every assistance: machinery at cost, designs by government draftsmen, and secret processes of fabrication developed since he had left Essonne. These processes, written out for him on official stationery, included new and speedier methods of refining saltpeter. He was also promised a

[53]

new graining machine which could be run by one man and would do the work of ten.

On April 21, 1801, articles of incorporation were drawn up in Paris "for the establishment of a manufacture of military and sporting powder in the United States of America" to be directed by "Citizen E. I. du Pont," who was to receive a yearly salary of $1,800.

The company was capitalized at $36,000, in eighteen shares of $2,000 each. Yearly inventories and reports were to be made but the determination of dividend payments rested entirely with the director and the firm of *Du Pont de Nemours Père, Fils et Cie*, which was to subscribe for twelve shares.

Profits, if any, were to be split into thirty parts: eighteen to the shareholders, nine to the director and three as a promotion fund to be used in obtaining government contracts. This promotion fund was to be suppressed if found unnecessary. One year in advance of January 1, 1810, the shareholders could decide, by a two-thirds vote, whether or not to continue the enterprise.

When Irénée returned to America in mid-July, 1801, he found his father in favor of locating the powder works near the new capital, Federal City. Proximity to the capital, the elder Du Pont diplomatically reasoned, would be advantageous in obtaining government orders. Irénée, however, was undecided and started out to find a suitable site. He explored the Hudson River country and New Jersey. Then he went to Philadelphia and made an offer to Lane and Decatur for the Frankford plant. They refused to sell.

September found Irénée in Federal City, from whence

ιε scoured nearby points in Virginia and Maryland on
ιorseback. "The country, the people, the location are
ιll worthless," he wrote his father, disgustedly, on
ͅeptember 19th. "I shall stop off in Wilmington for a
ιay to see the Brandywine."

Wilmington was a quiet little Quaker-influenced community on the Delaware River, some twenty-six miles
ιouthwest of Philadelphia. Flowing into the Delaware,
ιear the center of the village, was a small stream, the
ͅrandywine. Though a river, it was called Brandywine
ͅreek. Not far from the Creek and the historic Brandywine battlefield where young La Fayette, in September,
ι777, had fought and been laid low by a ball in the leg,
ιived a small colony of Frenchmen. Among them were
ιany friends of the Du Ponts, including Colonel Tous-
ιard, Irénée's companion on the memorable hunting
ιrip, and Peter Bauduy.

Peter Bauduy, a bluff, hospitable person, was the
ιropertied man of the group. He had already promised
ιo subscribe to the powder project and he now offered
ͅurther backing if Irénée would locate the plant near
Wilmington. Bauduy's promise meant cash, which
Irénée was discovering was not always true in the case
ιf his other subscribers. So, after testing the water
power on Brandywine Creek, he and Bauduy searched
ιhe local country for a site, and finally decided upon
ιhe ninety-five acre farm of Jacob Broom, which lay
ιlong the south bank of the Brandywine, four miles
ͅrom Wilmington.

Here, in 1795, Broom had built the first cotton mill
ιn the United States, which had later been destroyed
by fire. The tract, however, was well stocked with

[55]

willow trees, the best variety for charcoal; had sufficient land cleared for farming; and, best of all, there was a fast and steady flow of water in the Creek at that point.

The price finally agreed upon for the farm was $6,740, of which $2,000 was paid at once. Delaware statutes did not permit alien ownership of land, so the deed was recorded in the name of William Hamon, Bauduy's brother-in-law. The date was April 27, 1802.

It was decided to name the powder plant the Eleutherian Mills and to call the product Brandywine Powder. One wonders if perhaps Turgot did not twinge a bit beneath the sod over this use of his well-intended name for his god-son: Eleuthère Irénée—"for liberty and peace."

If Irénée had any twinges, they were strictly monetary in nature. His capital was exceedingly slender. The $24,000 pledged by his father's firm was still only a paper subscription. But his machinery was paid for, his site chosen and he still had $2,000 left of the $4,000 Bauduy had paid for two shares. He went to Bergen Point to collect his wife and children.

Meanwhile, Du Pont de Nemours had managed to get into further tangles. While his sons were away, he had sent Bureau de Pusy to Holland in an effort to enlist more capital. De Pusy had failed and, when offered a government position in France, accepted readily. His defection did not help the credit of the firm nor make life happier at Good Stay. After Madame de Pusy, with her two children, sailed to join her husband, Madame Du Pont became utterly dejected over the separation from her daughter and grandchildren, and she beseeched her husband constantly to take her back to France.

When Victor returned, early in 1802, he found the family atmosphere decidedly strained.

Nor had Victor's long absence yielded any financial fruit. He had, however, brought letters from Talleyrand and several other high officials to the French Consul General in Washington, Louis André Pichon. The letters recommended cooperation with *Du Pont de Nemours Père, Fils et Cie* in the purchase of supplies for the French troops in Santo Domingo. Napoleon, determined to conquer the indomitable negro dictator of Santo Domingo, Toussaint L'Ouverture, was sending his brother-in-law, General Leclerc, with 25,000 men, to reestablish slavery in the colony—all in the name of Liberty, Equality and Fraternity. The troops, as well as the supporting naval craft, were to be provisioned from American ports.

The contracts would, of course, be enormous. Victor visioned a fortune in commissions. What was his consternation to learn that his father, seeking the same business on behalf of the firm, had bitterly antagonized Pichon. Victor hastened to Washington where the Consul General told him that the elder Du Pont had tried to dictate to him.

"Why, he treated me like a little boy!" exclaimed the indignant Pichon, and then he made a surprising proposition to Victor. He offered to divide with him on an equal basis the entire profits of all Santo Domingan purchases—if he, Victor, would completely sever connection with his father's firm. Such an opportunity was too seductive for Victor to resist. He signed a contract with Pichon at once and then notified his father.

Du Pont de Nemours took the decision astonishingly well. In fact, he seemed relieved. Now he could go back to France, perhaps to a high post in the Government, where, he felt certain, Bonaparte would welcome his ripe experience. Friends wrote constantly urging his return, insisting that his varied talents should not all be devoted to commercial business. His firm, he decided, should have its headquarters in Paris. Besides, in France he would be able to expedite the payments of the fat drafts on the Treasury which Victor would receive for the Santo Domingan deals.

A little juggling took care of Victor's pledge to Pichon. The firm of *Du Pont de Nemours Père, Fils et Cie*, of New York, was dissolved and its assets transferred to *Du Pont de Nemours Père, Fils et Cie*, of Paris. A new firm, *V. du Pont de Nemours & Company*, of New York, was formed.

Nominally, each company was independent of the other. The twelve shares of Irénée's powder company were transferred to the elder Du Pont's French firm, the greater part of the pledged $24,000 still owing.

When Jefferson, who had become President, learned that his friend was returning to France, he enlisted Du Pont's services in that series of momentous events, summarized in two words, "Louisiana Purchase," which carried the American flag from the mouth of the Mississippi to the Rockies. Jefferson asked his friend "to impress on the Government of France the inevitable consequences of their taking possession of Louisiana."

Accompanied by thirteen bales of household goods and numerous trunks, Du Pont and his wife waved farewell to New York from the comfortable sailing ship *Virginia*, June 1, 1802. During the voyage Du Pont had planned to draw up a full report of his operations in

A FOOTHOLD

America for the benefit of the men and women in Europe who had invested in his company. Finding that he had left the necessary data behind, he busied himself instead with an essay on *Instinct* for the French Institut.

The new financial shuffle left Irénée pretty much in the same position of fending for himself as he had been. However, he was convinced that Victor's new alliance and his father's return to Paris would soon be beneficial to him.

Already crates of machinery from France, consigned to the powder works, lay on the landings at Philadelphia. Irénée and his family hastened their departure from Bergen Point as rapidly as possible. Boxes, barrels, trunks, bales of bedding and furniture, a small flock of merino sheep and several dogs went first in charge of Charles Dalmas, Sophie du Pont's young brother. Irénée, Sophie and the children followed, arriving on the Brandywine July 19, 1802.

Their first home was a two-story log cabin. It was hot, stuffy, crowded. Their great venture was begun.

Chapter Two

DISSENSION

THE position of our house at the very bottom of
the valley and in the damp air of the Creek is
not a healthful one," Irénée du Pont, in February, 1803, wrote from the Brandywine to his father in
France. "But I think that when spring comes and we
live on the hill I shall be quite strong again."

In the same letter he reported his progress with the
powder plant:

"We have accomplished an astonishing amount of
work since August, but I am dismayed when I think
of what is still before us. Within three months we have
built a large house and barn of stone and the greater
part of the refinery; we have repaired the water-course
and the sawmill in which we prepare the wood for our
framework and a part of that used for the machines.
This month we have still to build three mills and one or
two other buildings; to dig a new race for one of the
mills; to make the drying place, the magazine, the
workmen's quarters. It is evident that we cannot make
powder before the autumn."

Autumn came and went and still not a millwheel
turned on the Brandywine. Skilled carpenters and stone

nasons were difficult to obtain. Those workmen who were lured from Wilmington and Philadelphia wondered why the tall, unsmiling "Monseer" du Pont, forever bending over his blueprints, insisted upon walls of triple thickness and light roofs that sloped toward the Creek. "Monseer" did not explain that, in case of explosions, the flimsy roofs would sail like scattered cardboard into the water while the stout walls of native stone *might* remain undamaged. The least said about explosions the better.

The cost of the plant far exceeded original estimates. Unable to obtain substantial sums from his father and brother, Irénée called on Peter Bauduy for more and yet more money. Almost before he realized it, Bauduy had signed and paid for two more shares and, in addition to his total outlay now of $8,000 in cash, he had arranged bank loans, secured by his personal notes, for $18,000. The sum eventually staggered him and he decided to call a halt.

Soon Irénée and Bauduy were at daggers' points. The two hurled charges and counter charges at each other, as Frenchmen can, in bitter letters to Victor du Pont who, as mentor, had been able to patch up previous disputes between them. Bauduy complained that Irénée was wasting money in stocking a farm, in feeding the workmen and in purchasing materials. Irénée charged that Bauduy had cozened him into signing a paper written in English which he, Irénée, imperfectly understood, and certainly did not intend; that this paper gave Bauduy a full partnership in the business; and, furthermore, that Bauduy was signing letters "Du Pont, Bauduy & Company."

Bauduy became infuriated and threatened to institute suit and tell the newspapers and the public how he had been defrauded and rooked.

Victor, who had always been congenial with Bauduy, now employed all his charm and tact to bring the feud to an end. Finally it was agreed that Bauduy should be given certain commissions on sales and the three parts in the profits originally set aside as a political "acceleration" fund. With the elder Du Pont's friend, Jefferson, in the White House, this fund, it was thought, would not be necessary.

The name of the firm was definitely settled as E. I. du Pont de Nemours & Company. On this point Irénée was inflexible. He notified Bauduy in writing that if the plant "earns a reputation greater than that of others, and if it makes a name—that name should be mine."

Though self-interest held Irénée and Bauduy together for years, from this time on they thoroughly distrusted and disliked each other.

At last, in the spring of 1804, E. I. du Pont de Nemours & Company produced its first run of powder. A few twenty-five pound sacks were sent to Victor's firm at 101 Greenwich street, New York. Victor proudly wrote out a newspaper advertisement:

E. I. Du Pont De Nemours Gun Powder Manufactory
Wilmington, Delaware

THIS NEW AND EXTENSIVE ESTABLISHMENT IS NOW IN ACTIVITY AND ANY QUANTITY OF POWDER, EQUAL IF NOT SUPERIOR TO ANY MANUFACTURED IN EUROPE, WILL BE DELIVERED AT THE SHORTEST NOTICE.

Samples to be seen at
V. Du Pont De Nemours Et Cie
New York

DISSENSION

It was good powder, fine, dry, well grained. Irénée knew his business. Orders began to come in gratifying quantity. Sales for the remaining months of 1804 totaled $10,000. In 1805 they jumped to $33,000. The increase was largely due to a sale of 22,000 pounds for the American frigates sent to Algeria to suppress the Barbary pirates. The first order was for 14,000 pounds at 39 cents a pound.

"This powder was tested several times at Federal City," Irénée reported in a buoyant note to his father, "and was compared with powder sent by all the manufacturers, as well as with some lately secured from England, and it proved so superior that old Mr. Dearborn, in spite of his unwillingness, sent us about 120,000 pounds to remake and a part of his saltpeter to refine, and he announced publicly on the Fourth of July before the officers, who were delighted with our powder, that in future we will do all the government work. Besides that, I have in the past month made 40,000 pounds for the Spanish Minister."

"Old Mr. Dearborn" was Major General Henry Dearborn, of Massachusetts, Secretary of War. His "unwillingness" was due to official prejudice against ordering essential military materials from alien-owned concerns. The Du Ponts were to feel this resentment for years.

In 1805, though, their first war-born prosperity came in the nick of time. Victor's firm in New York was in a very precarious position. Its very existence depended upon the payment by the French Government of Victor's commissions on the Santo Domingan supplies, as per arrangement with Consul General Pichon. The payment, in turn, rested entirely upon the whim of Napoleon Bonaparte, now Emperor.

Hence Du Pont de Nemours, in Paris, pulled every wire, used every artifice (and he was no novice) to gain favor at the court of Napoleon. With the Empress he succeeded admirably. Josephine found his drolleries amusing (he could usually amuse the ladies), gave him a card to the Tuileries and accepted seeds and plants which he had Irénée send her from America. However, he failed dismally with Napoleon, who wanted young blood about him.

Nor was Napoleon unaware of the colossal fortunes which could be garnered by profiteers from his campaigns. Regarding most purveyors of supplies as leeches and parasites, he questioned their bills with both suspicion and a microscopic knowledge of detail. Du Pont, unaccustomed to such raking cross examinations, became confused. Napoleon was frankly bored by the old gentleman's long-winded explanations of Victor's Santo Domingan transactions. The drafts were paid haltingly, then only in part.

"An opinion is growing that is very bad for us," Du Pont de Nemours reported to Victor. "Everyone who holds Santo Domingo drafts is *suspected of trickery* and his honor is more or less questioned! And if my own reputation lifts me a little above that class, I have been made to feel it. Ith as kept me out of the Senate and out of the Legion of Honor."

At this dubious moment Napoleon's dashing younger brother, Jérôme Bonaparte, a youngster of nineteen, with more charm than principle, deserted a French naval vessel in New York and embarked upon a round of gaiety, climaxed by his marriage to Elizabeth Patterson, a Baltimore belle. Jérôme applied to Pichon and Victor du Pont for funds, promising, with his hand on his heart, that he would persuade his august brother to pay their requisitions. It turned out he was talking through his hat, but Pichon and Victor swallowed the bait and agreed to finance him. He proved an expensive luxury. Jérôme and his bride passed the summer of 1804 at a watering place and Victor wrote to Irénée that they were spending about $8,000 a month, adding that "if Pichon pays I have no objection to keeping them there."

Pichon paid Jérôme's bills but he so juggled his accounts in the process that he was recalled to France, accused of defrauding his Government and dismissed in disgrace. The repercussion ruined Victor who had $140,-000 in Pichon-endorsed drafts waiting payment. In August, 1805, Victor's firm failed. Irénée begged him to come at once to Delaware. But Victor took his family into the wilds of the Genesee Valley, in the western part of New York State, where there was a settlement of sixty families called Angelica. For three years they lived in a log cabin and Victor earned a fair income as proprietor of the general store.

Meanwhile the mill on the Brandywine was steadily rolling out its kegs of black powder. Sales in 1806 totaled $32,000 and in 1807, despite the plant's first explosion, jumped to $43,000. Irénée described the explosion in a letter to his father:

Tired of building and forced by the demand to start manufacturing as soon as possible, I was obliged to use a house that was already built, sixty feet from the graining mill, to make

[65]

a heated dry-house. Attached to this was another building that was formerly used in the cotton manufactory and that I use for a charcoal house, having no other. I knew that the charcoal had several times lighted spontaneously at the Essonne mills and at other mills in France; I knew the danger of thus having powder and charcoal under the same roof; but my partner did not think as I did; we were tired of building and we had to start.

On the 18th of August we had taken the charcoal out of the furnace with the fire absolutely extinguished. When we stopped work in the evening Dalmas and I went to look at the charcoal to be sure that there was no appearance of danger; we saw none. After supper Dalmas said, "We should go back and look at the charcoal—it is too dangerous. Will you go or shall I?" Then he added, "You are tired, I will go." In less than fifteen minutes after he left the drying-house exploded with a tremendous crash. I ran down, convinced that Dalmas was lost. Imagine my joy when he was the first to answer my call.

We spent the rest of the night putting out the fire and preventing it from spreading to other buildings. All of the windowpanes in my house were broken and some of the windows blown in. What proved most fortunate for us and really seemed help sent from Heaven, was the light wind, cold and damp, that was blowing from the northeast and had thoroughly wet all the roofs.

In the same letter, Irénée cautioned his father against undue optimism. He still had $11,000 in bank loans outstanding and, owing to the necessity of selling the powder on long-term credits, collections were slow.

Such warning was of course futile to one of Du Pont

le Nemours' temperament. He scented success. Bustling
about Paris, he magnified Irénée's figures and assured
everyone that the powder company would more than
make good the shareholders' losses in the other Du Pont
firms.

Beaming, he told his principal backer, Jacques Bidermann, the banker, that each share of the powder bonanza
would soon be paying $600 a year, which would thereby
give each share a real value of $6,000. "For," added the
sanguine Du Pont, "one cannot estimate the capital of
so hazardous a manufacture as gunpowder at more than
ten times its profit. But even that would be three times
the original cost of each share of my own company.
And it follows that the twelve shares that my company
owns in the powder company would equal thirty-six
shares in the company that bears my name."

Bidermann, who had sunk large sums in the various
Du Pont enterprises, fervently hoped that this time the
old gentleman's calculations would prove correct.

Irénée had agreed to give his stockholders a complete
accounting and inventory on or before December 31,
1809. This accounting was long delayed. When finally
presented, however, it showed sales of $243,554.79 for
the first six years of operation and profits of $43,613.68.
The ratio of profits to sales amounted to almost twenty
per cent, a ratio that was to become a guiding principle
of Du Pont investments over the years.

The document follows:[1]

[1] From *E. I. du Pont de Nemours & Company, A History, 1802–1902*, by B. G. du
Pont, Houghton Mifflin Company, 1920.

THE DU PONT DYNASTY

STATEMENT OF GUNPOWDER SOLD BY MESSRS. E. I. DU PONT
DE NEMOURS & CO. AND THEIR AGENTS UP TO THE
31 DEC., 1809

SOLD BY THEMSELVES	QUANTITY IN POUNDS	KEGS	
1804............	11,350	454	$ 4,368.00
1805...................	80,720	3228	29,581.00
1806.......	38,269	1527	14,239.00
1807......	38,551	1541	13,495.00
1808......	53,900	2156	22,523.00
1809......	25,456	1018	12,694.00
			$96,900.00

SOLD BY THE FOLLOWING AGENTS		
Mitchell & Shepherd.	330	2,927.65
Delaire & Canut..................	249	2,552.07
V. du Pont de Nemours & Co.......	96	787.52
Aubin Laforest.................. ..	550	5,829.36
John Sullivan.		253.27
Anthony Chs. Cazenove.......	975	10,213.10
Anthony Girard.........		33,972.55
Richard Bowden & Co.... .. .	302	2,545.98
Archibald McCall.......		36,486.16
Brujiere & Teisseire.............. ...	490	5,505.85
Suydam & Wickoff		674.96
D. P. Dows & Co..........		465.79
Thomas Shewall......		4,548.39
Benjamin Herr..........	32	
John Hancock....................	470	4,987.32
Samuel Hastings		410.00
John Strong..................		472.10
Watkinson & Co................		716.78
John Chew............		426.50
John Thurston.............		300.00
Anthony Buck..		184.04
Mein & Rodgers..................	66	570.24

DISSENSION

SOLD BY THE FOLLOWING AGENTS

John Whipple..		$854.75
Richard Drummond & Co...............	140	1,630.51
		$214,214.79

$5,355.37 P. Bauduy's Commission @ 2½ pr. ct.

Brought forward $214,214.79

*Gunpowder manufactured & remanufactured
with the saltpetre of the U. States*

	LBS.	
In 1805....................	35,000	2,800.00
1806.............	67,200	5,376.00
1807........................	29,500	2,360.00
1808.............	98,400	8,116.00
1809....................	93,800	10,688.00
$29,340 00		$243,554.79

$1,467.00 P. Bauduy's Commission @ 5 pr. ct.

5,355.37 *Brought forward.*

$6,822.37 *Carried to account current.*

Inventory of the money, prime materials, gunpowder manufactured, goods, land property, improvements on the same; and debts belonging to E. I. du Pont de Nemours & Company: as also of the debts due by Them to Others on the 31st day of December, 1809, when the term of their original association expired, as per Statements in waste book No. 6, folios 1 and 24; and in Journal No. 7, folios 1 and 26:

To Wit

BELONGING TO THEM

Cash in the Delaware Bank......................	$ 1,911.66
Prime materials outstanding: valued at...	4,028.34
Gunpowder unsold: valued at....................	21,780.64
Bills receivable...............................	1,130.00
Goods and land property mortgaged to them.........	5,712.97
Real estate of their own, buildings thereon, machinery and utensils: valued at.................	42,750.00

BELONGING TO THEM

Book debts due to them . . . .$ 31,504.31

$108,817.92

Brought over $108,817.92

They are indebted as follows:

Book debts due by them $22,304.24

Promissory notes due by them 6,900.00

18 shares due to the stockholders 36,000.00 $65,204.24

*Profit made since the 21 April, 1801, to the 21 Dec.,
1809, and divided as stated in waste book no 6,
folio 24* $43,613.68

SHARES OF STOCK			SHARES OF PROFIT
1 J. Bidermann	1 placed to a/c ct.		1,453.78
12 Du Pont Father & Co . .	12 " " "		17,445.47
4 Peter Bauduy	7 " " "		10,176.52
1 E. I. du Pont	10 " " "		14,537.91
			$43,613.68

Most of the profits went back into the business. Some of the surplus, however, went into the establishment of woolen mills. Both Irénée and Bauduy grazed fat flocks of merino sheep. They decided to pool the wool, build mills on some land Bauduy owned on the north bank of the Brandywine, opposite the powder plant, and to offer Victor du Pont the management of them. Back of the offer was mutual realization that Victor's presence might lessen somewhat the friction and irritations which continued to crop up between them. Victor, weary of the wilderness, accepted.

The spring of 1810 found the brothers, with their increased broods, together on the Brandywine. It was a glad gathering. Victor, though he had grown even stouter, was still the beau ideal of shy, unemotional Irénée. And now Victor's admiration grew for the gaunt strength, sturdy independence and silent efficiency of his younger brother.

Both families piled into Irénée's big stone house on the hill, which had kept the name of Eleutherian Mills. The woolen factory and a home for Victor were still under construction. Victor now had two boys and a girl, Irénée a son and four daughters. Irénée's boy, Alfred Victor, was twelve; Victor's oldest son, Charles Irénée, thirteen.

To Du Pont de Nemours in Paris, this happy reunion of his sons brought fresh difficulties. Irénée's use of the powder company profits to establish his brother in business caused an uproar. Shareholders of Du Pont's firm became pressing. Then a frightful financial panic swept France. Jacques Bidermann failed for 4,000,000 francs.

Du Pont de Nemours decided the only thing to do was to liquidate his firm. Without consulting either of his sons, he hit upon a plan that seemed to him very feasible. Since his company's only assets were the twelve shares in Irénée's powder plant, he would give each of his thirty-six stockholders one-third of a share. It seemed really very simple, in spite of the fact that Du Pont had never completed the purchase of these shares. He made a formal assignment, May 10, 1811, and issued this explanatory statement:

The misfortunes from which the Company has suffered and which I have explained, have reduced its assets to twelve shares in the Powder factory founded by my son, Eleuthère Irénée du Pont and of which he is Director and a shareholder; the liquidation is therefore very simple, each share in my Company being represented by one-third of a share in the Powder Company.

[71]

In consequence:—

I ask of my son, living at the said factory called Eleutherian Mill on the Brandy Wine River near Wilmington in the State of Delaware, and I exact of him that he divide the Twelve Shares held by my Company in his, into shares and parts of shares of the said manufacture, in such a way as to satisfy in accordance with their rights all my shareholders, as is arranged in the following list with the statement of their shares in the Powder Company—they being required to return to him as proof of their claims their shares in the Company Du Pont (de Nemours) called d'Amerique and in agreement with the following list:

NAMES OF THOSE NOW INTERESTED IN THE COMPANY KNOWN AS DU PONT (DE NEMOURS) PÈRE ET FILS ET COMPAGNIE AND THE NUMBER OF THEIR SHARES IN THE COMPANY.		NUMBER OF SHARES TO BE GIVEN THEM IN THE POWDER COMPANY ESTABLISHED AT ELEUTHERIAN MILL.
M. Bidermann	13	$4\frac{1}{3}$
M. Johannot	5	$1\frac{2}{3}$
Mme. de Pusy	5	$1\frac{2}{3}$
Du Pont de Nemours	3	1
Mme. de Staël	2	$\frac{5}{6}$
M. de Crillon	$1\frac{1}{2}$	$\frac{1}{3}$
Mme. Du Pont (de N)	1	$\frac{1}{3}$
M. Lescalier	1	$\frac{1}{3}$
M. Ochs and children	1	$\frac{1}{3}$
M. Wischer	1	$\frac{1}{3}$
M. Forcard Weiss	1	$\frac{1}{3}$
M. Reinhard	1	$\frac{1}{3}$
M. Hom	$\frac{1}{2}$	$\frac{1}{6}$
	36	12

And until such new shares and parts of shares are issued by the Powder Company, I hereby declare that the Shares of my Company shall be valued according to the said proposition and I require my son to honor them.

[72]

DISSENSION

Du Pont de Nemours was no doubt within his legal rights, but this precipitate action of his unleashed a hornet's nest about Irénée's head.

The new shareholders of the powder company demanded full and immediate payment. Many had been shown letters from Irénée reporting the 1810 profits at more than $30,000 and estimating the net returns for 1811 at between $40,000 and $50,000.

Mme. Du Pont's daughter, Julienne de Pusy, now a widow with two young children, living on a small pension, was particularly insistent. Her late husband's entire fortune had been invested with her stepfather. She hopped aboard the first boat for America. In October, 1811, she arrived in Wilmington, a thunderbolt in petticoats. Straightway, she demanded that Irénée pay her $20,000 at once as the value of her interest. Refused, she settled down in Philadelphia and conducted a bitter campaign of propaganda against both Irénée and Victor.

Peter Bauduy joined the attack and they both wrote letters to the French stockholders assailing the integrity of the brothers du Pont. Du Pont de Nemours was informed that his sons would not honor the agreement he had made with his creditors and that they wished no further financial relations with him. This inflamed the harassed old gentleman beyond endurance. Dipping his pen in vitriol, he denounced Victor and Irénée as thieves and unnatural sons and informed them that he would soon come to America for the sole purpose of suing them. He quickly regretted this intemperate outburst, however, and posted a remorseful apology.

The woolen mills were completed early in 1812, but the promoters soon realized that they could not operate them on theory alone. A practical weaver was required, and one was found in the person of William Clifford, a young Englishman. Clifford, who had come to America to make his fortune, said his father, a woolen manufacturer of Gloucester, had died following the falling off of manufactures in England, and that he, himself, would inherit a considerable fortune upon the death of his mother.

Clifford proved a jewel. He revamped the machinery and methods, taught Victor's oldest son, Charles, to spin, and made himself so useful generally that he was appointed manager of the mills, with a good salary, and promised a percentage of the profits. He lived with the Victor du Ponts, in their roomy new house, Louviers, and soon was looked upon as one of the family. Victor and Josephine were rather flattered when he asked the hand of their eldest daughter, Amélie.

Amélie, though a gentle little soul and accomplished, was the ugly duckling of the family, dumpy, with a short nose and irregular features. She loved music. At Angelica the shy child often played for hours on her mother's tiny piano, sometimes looking up to find the face of an Indian pressed against the windowpane. Clifford, the first man who had ever courted or looked at her with proprietory eyes, won easily her fluttering consent to become his bride. The marriage took place September 12, 1812, a few months before Amélie's seventeenth birthday. Clifford was twenty-seven.

In due course, a round-faced, chubby infant graced the union. The baby, Gabrielle, was but a few months old when the tragic dénouement came. A new workman in the factory, an English weaver, looked long and hard at

Clifford. He recognized in Amélie's husband a man who, under another name, had deserted a wife and child in England. Clifford did not deny the charge. That day the factory lost a manager and Amélie a husband. Her father took legal action to legitimatize the baby and restore his daughter's maiden name. For the rest of her life Amélie, never complaining, lived with her family.

Sorrow, too, invaded Irénée's home about this time. His eldest daughter, Victorine, and Peter Bauduy's son, Ferdinand, had been in love since childhood. Both families opposed the match but the young people persisted and, in November, 1813, were married. Eleven weeks later, young Bauduy died of pneumonia in his bride's home. His death foreshadowed a final break between his father and the Du Ponts.

Meanwhile, the United States and Great Britain had gone to war. Orders for ammunition poured in upon E. 1. du Pont de Nemours & Company. The clashing factions concentrated upon the profitable job in hand as though there had never been a ripple of dissension.

CLEARING SKIES

THAT lengthy, wearisome and inconclusive struggle, misnamed the War of 1812, touched the very doorstep of the Du Ponts.

Delaware was harassed and bedeviled by the enemy. The tiny state's entire eastern shore line—the one-hundred-and-ten-mile strip lying along the Delaware River and Bay and the sea from Wilmington, on the north, to Lewes, Cape Henlopen and the Maryland border, on the south—was exposed to attack. Upon the declaration of war, in June, 1812, banks in Wilmington and New Castle moved their funds to Philadelphia.

Privateer fleets were soon darting out of the Delaware River to prey on British commerce. The Du Ponts did a thriving business with them. These "Skimmers of the Sea" became such a scourge that one British journal was moved to pose an indignant rhetorical question: "Shall England, mistress of the seas, be driven from her proud eminence by a piece of striped bunting flying at the mast heads of a few fir-built frigates manned by a handful of bastards and outlaws?"

In the spring of 1813, the British concentrated a powerful fleet in Delaware waters. Irénée du Pont, at his mill on the Brandywine, was handed a rather casual note one day in March:

WILMINGTON, MARCH 19, 1813.

DEAR SIR:

I this morning received a letter from Governor Hazlet stating that considerable depredations in Burning of Vessels &c are committed by the British Vessels of War about Lewes Town in Sussex and requests of me to forward him six kegs of your best rifle powder or such as is used for musketry. perhaps one or two of the kegs had best be of Cannon powder. I wish you to have it sent in to Paul McGin's this evening or early in the morning, as we wish to forward it tomorrow with some lead I am procuring.

YOURS SINCERELY,
JOHN WARNER

P. S. Send me a bill of the powder.

The British became more active. From his impressive flagship, the *Poictiers*, Commodore Beresford wrote to "the first magistrate of Lewes," demanding that "twenty live bullocks, a quantity of vegetables and hay be sent to the *Poictiers* for use of his Britannic Majesty's squadron, which shall be paid for at the Philadelphia prices. If you refuse to comply with the request, I shall be under the necessity of destroying your town."

The demand was defiantly refused. Delawareans, though but seventy-odd thousand strong, did not scare easily. Before the Quakers had poured into their valleys and villages, they had been, since the early seventeenth century, quite accustomed to the violent and successive struggles of the Swedes, Dutch, England, Baltimores and Penns for possession of the territory known as the "Three Lower Counties on Delaware."

[77]

In every town and hamlet along the coast, the drums beat to arms. Farmers, tradesmen, old soldiers of the Revolution came forward with rusty muskets and snarls of defiance.

The British repeated their demand for food and water. Otherwise, they warned, the bombardment would begin and they therefore advised removal of all women and children. The ladies of Lewes, one may be certain, left their brave defenders plentifully supplied with fried chicken, potato cakes and the famous Delaware peach brandy before they departed.

Irénée du Pont received another order:

THURSDAY, APRIL 8, 1813

DEAR SIR:

By express from Governor Hazlet this morning at one o'clock the enemy's Ship Belvedier had commenced cannonading Lewes Town.   In addition to the number casks of powder, I am directed to get ten more of Cannon powder, please to send them this day to Mr. Dixson's store.

JNO. STOCKTON.

The attack on Lewes lasted for twenty-two hours. The British had to keep well out of rifle range and the aim of their gunners was poor. The houses of Lewes were damaged to the extent of about $2,000 but there were no casualties. In fact, the bombardment, according to a contemporary historian, had a comic accompaniment: "The people of Lewes are merry. They enumerate their killed and wounded as follows, one chicken killed, one pig wounded—one leg broken."

Financially, however, the War of 1812 came much closer to the Du Ponts. It marched right into their pocketbooks. They sold more than 1,000,000 pounds of powder, at a price averaging close to 40 cents a pound, to the United States Government and to individual naval and military units. There were other good customers, including John Jacob Astor, whose trappers and hunters were pushing everywhere into the wildernesses. Astor's American Fur Company consumed 25,000 pounds of rifle powder a year.

For 1812, the books of E. I. du Pont de Nemours & Company showed gross sales of $148,597.62 and for 1813 the figure was $107,291.20. In 1813 the firm bought for $47,000 a nearby tract known as the Hagley property and rushed to completion a new powder plant on the site of an abandoned iron and slitting mill. The Hagley mills, first of numerous expansions, doubled the company's capacity, doubled, also, Irénée's responsibilities.

Day and night, two shifts of workmen packed the military powder in canisters, kegs and barrels and piled them gingerly into stout wagons, lined with straw, which hurried them to nearby arsenals and magazines. Most of the wagons were supplied either by the Government or by private contractors. From the arsenals the ammunition was shipped by canal or horse-drawn freight lines, which now ran as far south as Baltimore, as far north as Boston, as far west as Pittsburgh. By this means, or by its own direct overland caravans, the Government filled the needs of widely scattered naval and military commands.

Transportation by sea, during most of the thirty months of conflict, was seriously interrupted by the British blockade. Moving powder by sea was uncertain even in peace time. During electric storms nervous captains often dumped consignments of inflammable material overboard. Perry's victory on Lake Erie and Macdonough's on Lake Champlain were both aided by hardy teamsters who hauled ammunition to them over miserable country roads and tangled forest trails.

The war brought one relief to Irénée du Pont. His most irritating creditor, Julienne de Pusy, took herself and her maledictions back to Paris, where she made the home of Du Pont de Nemours woeful with lamentations over her misfortune of ever having been connected with him or his sons.

In April, 1814, Napoleon, shattered in health and prestige, abdicated and the Bourbons returned to power. Du Pont de Nemours' mentor, Prince Talleyrand, leaped lightly on the new bandwagon. Du Pont, seeking to follow, found that vehicle already laden with returned *émigrés*, hungry for their old privileges.

Most of them had more influence than Du Pont could command. His efforts to be appointed Minister to the United States, or even to a minor consulship, were pushed aside. And, at home, Julienne de Pusy continued her taunts. Gouty, disillusioned, low in funds, he wrote his sons, mournfully: "One should avoid founding business associations and should never form them with one's family. It weakens affection and sometimes destroys fortunes."

One result, however, of the widow Pusy's plaints was that banker Bidermann, weary of bickerings and conflicting reports, sent his son, Antoine, to America to find out what all the fuss was about and to protect his interests. Antoine, a cool, capable young man of twenty-four, was inclined to be critical, even hostile at first.

Long talks with Irénée and Victor du Pont, with Peter Bauduy, and a thorough examination of the accounts, finally convinced him that Irénée had been cruelly libeled. He became even more convinced that Evelina du Pont, Irénée's second daughter, was the loveliest creature he had ever known. It was not long before Irénée had a new son-in-law, one who proved an invaluable asset to the family.

Young Bidermann aided the Du Ponts in forcing Bauduy out of the firm. Under protest, and pending negotiations for a settlement, Bauduy withdrew and, in February, 1815, Bidermann took his place in the partnership.

Bauduy also withdrew, and willingly, from the woolen mills, which had been a losing venture from the start. Victor's eldest son, Charles Irénée du Pont, not yet eighteen, had been alone in the management of the mills since the departure of the faithless Clifford. Victor had decided to try his hand at politics and had won election to the lower house of the Delaware Legislature. The move he thought was expedient in view of constant criticism that he and his brother were more loyal to the land of their birth than the country of their adoption.

This insinuation had lost the powder company many lucrative contracts. The brothers continually urged their father to rejoin them. His wide acquaintance and facile pen could be turned to better advantage here than abroad, they thought. While Du Pont de Nemours hesitated, history made up his mind for him.

On March 1, 1815, Napoleon landed at Cannes from the island of Elba and commenced his amazing march on Paris. The city was plunged into panic. The trembling

Bourbons and their supporters fled, Louis XVIII taking refuge in Belgium.

A few hours before Napoleon entered Paris, March 20th, a stocky, partly bald old gentleman was galloping toward Havre behind foam-flecked horses. His passport, hastily obtained from William H. Crawford, the American Minister, described him as "Monsieur Du Pont (Peter), american, citizen of Louisiana, carrying despatches from the American Legation to his Excellency the President of the United States." He was alone. Madame Du Pont, confined to her room with an injured hip, was unable to accompany him. They were never to meet again.

Six weeks later found Du Pont de Nemours settled in the best room in Irénée's house, telling the tale of his adventures with vast gusto to his admiring sons and their wives and bouncing upon his knee his great-grand-child, Amélie du Pont's (Clifford) little Gabrielle. Four generations under one roof! The knowledge stimulated "*Bonpapa*" into gale after gale of fascinating reminiscences. Six of his eleven grandchildren he had never seen, including Irénée's second son, chubby little Henry, now three.

In letters to his wife he summed up his impression of the children: Irénée's oldest boy, Alfred, now seventeen, was a little slow of wit but kind and fond of mathematics. Victor's oldest boy, Charles, eighteen, was of a good and sound nature, while the curly-headed, large-eyed younger boy, Samuel Francis, was handsome and promising at twelve.

He noticed one curious thing in the family: *Charles*, Victor's son, and in Irénée's family, *Victorine, Evelina,*

Alfred and *Eleuthera* had long, serious faces—thin and pale excepting Evelina. But *Amélie* and her *Gabrielle*, *Samuel Francis* and *Julia*, *Sophie* and *Henry* had fat, round faces—gay, pink and white. The long ones looked like brothers and sisters, so did the round ones.

The chieftain of the clan Du Pont was astonished and delighted, too, with the powder plants. After inspecting the original mills and the new Hagley Works, he wrote his wife: "It is amazing, inconceivable that one man could design and execute such works and such mechanical and hydraulic machines. Irénée is a great man with capability, courage, perseverance ten times greater than I would have dared to expect, though I have always thought highly of him."

The ceaseless strain under which Irénée labored was strikingly demonstrated to the father a few days after his arrival when an explosion killed nine workmen and destroyed $20,000 worth of material and machinery. In the weeks that followed the old man also gained some understanding of Irénée's financial problems. Money was tight. Every business man had to scratch for credit. Du Pont de Nemours summed up the situation in a note to Johannot, one of his original backers in Paris: "Houses without number have been built of paper; water power for factories and the factories themselves—of paper; canals and roads—of paper; beautiful and useful steamboats—of paper."

Shortly after the elder Du Pont's arrival, the Irénée-Bauduy conflict flared again into the open. Bauduy broke off negotiations for a settlement and sued Irénée for an accounting of their involved business affairs. He placed high, and yet higher, valuation upon his four shares of stock. He demanded accrued interest and gains on that portion of the profits, three parts out of thirty, originally held in reserve for use in promoting public contracts. Charges of chicanery and fraud flew back and forth. Bauduy asserted that Irénée had used his (Bauduy's) money, credit and services in time of need, then discarded him with the coming of prosperity. Irénée retorted that, since 1804, Bauduy had drawn more than $100,000 in salary, profits and commissions from the powder company.

After years of tugging and hauling in various courts, Bauduy lost his suit. Not until 1824 did he fade finally from the Du Pont picture.

While the case was pending, Bauduy put up a powder plant of his own, lured away many Du Pont workmen and entered active competition with the mills on the Brandywine. "Though he uses almost the same machinery and methods of mixing," the elder Du Pont wrote Johannot, "no powder compares with ours. All because of Irénée's skill and his marvelous industry." The Bauduy powder venture also failed.

The last years of Du Pont de Nemours' life were happy. He wrote much, received occasional visitors and maintained an indefatigable correspondence with Jefferson, Talleyrand, La Fayette and other friends on both sides of the water. He asked Jefferson's intercession with President Madison to have his grandson, Samuel Francis, appointed a midshipman in the Navy. Voicing the hope that his descendants would always prove "loyal Americans and valiant Republicans," he added a priceless Nemourian touch:

"The Du Ponts, beginning with Pontius Cominius

who carried letters from Camillus to the Capitol and crossed the Tiber without a boat and without knowing how to swim, have always been men of decision and resource. I do not want them to be valueless or a poor acquisition for any country, least of all for yours."

Jefferson replied, expressing hope that peace would prevail for the next twenty years. "At the end of that time," wrote the Sage of Monticello, "we shall be 20 million in number and 40 in energy, when encountering the starved and rickety paupers and dwarfs of English workshops. By that time, I hope your grandson will have become one of our High-admirables, [sic] and bear distinguished part in retorting the wrongs of both his countries on the most implacable and cruel of their enemies."

The appointment was prompt. Samuel Francis returned to Mr. Constant's boarding school, at Mount Airy, near Germantown, Pennsylvania, proudly sporting a cockade which indicated that he was a cadet-midshipman awaiting a call to a training ship. The Naval Academy was not yet in existence.

Under recurrent attacks of nephritis and gout, the strength of Du Pont de Nemours began to fail, though not his roguish spirit. During the Christmas holidays in 1816 he decided to surprise the Victor du Ponts by rowing across the Creek and dropping in for dinner. The boat capsized as he was stepping into it. He was thrown into the water and, unlike Pontius Cominius, who, presumably, kept his letters dry, Du Pont de Nemours was thoroughly drenched. "Ah, my children," he exclaimed gaily, as he was put to bed with hot bricks at his feet, "your old father never before went through the Ordeal

[85]

by water but he came out victorious!'' After this experience, however, his decline was rapid.

In July a charcoal house caught fire in the middle of the night. When the watchman's whistle sounded its familiar and dreaded warning, all hands rushed to the powder yards. Despite his seventy-seven years, *"Bonpapa"* was in the midst of the mêlée. The next day he was desperately ill, suffering acutely. Early in August he lapsed into a coma.

At three o'clock on the morning of August 7, 1817, with his sons and eldest grandson, Charles, at his bedside, the turbulent career of Pierre Samuel Du Pont, the First, came to an end.

Chapter Four

THE BATON PASSES

LIKE a Damoclean sword, hanging over the head of every powder man, was the dread of explosions. It was a nameless terror, waking men at night to prowl at odd hours about the yards, observing things that would have drawn scarcely a glance from less anxious eyes—random sparks from chimneys, wind direction, faintest indication of heavy skies that might bring thunder and lightning.

The experience and keen watchfulness of Irénée du Pont had held accidents to a minimum in his mills. His workmen were sober, reliable, carefully trained. But no one could foretell when some small particle of saltpeter, sulphur or charcoal would erupt in rebellion against the grinding, rolling and pounding that processed it into black powder. Then, with no warning, would come the rumble, crash and flare of flame, the billowing black cloud and flying débris, and later the utter desolation of chaos—demolished buildings and sometimes torn and mangled bodies that, but a moment before, had been moving, living creatures.

One day in March, 1818, the master of the Brandywine mills was in Philadelphia when a pallid, sweat-streaked messenger brought word of an overwhelming disaster. An explosion had torn the old, or Upper Yard, to pieces, destroying five of the six mills and 85,000 pounds of powder, killing thirty-four persons and wounding many others, including his wife and brother-in-law, Charles Dalmas. Galloping madly, Irénée du Pont was at the scene within a few hours.

He found his home, Eleutherian Mills, and those of many workmen, reduced to ruins. His wife and Dalmas were bruised and cut. Two-year-old Alexis, the youngest child, had miraculously escaped hurt amid caving walls and flying stones. Windowpanes were smashed even in Victor du Pont's home, Louviers, many hundreds of yards away across the Creek.

Victor, with his guest, Marquis de Grouchy, the famous marshal of Napoleon, who had been banished from France for treason, and de Grouchy's two sons had taken charge of the yards and were doing what they could for the wounded and the bereaved. When he beheld the scene of destruction and the distress of widowed women and orphaned children, Irénée du Pont must have been shaken to the core. But, with outward calm, he moved his family into his brother's house, where they slept on pallets in the library, and began the tedious task of rebuilding. By fall, the mills were again humming.

Coming at a time when business conditions were intolerably bad, the catastrophe was a serious blow financially. In cases of death by accident, the widows and minor children of the workmen were each guaranteed $100 annual income. Losses for 1817, '18 and '19 from bankruptcies, explosions, etc., were $140,000.

The French creditors, however, learning of the disaster, ceased their clamors for immediate dividends and accepted long-term notes. Irénée's life was plagued with notes. His own personal pledges were constantly falling due, necessitating frequent trips to Philadelphia. "It is cruel," he wrote his wife one evening from Philadelphia, "to ride sixty miles every five or six days to meet one's notes, and so to waste one's time and one's life. God grant that some day I may get to the end of it."

The fervent wish was never fulfilled. The load he pulled was too heavy to ever fully clear his obligations. However, there were compensations. His reputation and that of his product grew. Men consulted him as an expert on manufacturing and agricultural problems. He was always welcome at Washington and became a director in the Bank of the United States, depository of public funds and crude forerunner of the present Federal Reserve system. Although he gave little thought to politics, he was in broad sympathy with the Federalist, later the National-Republican Party and believed, of course, in a protective tariff.

The powder maker's keen interest in government policies that bore upon his business is shown in a communication to a Baltimore editor in 1827. The letter also contains a summation of his first quarter century of business activity:

E. I. DU PONT TO HEZEKIAH NILES, EDITOR *Niles' Weekly Register, Baltimore.*

AUGUST 29, 1827

The amount of Gunpowder manufactured at du Pont's mills near Wilmington Delaware has been of late years from 6 to 700,000 lbs. with the new mills lately added to the establishment the quantity manufactured this year will be upwards of 800,000 lbs.

The raw material annually imported for manufacturing this quantity of Gunpowder are 712,000 lbs. of crude saltpetre imported from the East Indies, and 94,000 lbs. of Brimstone from france or Italy.

The number of persons employed at the factory are
Overseers, clerks and workmen. 99
Blacksmiths. 3
Mill wrights. 8
Carpenters. 6
Masons. 5
                                                                          121
to which are to be added Coopers for making kegs. . . . 17
Tin men for canisters. 2
                                                                          140
and also Waggoners, Shallop men &c., &c.

The whole amount of pounds of Gunpowder manufactured at du Pont's mills since their first establishment in 1803 up to the 1st of June, 1827, has been 9,718,438 lbs. When this manufacture was first erected the greatest part of the gunpowder consumed in the United States was imported from England. Had the above quantity continued to be imported, the average cost in England would not have been less than 21 cents pr. pound; so that this establishment alone has already saved to the nation upwards of two millions of dollars, which have been kept at home to circulate among ourselves, instead of being paid as a tribute to European industry.

The encouragement afforded by the last war, had upon Gunpowder manufacturers the same effect as protecting duties would have upon all other branches of National Industry; Large Capitals were involved, and a competition created which not only forced the manufacturers to improve in their art but at the same time reduced the price of the article very considerably. the cost of Imported Gunpowder of a good quality, without any profit to the merchant, is at present from 26 to 30 cents per pound, while american powder of the same kind sells at 16 & 20. if the american manufactures had not been encouraged there would still be a few in the country and the importers would still have it in their power to fix the price in the market, which with a reasonable profit to themselves could not now be less than 32 to 36 cents per pound; previous to the last war the regular price was 40 cents—so that the encouragement given and the competition created, united with the enterprise and skill of the American manufacturers have reduced the price of the article to be forever cheaper than it can be imported.

It is however to be observed that the government by allowing the drawback of duties upon Imported powder encourages the importation of inferior and of damaged Gunpowder, which as it could not sell in Europe continues to be imported here to be re-exported to South america, and thus contribute in part to the supply of a market which otherwise would be furnished by the produce of our own manufacturers.

It ought also to be noticed that the importation of Crude Saltpetre, one of the principal raw materials for the manufacture of Gunpowder, is taxed with a duty of 15 pr. ct. Saltpetre is not manufactured in this country in time of peace, and should not if it could as it is of great importance to keep for time of war all that the country may contain. The duty on crude saltpetre acts consequently only as a tax on Industry and as an obstacle for the american manufacturer to meet foreign competition in foreign markets. Crude saltpetre ought to be imported free of duty as it was formerly, but the tariff of 1816 subjected it to a duty of $7\frac{1}{2}$ pr. ct. which in 1826 was increased to 15 pr. ct. The duty of 3 cents pr. lb. on refined saltpetre which was laid by the tariff of 1824 acts on the contrary as an encouragement to Industry, and has already had the good effect of every other encouragement on domestic manufactures. There are now several large establishments for refining saltpetre and the price which had never been previous to the duty less than 10 cents pr. lb. is now reduced to $7\frac{1}{2}$ pr. pound.

The writer did not consider it worthy of note that his firm also sold refined saltpeter, charcoal, pyroligneous acid, iron liquor (a red dye) and creosote—a very considerable line of chemicals; nor that a tanning process had been developed by which leather became fit for use in three weeks.

In the development of these products and in practical research work, Irénée du Pont found a capable assistant in his oldest son, Alfred Victor. Alfred, too, was of the plodding, bulldog type, not quick but thorough and dependable. He knew every crevice and corner of the yards and mills and had made himself useful since boyhood, running errands and helping retrieve shot fired from the crude *éprouvette* mortars, by which means the strength of powder was then tested.

After attending boarding school in Carlisle, Pennsylvania, Alfred specialized in chemistry under Thomas Cooper at Dickinson College. It was a fortunate association. Cooper was a painstaking scientist and a master who encouraged his pupils to venture off the beaten path. At Dickinson, young du Pont made a study under Cooper of the colors imparted to flame by metallic salt solutions. This was a pioneer attempt to recognize metals by colored flames. The procedure consisted in dipping a bit of cotton in a solution of some chloride, pressing the cotton, then dipping the alcohol and holding the cotton in the flame of a lamp, to which the color was imparted.

When he took his place in the mills at nineteen, Alfred spent much of his time in a small laboratory his father had fitted up in a corner of the saltpeter refinery. In 1823 his father wrote of him: "Alfred has just contrived a new instrument as simple as it is ingenious and has proved an interesting fact, that there is no relation between the strength and quickness of gunpowder."

In the fall of 1824, General La Fayette, now sixty-seven, toured the United States as the guest of the nation and nowhere was his welcome warmer than in Delaware. On October 6th, a troop of horsemen in blue and black coats, black stocks and white pantaloons, and a band of music, met La Fayette's barouche at the Pennsylvania-Delaware line and escorted him through the streets of Wilmington under arches decorated with flowers.

From Wilmington the distinguished visitor went to New Castle to attend the wedding of Victor du Pont's oldest son, Charles Irénée, and Dorcas Montgomery Van Dyke, daughter of Nicholas Van Dyke, who had been president of Delaware State in colonial times. La Fayette gave away the bride and by his presence made the wedding an even more gala event.

The following summer La Fayette spent a night at Eleutherian Mills and was escorted by a committee to the spot near Chadd's Ford where he had been wounded in 1777. In the album of one of the Du Pont girls, he wrote: "After having seen nearly half a century ago the banks of the Brandywine a scene of bloody fighting, I am happy now to find upon them the seat of industry, beauty and mutual friendship."

Victor du Pont headed the committee of escort. It was Victor's last public appearance. Though gout and rheumatism bothered him, he occasionally went to Philadelphia for an evening of whist or a day of jollity. He was in the Quaker City on January 30, 1827, when a friend stopped him and remarked upon his apparently ruddy health. "I never felt so well," assured Victor, beaming at the compliment. Half an hour later he dropped dead. "Rupture of a cavity in the artery of the heart," was the doctor's report. He was in his sixtieth year.

With the passing of Victor and Du Pont de Nemours, these Wilmington Du Ponts lost contact with the world of "grand" society both in France and America. Save for an occasional individual of Victor's temperament, the family became clannish, reserved, self-contained, and utterly absorbed in powder making.

Loss of Victor was a shattering blow to Irénée du Pont. Once, when Victor had reproached himself as a financial burden upon his brother, the latter had stopped him with a solemn sentence: "We are as twins—when one dies, the other dies."

Now Irénée grew grayer, more melancholy. Waves of nostalgia swept over him. His wife, too, longed for another sight of France, where three of her seven children had been born. The two dreamed of a long visit back home, and often discussed the homecoming as they sat together in the evenings, the clangor of the mill machinery stilled. But it was not to be. Scarcely a year after Victor's passing, Sophie Dalmas du Pont died. Quiet, strong, reliant, she left a void that none could fill. Deep as her love was for France, she was loyal, too, to the land where her family had found asylum and opportunity. Her second son, Henry, was preparing for West Point and she had encouraged his ambition.

After his wife's death, Irénée buried himself in his business with more absorption than ever.

The steady supply of saltpeter was a major problem of powder manufacturers. Reports began to filter into the United States of the discovery of saltpeter deposits in Peru and Chile. Fortunately the family had a representative in Chile in the person of Lieut. Irvine Shubrick, of the United States Navy, who, in 1824, had married Victor du Pont's youngest daughter, Julia. Shubrick readily agreed to investigate the new deposits.

"The saltpeter is produced in the province of Tarrapaca," he wrote from Valparaiso. November 18, 1832, "and embarked at the port of Iquique, a small port in the latitude of 21° 40' south and longitude 70° 00' west, a little more than halfway between this place and Callao. It is said here that its basis is nitrate of soda and unfit in the composition of gunpowder, and that in France it is principally used for acids, glassware, soap, &c. It is thought that the province of Tarrapaca could produce as much as might be demanded for all Europe or any other destination, but the present establishments do not yield more than 80,000 quintals annually. The principal mines are about eight, ten and twelve leagues from the sea, and it may be said are productive from the surface of the earth.

"It is subjected to a simple process of purification which consists only in separating the salt from the earth. What is generally sold contains about four per

[95]

cent extraneous parts, whereof one and a half and two per cent humidity. The quantity exported June, 1830, to the present time is computed at 90 to 95,000 quintals. The present price is $4 per quintal in bags delivered into the ship's boats, which in addition to the freight from this to the United States would make the cost greater than the amount stated in your letter of August, 1831. The saltpeter now is a regular business, and all French ships from this to France are freighted with it."

Long and exhaustive experiments with samples of the "Peruvian saltpeter" convinced Irénée du Pont that, as powder was then made, the South American product would be of no use to him. However, with characteristic exactitude, he wrote a detailed report of his tests. A generation later this report was to form the basis of further experiments by a grandson—with astonishing and revolutionary results.

During successive administrations in Washington, the Du Ponts' relations with the United States Government grew closer and more profitable. Irénée du Pont neglected no opportunity to demonstrate his loyalty. In 1833 South Carolina threatened secession from the Union in protest against the "Tariff of Abominations" which Congress had enacted in 1828, and which the state maintained favored northern manufacturers. President Andrew Jackson met the challenge by ordering General Winfield Scott and a naval force to Charleston.

At the height of the furore, Irénée du Pont received an offer from individual South Carolinians of $24,000 for 125,000 pounds of cannon and musket powder. He promptly declined the order, explaining: "The destination of this powder being obvious, we think it right to decline furnishing any part of the above order. When our friends in the South will want sporting powder for peaceful purposes, we will be happy to serve them."

A few weeks later, when peace again reigned, through the speedy passage by Congress of a compromise tariff act, the proprietor of the mills on the Brandywine wrote a bit ruefully in French to Pitray, Viel & Company, his Charleston agents: "Our E. I. du Pont has been in Washington assisting at the treaty of peace between your friends, the Nullifiers, and ours, the monopolist manufacturers of the North. Now that the affair has ended so amiably I almost regret that we refused to supply the powder. We should be very glad to have that twenty-four thousand dollars in our cash box rather than in that of your army."

Later that same year, June 27, 1833, Eleutherian Mills was the scene of the wedding of Samuel Francis du Pont and his first cousin, Sophie Madeleine du Pont. This union of Victor's youngest son and Irénée's youngest daughter was a private, strictly family affair. Samuel Francis, twenty-six, six feet one, wore the uniform of a lieutenant in the United States Navy. Sophie was a delicate, gentle girl of twenty-two. There was a significance, a solemnity bordering upon the sacerdotal in this first consanguine marriage of the American Du Ponts.

Irénée du Pont's mind must have gone back, inevitably, to the feudal ceremony, almost half a century before, when his father invested him with his first sword and made Victor and himself promise "to be always firmly united, to comfort each other in every sorrow, to help each other in all efforts, to stand by each other in all difficulty and danger."

This mating of his daughter and nephew was the last event of note in Irénée du Pont's life.

On October 31st, 1834, during one of his periodical visits to Philadelphia, he was stricken with a heart attack and died within a few hours in a hotel room. The circumstances of his death were strikingly similar to that of his brother. He was sixty-three.

For thirty-two years he had struggled, against mountainous odds, to build a business that would provide for his populous family. From modest beginnings, in two tiny buildings of Brandywine granite, this business had grown into a cluster of fine mills, spread over many acres, and with annual capacity of more than one million pounds of powder. It was, at last, emerging clear and free of debt.

Part Three

EXPANSION HORIZONTAL

Chapter One

SONS AND GRANDSONS

DURING its entire history, with but a single exception, the executive direction of E. 1. du Pont de Nemours & Company has rested, in unbroken line, in the hands of a Du Pont.

For a brief period, following the death of the founder, the firm was headed by one who was a Du Pont only by marriage.

From November 1, 1834, until April 1, 1837, Antoine Bidermann was boss. The choice was inevitable. For twenty years this son-in-law had worked constantly at Irénée du Pont's side. He knew every detail oj the business. Irénée's three sons were not yet prepared to assume the full responsibility of their heritage. Alfred, although a man of thirty-six, was not robust and was more absorbed in the scientific aspects of powder making than in management. Henry, the second son, now twenty-two, had entered the mills only a few months before his father's death, reluctantly resigning a commission in the army engineering corps he had just won at West Point; while the remaining son, Alexis I., was a mere lad of eighteen.

Irénée du Pont had entrusted to Bidermann the double

mission of conditioning the sons to carry on the business and of paying as soon as possible the notes held in France by the original shareholders or their heirs. In 1836 Bidermann went to France, paid the notes in full and received quit claims. Then he stepped gracefully out, retiring from active business, and on April 1, 1837, the company became a partnership, American-owned, American-controlled. The partners were Alfred, Henry and Alexis du Pont.

It was a peculiar form of partnership, a form that lasted for sixty-two years. There were no officers, no president, secretary or treasurer. In correspondence the partners were referred to merely as "Our Alfred du Pont," "Our Henry du Pont," etc. By virtue of seniority and rigid family discipline, Alfred became the senior partner. His position was very much like the Old Man of ancient tribes. He wrote and signed all letters and his decisions were unhesitatingly accepted as final by his brothers.

All property was communal. Even the farmlands that now comprised several hundred acres, running far back into the rolling country on both borders of the Creek, were owned jointly. As each partner married, the company built a house for him, exacting no rent. They did not even own private carriages or horses. If a trip to Wilmington or elsewhere was necessary, a message to the company stable eventually produced a mount or a horse and buggy.

The partners drew no salaries, each being credited on the books with a proportionate share of the profits. Sums for personal needs were drawn as required from the cash box. A single clerk combined the functions of bookkeeper and cashier. He also paid the workmen and checked incoming and outgoing supplies. Most of the workmen were French, drawn from the original colony that had settled near Wilmington, and they were supplemented by relatives and friends from abroad. The others were of native stock, attracted by wages that were considerably higher than those of less hazardous occupations.

One of the most vexing problems was transportation. Agents in New York and other coastal points received their shipments by water. Sometimes the sloop or schooner arrived without its cargo. Cautious captains, as we have observed, had a habit of heaving powder overboard. Another difficulty was that powder had to be relayed to the ships by small boats in the Delaware River. In bad weather the transfer was a tough, tricky job.

Alfred du Pont solved this problem by building a pier and a magazine on the river three miles from Wilmington. He also insured uniformity in the kegs by putting up a cooperage and hiring a permanent force of carpenters. A special type of Conestoga wagon was designed to hold 150 twenty-five-pound kegs. On short trips these huge covered vans were drawn by four horses, on long hauls by six mules. And some of the hauls *were* long. Years after the railroads came, the picturesque six-mule teams, with the driver astride the lead mule, were a familiar sight as far west as Pittsburgh. Not only could the mule teams be operated at less cost than the rates charged by the railroads, but the mules were not so balky where explosives were concerned.

One railroad refused point blank to carry powder

under any circumstances. Another announced, with curious logic, that "friction matches will not be carried except in the cars that carry gunpowder." Consequently, Du Pont wagons covered regular routes in the coal and iron regions, where powder was steadily increasing in demand for blasting purposes in newly discovered mines.

In 1846 revolutionary changes in the composition and manufacture of explosives were heralded by Schoenbein's discovery of "guncotton" or "cotton gunpowder." The German, by treating cotton with nitric and sulphuric acid, created the most powerful explosive agency then known. Although England and France refused to purchase Schoenbein's patents, the European press was filled with colorful accounts. Long before news of the discovery reached America, Alfred du Pont had experimented with cotton soaked in acid. Thus, when agents all over the country began flooding him with inquiries, the Du Pont senior partner was ready with his report: "The discovery is brilliant and such as to create astonishment, but the introduction of guncotton in common use must be the work of time, because the cost of preparing it is high and it will require years before the application of machinery to its manufacture can make it cheap enough."

The writer pointed out that guncotton was more explosive than propellant, that its gases would corrode the interior of gun barrels and its nitrous vapors would make its use untenable in confined spaces, as between decks of ships.

"Many other reasons could be given," he added, "which would at once convince any person that guncotton cannot come into use for military purposes. There is, however, a trifling experiment which will show the merit of the new article. Take a small lock of guncotton between your thumb and finger, holding it with no more pressure than you would hold a pen in writing; fire one end and you will find that the fire will be cut off at the point of compression, the piece held between the fingers remaining unburnt. Now, what dependence can be placed upon a substance so easily affected by pressure?"

Alfred du Pont's conclusions proved correct. It was thirty or forty years before guncotton became useful for either military or commercial purposes.

The 1840's and 1850's were America's Age of Energy.

The great push across valleys and plains into the West was in mighty momentum. Other tremendous forces, social and economic, were in movement. Canals, steamships, railroads were transforming transportation. In communications, the telegraph; in agriculture, the mechanical reaper; in industry, new machines and ingenious contrivances of a thousand varieties foreshadowed incredible readjustment in man's relation with his fellows.

Young America strode lustily ahead, while its painfully inadequate financial system limped hopelessly behind. There was not enough currency or credit to float a fraction of the enterprises that were crying for capital. Andrew Jackson tried a drastic remedy, smashing the Bank of the United States and distributing public deposits among state banks. An eruption of speculation, inflation and wild cat schemes followed, culminating in the Panic of 1837. The effects were felt for years.

The Du Ponts suffered with the rest of the business

community. Agents went into bankruptcy; debtors repudiated. But, just when the pinch was particularly nipping, a war came along to fill their coffers. To the munitions makers of the Brandywine, the war god Mars was Santa Claus.

The sale of more than one million pounds of powder to the United States Government during the Mexican War, 1846-48, erased most memories of the late panic. Similarly, a few years later, profitable sales to the British for the Crimean War enabled the brothers to weather the Panic of 1857 nicely.

During the Mexican War, new mills were built on the other side of the Creek and a bit nearer to Wilmington. These were called the Lower Works. By 1848 the combined mills were producing 10,000 pounds of powder a day, working half the time by lamplight. The long hours, and the shock of an explosion that took eighteen lives, so sapped the strength of Alfred du Pont that, in 1850, he turned the active management over to his brother Henry. Alfred lived in semi-invalidism until his death in 1858.

Henry had been champing to take command. A peppery, positive person, he had developed into an all-around powder man and a cool, keen trader in matters financial. His régime was to be the longest in the company's history, and notable. Efficiency was his middle name, economy his battle cry. His initial act was to establish a branch sales agency in San Francisco to catch the dollars of the gold miners; his next, to break in a new junior partner in the person of Eleuthère Irénée du Pont 2nd, Alfred's oldest son.

Irénée 2nd had served a long novitiate in the mills

under his father and knew every employe by his first name. He proudly joined his uncle Alexis in taking charge of the manufacturing end, when Henry moved into the senior partner's office. Like his father, Irénée 2nd had an inventive streak. His contribution to the firm's progress was a patented metallic keg which became the company's standard container.

These new kegs minimized but did not eliminate explosions. The first explosion after their introduction was more harmful, from a cold business point of view, than those that had cost many more lives. For it occurred in Wilmington.

Wilmington was now a thriving town, climbing up the surrounding hills as it grew. With its neat little rows of red brick houses, each with its iron hitching post and spotless white marble landing block, with its carefully cultivated gardens, it had an air of genteel simplicity. Its industrious inhabitants, who went leisurely about their business, were quite unconscious of their dangerous proximity to the sinister product of their Brandywine neighbors.

Then, one day in May, 1854, three of the Du Pont covered wagons came clomping down the cobblestone streets on their way to the pier with four hundred and fifty kegs of powder. Suddenly there was an explosion, cause unknown. The three drivers, the wagons and their twelve horses were blown to bits. Houses for hundreds of feet were damaged. Worst of all, two passersby were killed.

The story of this spectacular tragedy spread to every part of the country. The Du Ponts were bitterly assailed for permitting their wagons to traverse busy thoroughfares. Powder wagons were banned from the streets of practically every city and town in the nation. The accident, it may be needless to remark, did not add to the popularity of the Du Ponts in Wilmington.

The next tragedy was more personal. On August 23, 1857, Alexis du Pont was directing a gang of half a dozen workmen, dismantling a mill in the Hagley Yard. The moving of a heavy bin caused a small friction explosion, sparks from which set fire to an adjoining mill. Before the men could stamp out the fire, the mill blew up, killing all of them and fatally wounding Alexis. Conscious, but in agony, he was carried to his home. Sensing that his injuries were fatal, he asked to bid goodby to those who had worked under him. A procession of grimy men, in overalls and boots, passed into the darkened bedroom and silently pressed the hand of the dying man. Some were gnarled old veterans of the powder line who had known "Mr. Alexis" all of his forty-one years.

It was a sad and touching scene. But the mills must grind on. According to tribal rule, when one Du Pont fell out, another must be ready to take his place. And one always *was* ready.

Lammot, second son of Alfred, was chosen to succeed Alexis in the triune partnership. This young man was the most promising of the twenty-four children of the three brothers, not to mention the numerous offspring of Irénée's daughters or the grandchildren of Victor.

Although Lammot never achieved the senior partnership, he was undoubtedly one of the most outstanding and brilliant men the Du Ponts produced. Upon graduation from the University of Pennsylvania in 1849, Lammot had made an enviable record as a chemical engineer. He was always referred to proudly as "our chemist" in the senior partner's correspondence. Carrying forward the experiments begun by his grandfather, E. I. du Pont, a quarter of a century before, Lammot, in 1857, introduced and had patented the use of nitrate of soda in place of nitrate of potash (saltpeter) in the manufacture of blasting powder. His discovery made possible at last the utilization of those vast deposits of soda nitrate in South America. It was of tremendous financial importance to the company and marked a big technological advance in powder making.

Lammot's new soda powder was cheaper and fully as effective as black powder in the mining of coal. Demand from the anthracite regions grew so rapidly that the company purchased its first outside mills in Luzerne County, Pennsylvania, on the Big Wapwallopen Creek, a tributary of the Susquehanna River. This was a first attempt to bring mills and market geographically closer. Also it marked a departure from the company's traditional policy of operating no plant which a member of the family could not personally supervise every moment. Although its initial output was but 250,000 pounds a year, "Wapwallopen" was a success from the start.

In 1858, Lammot spent several months in Europe, inspecting the arsenals and powder mills and noting the radical changes in manufacture wrought by the Crimean War. He returned enthusiastic over the possibility of improving military powder, and started to work on his new ideas with Captain Thomas J. Rodman, noted ballistics engineer of the United States Army Ordnance Department.

Guns of large bore had been built but were unable to resist pressure generated by the big powder charges they required. Captain Rodman worked out a method of measuring the pressure of the powder gases in the new artillery pieces. The problem now was to modify the explosive force within the gun. Using Rodman's formulas, Lammot du Pont solved the problem by increasing the density and size of the powder grains. Some of the new grains, round in shape, were as much as three inches in diameter.

This "Mammoth" powder, so-called, burned much more slowly than the usual cannon powder. It reduced pressure and increased velocity. Mammoth powder later proved its value in the battle between the *Merrimac* and the *Monitor*. With the iron clad ship and large cannon, it played its part in revolutionizing naval warfare.

Rodman and Lammot continued work upon improvements in ammunition for the big guns. Their joint labors came to a sudden halt with the Civil War. Experiments were forgotten in the rush of action.

Delaware was a hotbed of intrigue and excitement. The two lower counties, Kent and Sussex, sympathized with the South. In the upper county, New Castle, the pecuniary pull of the business interests—the Du Ponts among them—was toward the North. In the election of 1860, less than one-third of Delaware's votes were cast for Lincoln. The census that year listed the population as: white, 90,589; free negroes, 19,827; slave negroes, 1,798. By the narrowest of margins, the bankers and manufacturers held the state in line for the Union.

At the outbreak of hostilities, Senior Partner Henry du Pont requested the War Department to exempt his

workmen from enforced military duty on the ground
that they were of greater service to the Union in the
mills than on the firing line. Secretary of War Stanton
granted the plea on condition the men be trained and
held available for service in the event of invasion or insurrection within the state. Accordingly, Henry du Pont
was appointed Major General of Militia for home
defense.

General Henry was in his element—out came the old
West Point manual which had been so reluctantly cast
aside when it was "his turn" to carry on the mills. He
lined up his employes and made a short, sharp speech,
informing each man he could take the oath of allegiance
to the flag—or his hat. Few elected to leave. Fatter pay
envelopes were in the offing.

Two companies of infantry were promptly organized
and drilled rigorously by their sparky boss. The Du Pont
musket men were called to guard the Philadelphia, Baltimore and Wilmington Railroad during a Confederate
cavalry raid; again when Lee made his bold thrust into
Pennsylvania before the battle of Gettysburg.

Once the foe penetrated within fifty miles of Wilmington and grave concern was felt for the safety of the
powder works. Confederate spies were active along the
Brandywine. Two of them, Captain O'Keefe, and one
Ryan, were captured September 17, 1862, within half a
mile of the mills. In their possession were complete
plans of the plant and approaches. They were clapped
into Fort Delaware on Pea Patch Island.

Other Confederate agents were apparently more successful. A series of mystifying explosions racked the
works at intervals, taking thirty-nine lives and destroy-

ing valuable machinery.

Meanwhile, Lammot du Pont had a hectic adventure of his own. The war caught the Union short of saltpeter. By the fall of 1861 the supply of this essential ingredient was dangerously low. Lammot went to Washington and consulted the Secretaries of War and of the Navy. They authorized him to sail at once for England and purchase in his own name as much saltpeter as he could obtain, the transaction to be financed by the Government. The greatest secrecy was necessary, not only to keep the price of saltpeter from skyrocketing, but because England's sympathy was with the South.

Lammot reached London November 19th. After a bit of difficulty in identifying himself at Baring Brothers, the bankers, the young man worked fast. Within a day, acting through brokers, he corralled every pound of salt-peter in England—some two thousand tons—and obtained options on cargoes en route from East India. He contracted for freight space on ships in London, Liverpool and Greenock.

The ships were about ready to hoist anchor for America when a peremptory order from the British Government commanded them to halt. Mason and Slidell, Confederate envoys on their way to England, had been taken as prisoners from a British vessel, the *Trent*, by Union officers and whisked to Boston. Pending protest of this bold defiance of international law, the British declared an embargo on all shipments to America. This tied up Lammot du Pont's precious saltpeter, for which the Union had paid $400,000.

His mission was so personal and important du Pont did not dare wait to exchange letters with Washington.

He caught the fastest available ship and was in the capital the day after Christmas. Here he learned that Mason and Slidell had been released. On New Year's Day, he was on his way back to England, bearing a letter from the State Department to Charles Francis Adams, the American Minister, asking the latter to do everything he could "for the relief of E. I. du Pont de Nemours & Company."

In London the atmosphere had grown less tense. The British embargo was removed January 18, 1862. By the first of February, Lammot's saltpeter was bounding over the waves to America. He followed at once. It was a very relieved though weary young man who walked into his uncle Henry's office a fortnight later. During Lammot's absence, his cousin Eugene, oldest son of Alexis, had been helping out in the laboratory.

The cousins worked indefatigably in improvements on both military and blasting powder. Lammot also had the general supervision of the Wapwallopen works. The double task was extremely wearing. The summer following his return from abroad, he was stricken with typhoid fever. Again, in June, 1864, he was ill with acute rheumatism. His tall, spare frame lost flesh he could ill afford and gave him a gaunt, spectral appearance. His eyes became strained. He had to be pried, almost forcibly, from his laboratory.

Although 4,000,000 pounds of powder, at a price upward of $1,000,000, was sold to the Army and Navy during the Civil War, the company mourned the loss of its Californian, West Indian and Southern trade. Shipments to California were cut off due to risk of capture by Confederate privateers. Overland transport was not pos-

sible. By the fall of 1863 the miners were in desperate
need of blasting powder. The flow of gold was threatened. Weary of appealing to the Government, a group of
Californians chipped in $100,000 and built powder mills
of their own. Soon this plant, the California Powder
Works, was flourishing. Using Chinese labor and saltpeter imported from India across the Pacific, their prices
were lower than those of the Eastern manufacturers.
The Du Ponts sadly saw a fertile market slipping away
from them.

They were also exceedingly vexed over proposals, in
and out of Congress, that the Government manufacture
its own powder. This proposal had been recommended to
the War Department as far back as 1837. When it was
renewed in 1862, Henry du Pont wrote a resentful letter
to an army officer: "The market price was twenty cents
in December when we supplied the Government at eighteen cents; the present price compared to current rates of
trade is two dollars a barrel better for the Government
than it ought to be by present prices of materials. There
is no country in the world where the Government ob-
tains its powder on as favorable terms as in the United
States. When our Mr. Lammot du Pont was in England
in January and February last, the British Government
was paying its contractors, in time of peace, eighty shil-
lings per hundred pounds for cannon powder, one hundred and ten for musket, one hundred and twenty for
rifle—a good deal above the war prices here; the British
manufacturer having the benefit of free saltpeter and
brimstone, while the American manufacturer pays a
heavy duty on both."

The powder men were even more indignant over the

war taxes on their product—though with each penny increase in taxes, their charge in turn to the Government rose automatically, a little, it was suspected, being added for good measure. Though the manufacturers were always ready with elaborate schedules showing the increased cost of labor and materials, the Government was often lax in its payments, then paid only part in cash and the rest in certificates of indebtedness. The correspondence books of the company show that Henry du Pont put in many hours writing dunning letters to various Government departments.

During the Civil War, two Du Ponts did, however, see actual service outside the powder mills.

One was Henry Algernon du Pont, General Henry's eldest son, who followed his father's footsteps by entering West Point, graduating first in the class of 1861. He immediately entered active service in the war, emerging in 1865 as brevet-Colonel. As a Captain of Horse Artillery he won the Congressional Medal of Honor for gallantry in action. His most remembered act, however, was his refusal to shell historic buildings in Lexington, Virginia, during the sack of the Valley of Virginia by General David Hunter in 1864.

The other, Samuel Francis du Pont, risen to the post of Commodore in the Navy, had more harrowing experiences. A squadron of seventy-five vessels under his command captured Port Royal, South Carolina, on November 7, 1861. The victory broke the naval power of the Confederacy. Samuel Francis, grown into a stout, stately gentleman, with all the friendly charm of his father, Victor, was hailed as a hero. Congress lauded him in formal resolutions and, in July, 1862, he was promoted to the rank of Rear Admiral. He was given the choice command, the South Atlantic Blockading Squadron.

Nine months later, he failed to force a passage through the harbor of Charleston, South Carolina, with turret iron-clads, and, at his own request, was relieved of his command. Disappointed, derided, broken-hearted beneath his mask of dignity, as puzzled as a child over the twist of fate that clouded a distinguished career, he returned to the old family home, Louviers, and died two years later in the arms of his cousin-wife, Sophie.

The consensus of naval opinion was that Admiral du Pont was shabbily treated. By enactment of Congress, Du Pont Circle in Washington was named for him and, in 1884, a bronze statue of him erected there. A few years ago the statue was removed to make way for a fountain, but the Circle still bears his name.

Henry A. and Samuel F. were the first and last Du Ponts to appear prominently in the active military records of their country. The family has evidently found it more to its taste to make powder than to fire it.

THE REIGN OF HENRY

THE main and only office of the du Pont Company was a small, square one-story structure of stone containing four rooms and an annex. Built by the first Irénée du Pont, it lay midway between his dwelling on the hill and the gate to the original powder mill. The senior partner occupied the annex.

From this office, with a staff never exceeding four men and a boy, Henry du Pont, from 1850 to 1889, conducted a business of constantly increasing magnitude and complexity. He, alone, was master of its every detail. His junior partners, nephews, were engaged in gruelling and absorbing tasks in the mills or the laboratory. The juniors, in the years immediately following the Civil War, became three: Eleuthère Irénée 2nd and Lammot, sons of Alfred, and Eugene, eldest son of Alexis du Pont. Thus, each son of the founder was still represented.

In the floor, under Henry du Pont's desk, forty years of incessant work and scuffling of his feet wore a hole resembling very much the shape of a cobbler's seat. At that desk, his old-fashioned quill pen scratched out an average of six thousand letters a year. Even after the typewriter came in, he clung to longhand, scribbling his

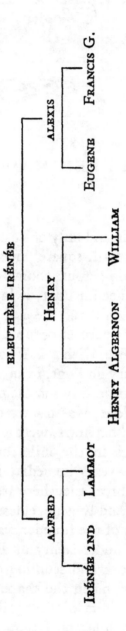

THE REIGN OF HENRY
1850–1889

ELEUTHÈRE IRÉNÉE

ALFRED — HENRY — ALEXIS

IRÉNÉE 2ND   LAMMOT   EUGENE   FRANCIS G.

HENRY ALGERNON   WILLIAM

letters in pencil before permitting the correspondence clerk to transcribe them on the newfangled device. By which it may be inferred that innovation irked this Du Pont, who was known to every man, woman and child for miles around as "Mr. Henry" or "the General." It did. Yet, during his unparalleled régime, the company grew steadily in power and prestige.

The General was a tall, erect person, with eyes that could blaze or beam, and with a fringe of beard that ran from ear to ear but did not conceal a cleft in his chin that had come straight down the line from his paternal great-grandmother, Anne de Montchanin. In manner he was decisive, to the point of gruffness. In business he could drive a shrewder bargain than the next man, and with as little compunction. But he preserved a certain primal simplicity. He knew every employe by name and he always listened to their problems. In his safe he kept a box where the workmen could deposit deeds, wills or other valuable papers.

Each day the General inspected some portion of the works or the company farmlands, using a horse and a single-seater buggy with a high, closed top. Usually a couple of hound dogs ran ahead. The outfit was easily recognizable and could be seen from a distance. Yet, occasionally, the boss caught someone napping. One warm day, he came upon a farmhand who was rubbing sleep from his eyes while the dogs frisked about him. "Ought to known you was coming, Mister Henry, when I saw the dogs," remarked the man, sheepishly. "Humpf, that's why I bring 'em along, to wake you fellows up," grunted the General, brusquely but without anger.

[119]

He had an eye for pulchritude and never passed up a chance to chat with a pretty woman. Many a girl, walking on the road, was surprised to hear a cluck behind her, followed by a jovial invitation to jump into the General's famous buggy. He had a fondness, too, for silk hats, always wearing one in the evenings when he came down to the office to write his letters, as was his custom.

The silk hat came in handy one night. About nine o'clock he heard a ringing or whistling sound somewhere along the powder line. The only mills in operation that night in the Upper Yard were the glazing mills. The senior partner lighted his little square lantern with its tallow dip and quickly made his way to the Upper Banks, the workmen's village nearby. He routed out Thomas Kane, foreman of the Upper Yard. In the flickering lantern light, they traced the whistling sound to the Eagle glazing mill near the dam breast. The main shaft where it entered the mill, had become overheated and was throwing off sparks. Not a moment was to be lost.

While Kane stopped the mill, the General rushed to the Creek, filled his hat with water and poured it over the red hot shaft. After several trips, the shaft cooled and danger of an explosion was averted. The hat was ruined but the General did not regret its loss, under the circumstances.

Henry du Pont's sway over the family was as absolute as his control of the business. When his nephew Lammot, in October, 1865, married Mary Belin, daughter of Henry H. Belin, bookkeeper at the mills, there were those who expected the walls to fall. For Mary Belin was one-quarter Jewish, and the Du Ponts were rather inclined to boast their hitherto unmixed blood.

However, Mary Belin had been born and reared in the Brandywine countryside and was popular. Her paternal grandfather, Augustus Belin, a Frenchman, had been employed by E. I. du Pont in the very early days of the business. So there was little surprise, on the next New Year's Day, when General Henry's modest rig halted at Lammot's house and he left a gift for the bride. It was a traditional custom for the men of the family, on New Year's Day, to call upon the women of the clan, bearing presents. The little ceremony meant that Mary Belin, by formal ukase, was now a Du Pont in good standing.

However, in those quick moving years following the war, Henry du Pont had many other things on his mind. Thousands of miles of railroad track were being laid, ore and iron deposits uncovered, great construction projects launched. Huge amounts of blasting powder were needed. The mills were working at a pace comparable to that of war days.

Suddenly there came an annoying interruption. The Government, by auction, began disposing of millions of pounds of surplus war powder. Speculators snapped up this powder, good, bad and indifferent, at bargain prices, and raided the markets of the large companies. The trade was soon sadly disorganized. Henry du Pont rushed his New York agent and right hand man, F. L. Kneeland, to Washington with a proposition to take over all the surplus government stocks. "I had a talk with Captain Crispin this morning," Kneeland reported. "He says he can see that it would be to the interest of the Government to have their powder handled by one large concern. But he does not think there is a man in the entire department, from the Secretary of War down, that would dare to make such an arrangement." A little later: "Your old friend Goodwin of the Empire Mills bought 1,000 barrels of government powder at St. Louis at seven and one-half cents a pound and shipped it to Pittsburgh, so look out for a raid on prices at that point."

The Du Ponts bought up what quantities of the government powder they could. Sometimes it was good and sometimes it was a distressing assortment of "percussion caps, fuses, ends of rope, old nails, spikes, paper and brass balls." The better powder was toned up—in fact the company was still "working over" Civil War powder in 1890—and sold at the best price possible.

For five years the powder trade was about as tranquil as a dog pit. Agents stole customers beneath each other's noses. Representatives of the same company undercut each other. Bribery and sabotage were common. The railroads openly gave rebates to the concerns that furnished powder for their construction work.

Though the Du Ponts held their own in the scramble, the unsettled conditions were equally offensive to General Henry's judgment and his pocketbook. Under his leadership, the larger powder manufacturers worked out an adroit plan to "stabilize" the industry through formation of a trade association.

On the morning of April 23, 1872, representatives of six gunpowder manufacturers met in the New York office of the du Pont Company at 70 Wall Street and organized the Gunpowder Trade Association of the United States, later more popularly known as the Powder Trust. Under the scheme of association, the three largest companies—Du Pont, Laflin & Rand, and Hazard—were given ten votes each; the Oriental Powder Company six votes; the American and Miami Powder companies four votes each. The Du Pont spokesman was F. L. Kneeland. A committee of four was appointed to arrange a schedule of prices "for the prominent markets of the United States." It was agreed that the members of the Association would not compete in the purchase of raw materials, would allocate markets where most convenient economically and would stop the devastating competition of individual agents.

The Gunpowder Trade Association lived longer than any similar combination with the exception of the Standard Oil Company. This powder pool operated with machine-like effectiveness, never once breaking down. Dominated from the beginning by Du Pont, Laflin & Rand, and Hazard, these companies used it with ruthless efficiency to eliminate or to gain control of smaller companies.

Thus, in 1875, by a campaign of underselling, conducted through the Association, the Du Ponts gained a substantial interest in the California Powder Works. The next year they bought heavily into the Hazard Powder Company, one of the original Big Three, which had barely staggered through the Panic of 1873. By 1880, the company owned two plants in the coal regions—Wapwallopen and mills at Tamaqua, Pa.—and listed its holdings "outside of the coal fields" as: the Brandywine Mills; the Hazard Powder Company; the Sycamore Mills; two-thirds of the Oriental Powder Company; one-third of the Austin Powder Mills; thirteen-twentieths of the California Powder Works.

No matter how hard times were for other concerns,

the Du Ponts always seemed to flourish. One key to their success was personal management.

"We build our own machinery," wrote Henry du Pont, in turning down an applicant for a job as engineer. "We draw our own plans; make our own patterns; and have never employed anyone to design or construct our mills or machinery, dams or races, roads or anything else; being our own engineers and superintendents of all work done at our mills, both here and in Pennsylvania."

To the men of Du Pont, in those laborious foundation years, the company was their religion and their life. The toil of the day, and the night, left no time or energy for lighter activities. The grind wore some of the partners down in their prime. Every few years another headstone appeared among the cluster about the grave of Du Pont de Nemours in the family cemetery—a shaded enclosure, quiet and secluded, on a little rise near the original mill.

In 1877, both Eleuthère Irénée du Pont 2nd, and his wife, Charlotte Henderson du Pont, entered this restful sanctuary. He had contracted tuberculosis from exposure and exhaustion; she had been in poor health for some years. He was but forty-eight. As factory superintendent, then partner for twenty-seven years, this eldest son of the eldest son of the founder had known no world save the colony on the Brandywine. Except for brief business trips, he was never far from the powder line.

Charlotte du Pont, a proud and temperamental Virginian, did not fit into the dull, drab routine of life on the Brandywine. She disliked the fetid odor of black powder and differed very decisively with her Yankee in-laws over the vital issues that culminated at Appomattox. After the Civil War, she traveled much in

Europe on a quest for health. Her three sons, Alfred I., Louis and Maurice were left at home in the care of an Alsatian nurse. As a result the youngsters escaped much of the rigorous discipline that conformed their numerous cousins to the traditional family pattern. Alfred, the oldest, was thirteen when his father died. Irénée 2nd's last words to the boy were to carry on in the family business.

After the death of Irénée 2nd, manufacturing operations were directed by the two sons of Alexis, Eugene du Pont, and his younger brother, Francis G. Two of the three groups of mills, the Lower and the Hagley Yards, were placed in the care of Francis G. Facilities at Hagley had now been expanded to include machine and millwright shops, carpenter and blacksmith shops, and a keg factory and packing house.

The Upper Yard contained the saltpeter refinery and laboratory where "our chemist," Lammot du Pont, worked out and patented improvement after improvement in military propellants and powder-making machinery.

Although he would not confess it, Henry du Pont, at sixty-six, began to bend under his burdens. He tacitly admitted as much in 1878, when he drew his sons, Henry Algernon and William, into the firm as junior partners. William, twenty-three, was placed in charge of the farmlands. The position suited him perfectly. Sturdy as a young bull, he was a slow, plodding type who seemed to belong to the soil.

On the other hand, Henry A., now a man of forty, who resigned his commission as Colonel in the regular army to come to the aid of his clan, was decidedly a man of the world. With his carefully waxed moustache, nicety of manners and drawing room accomplishments, Henry Algernon might have been a Parisian gallant, just off the Boulevards. Yet there was iron in his fibre and his military training had made him somewhat of a diplomat in handling men. His wife was more delighted than he at the opportunity to settle in a permanent home, after four years of army life. Before her marriage in 1874, she was Mary Pauline Foster, daughter of Herman Ten Eyck Foster, of New York.

Henry A. became a most decided asset to the firm. He took charge of traffic arrangements and negotiations with the railroads, a delicate and important mission in those days of rebates and drawbacks. These contacts later led to his becoming president of the Wilmington and Northern Railroad, a position that fitted in quite advantageously with his Du Pont tasks.

Subtly, Henry A. sought to inaugurate changes in his father's set methods. Though he was never able to persuade the old gentleman to hire a stenographer, he cagily won his way on other points. His diplomatic hand may have been behind a rather peremptory "suggestion" from the Ordnance Department of the Army that the mills, roads and yards on the Brandywine should be illuminated by more modern means than rows of lanterns. Electric lights were strung. Later a spur of the railroad was run into the yard. General Henry permitted the railways to supplement, but not to supplant, his pet mule teams.

J. W. Macklem, who was Henry du Pont's first office boy, recalls other innovations. "Everybody took chances in those days, members of the Du Pont family included," says Macklem. "In 1883, the graining mill was rebuilt after a fire. The new mill was of the high elevator type and equipped with horseshoe magnets, the latest safety device. The magnets were designed to withdraw any small piece of iron or steel that might accidentally get into the powder and, in passing through, strike a spark and cause an explosion. Eugene du Pont, his brother, Francis G., Colonel Henry A. du Pont, George Mathewson, the millwright, and others tested the mill in September. After safely putting about fifty kegs of rifle powder through the mill, the Du Ponts left. In a few moments, Mathewson called me over and pointed out one of the magnets, which was firmly clutching a large iron nail. In some unaccountable manner, it had escaped detection by the workmen. Magnetic attraction had pulled it out of the powder mass. If the magnet had not done its work, and the nail had passed on through the rolls and cutters, well, I might not be here to tell the story."

Throughout the world, since Schoenbein's invention of guncotton in 1845, and Ascanio Sobrero's invention, in 1846, of nitroglycerin, chemical engineers had sought a safe way to make military and commercial use of these super-powerful agencies. In 1865, the key was found.

Alfred Bernhard Nobel, a Swedish chemist and engineer, patented a process for detonating nitroglycerin with fulminate caps. The discovery was not only to revolutionize the explosives industry but to change the very face of nature itself, leveling mountains, deepening harbors, boring tunnels, uncovering new vast deposits of minerals.

Henry du Pont, at his desk on the Brandywine, scoffed at Nobel's process, which he contemptuously labeled "blasting oil." The General minced no words in his correspondence with his agents: "Since writing to you on the subject of Blasting Oil, we have seen an interesting article on the subject in the last number of the *Scientific American*, taken from some European paper, which confirms the impression we had and proves that its use would be much more dangerous than gunpowder." And a few weeks later: "We thank you for the slip containing account of the explosion at San Francisco. We think that will be the end of Nitro-Glycerin in this continent."

In fact, there were many terrible explosions and the end predicted by the General seemed at hand in 1868, when Nobel's own plant near Stockholm blew up, and the importation or use of nitroglycerin was forbidden in England and Belgium. However, that year Nobel combined nitroglycerin with an inert, absorbent substance, kieselguhr, and succeeded in reducing the sensitiveness of the explosive. He patented his new mixture and called it "dynamite."

Some American companies began to market the new "high explosive" under all sorts of picturesque names but Henry du Pont stuck to his guns. One can see his quill pen biting into the paper as he wrote: "The California Company are selling in Colorado a new article which they call Hercules, which is blasting powder soaked in Nitro-Glycerine. It is only a matter of time *how soon* a man will lose his life who uses Hercules, Giant, Dualin, Dynamite, Nitro-Glycerine, Guncotton, Averhard's Patent, or any explosive of that nature.

They are all vastly more dangerous than Gunpowder, and no man's life is safe who uses them." In 1873 he warned the Pennsylvania Railroad against transporting any "compounds of nitro-glycerine," adding: "We have sent circulars to all our agents cautioning them against allowing any such to be stored in our magazines."

Three years later, the head of the House of Du Pont began to weaken, permitting the California Powder Works, in which the Du Ponts were now the largest stockholder, to put up a plant for Hercules powder near Cleveland. "We know nothing about the prices of the Hercules powder," the General grudgingly wrote an agent late in 1877. "But please write or telegraph J. W. Willard, Hercules Powder Company, Cleveland, Ohio, and he will post you. On August 1st last he wrote to know if our agents could help in the sale of Hercules, to which we consented, provided they do not store it in our magazines. It is the best of all patent explosives."

Two years later General Henry's conversion was complete. Lammot du Pont, after thorough experiments, became convinced that dynamite, as a substitute for blasting powder, was on the scene to stay. Lammot's dander did not often rise. When it did, nothing could move him. His was the most original, perhaps the only, really original scientific mind produced in the family. His conviction upon the future of high explosives was so strong that he determined to manufacture dynamite in a plant of his own, if the company would not. He had actually obtained an option on a site near Wilmington when Henry du Pont gave in and, on January 29, 1880, announced laconically: "We are going into the high explosive business—that is, we are forming a company in which we are heavily interested to manufacture the same, and have not as yet fully determined on the name."

The new company, destined to become the largest high explosives plant in the world, was located at Gibbstown, New Jersey, at the junction of the Repauno Creek and the Delaware River, opposite Chester, Pennsylvania. It drew its name from the Creek—Repauno Chemical Company. Lammot du Pont became president, young William du Pont secretary and treasurer. Their headquarters, it was decided, should be in Philadelphia. Mary Belin du Pont went looking for a house in Philadelphia large enough to accommodate the numerous progeny that had blessed her union with Lammot.

The owners of Repauno were the Big Three of the Gunpowder Trade Association—Du Pont, Laflin & Rand, and Hazard—each subscribing one-third of the capital. Through Du Pont's ownership of majority stock in the Hazard Company, the Delaware men controlled Repauno. When, in January, 1882, Lammot du Pont left the du Pont Company in order to devote his entire attention to Repauno, he took over the stock in the dynamite plant owned by Du Pont, though not the shares it controlled through Hazard.

"Lammot du Pont resembled Lincoln in a good many ways," recollects his first secretary in the Repauno venture, George H. Kerr. "His unusual height, angular figure, beard and deep set eyes heightened the resemblance, as did his shrewdness and remarkable sense of humor. My first morning on the job he told me to meet him on the steps of the Philadelphia National Bank. He introduced me to the cashier as his secretary and drew out $1,000 which he handed to me, explaining that he was going West for a couple of weeks and that he wanted me to furnish an office he had taken at 305 Walnut street. Then he shook hands and evaporated.

"I located the office, bought a handsome carpet, desks, chairs and what was quite a rarity in those days, a typewriter, and had the walls rather gaudily painted. Mr. du Pont walked in one morning and looked around. 'Have you any of that money left?' he asked. 'No,' I replied. 'Didn't think you had,' he remarked quizzically. 'You're certainly hell for pretty.'

"The office staff consisted of seven clerks in one room, and the president and myself in another. One morning he wanted to send a telegram and rang the bells of both telegraph boxes to call the messengers. I asked him why he rang both and he merely smiled and said: 'Wait and see.' In a short time the door opened and one little messenger boy rushed in and came to a halt before Mr. du Pont.

" 'You got here first, didn't you?'

" 'Yes, sir. I caught the elevator.'

" 'Well, here's a dollar for getting here first,' said Mr. du Pont.

"Just then the second little messenger came in. He was puffing and panting.

" 'Well, you came last, didn't you?'

" 'Yes, sir,' replied the second youngster, 'I missed the elevator and had to run all the way up.'

"Mr. du Pont smiled broadly as he reached into his pocket. 'Well,' he said, 'here is a dollar for coming last.' "

Lammot du Pont held that anyone who visited an

explosives plant, without having to do so, was a fool. Violation of this dictum cost him his life on March 29, 1884.

One morning a salesman named Ackerson, representing Laflin & Rand and the Meachem Arms Company, of St. Louis, brought to Philadelphia a cartridge of competitive dynamite which, it was suspected, infringed on Du Pont patents. Ackerson had a hankering to see the Repauno Works and asked Lammot du Pont to show him around. The latter reluctantly made an appointment for the following morning. The rest of the story is told in a letter written by Henry du Pont, March 30, 1884, to Bernard Peyton, of the California Powder Company, with whom Lammot du Pont had conducted many experiments in high explosives:

"We have just advised you by telegraph of the death of Mr. Lammot du Pont, who was killed by the serious accident which occurred about 10.20 a.m. yesterday at the works of the Repauno Chemical Company.

"Something went wrong in the Nitro-Glycerine house, the person in charge—Mr. Norcross, who was there with two workmen, sent for Mr. Hill, the chemist. Mr. du Pont, who happened to be at the works that day with Mr. Ackerson, of the Laflin and Rand Co., went with Mr. Hill, as did Mr. Ackerson.

"All of these were at or near the house when the explosion took place, and all were instantly killed by the shock;—the bodies being very slightly mutilated.

"The damage to the other buildings was practically nothing; a few panes of glass being broken and a few weather boards knocked off. The most serious part of the accident was the sacrifice of so many useful and valuable lives—but we will not enlarge upon this, knowing how thoroughly you will appreciate the magnitude of our loss.

"As nearly as can be ascertained about 2,000 lbs. of nitro-glycerine exploded."

Lammot du Pont left five sons and six daughters. The night of the tragedy, in a silent, stricken house in Philadelphia, Mary Belin du Pont went to pull down the living room shades. Her eldest son, Pierre Samuel, fourteen, stopped her, saying: "Let me do that, Mother. I am the man of the family now."

After the death of Lammot, the company purchased from his estate most of his stock in Repauno and reorganized the Repauno Chemical Company, with young William du Pont as president. The Repauno offices were removed to Wilmington.

Two youthful members of the family donned overalls and went to work in the mills: Charles I. du Pont, a great-grandson of the original Victor, and the first of Victor's line to become importantly connected with the business; and Alfred I., oldest son of E. I. du Pont 2nd. Alfred I. became assistant to his uncle, Francis G. du Pont, in the Hagley and Lower Yards. He was a clean-cut, slender stripling of twenty, filled with nervous energy and self-confidence. The first member of the family to attend Massachusetts Institute of Technology, he had cut short his chemical courses in his eagerness to be doing practical things.

In 1886, while visiting his brother Louis at Yale, young Alfred met Bessie Gardner, daughter of a prominent New England family, and was dazzled by her wit and beauty. The next year he brought her, as his bride, to the house near the mills where he was born and where his parents had died a decade before. Bessie du Pont was infectiously gay and fun-loving. Wilmingtonians still remember her fine performances in amateur theatricals.

Those happy years, though, did not last. They were clouded even then by a tragedy: Louis du Pont, who had gone from Yale to Harvard Law School, broke down from overstudy and shot himself.

In 1888, Alfred I., as Francis G. du Pont's aide, helped direct the construction of a great new plant for blasting powder, the Mooar Mills, near Keokuk, Iowa. The young man's first individual mission for the company was more delicate. Early in 1889, he spent several weeks in France, Germany, England and Belgium investigating upon request of the United States Army Ordnance Department, a new brown or cocoa prismatic powder developed in European factories.

Alfred 1.'s reports were not overly enthusiastic. However, the United States Government offered to foot the royalty bills and the Du Ponts contracted with Coopal et Cie, of Belgium, and the Rhenish Westphalian Company, of Germany, for the right to manufacture their brown prismatic powder in this country. The German company also granted the Du Ponts a license for its nitrate of ammonia powder.

It was an open secret that the French had now succeeded in making smokeless powder for small arms. Alfred I. did his best to ferret out the formula, but failed. The Frenchmen, though courtesy itself, would not permit him to examine a pound of the new powder. Entirely lacking now was the spirit of eager coöperation, and the motives therefor, which had been so helpful to the young man's great-grandfather in 1802.

Alfred I. returned to the Brandywine in July, 1889, to find his grand-uncle, Henry du Pont, feeble and failing rapidly. The old gentleman had struggled against an overwhelming load of care since the death, five years before, of F. L. Kneeland.

Kneeland, able and forceful, had made himself invaluable as the company's general agent and Henry du Pont's confidential counselor. Constantly on the go, he knew the strength and weakness of every powder manufacturer in the country. He guided each investment the company made of its surplus funds, and seldom pointed it into a loss. To his adroit manipulations could be traced the growing influence of the Du Ponts within the councils of the Gunpowder Trade Association.

The Association now was dominated by the Du Ponts and Laflin & Rand, the latter a combination of several formerly competing manufacturers. The two groups had overlapping interests in many supposedly independent mills, which operated under secret and rigid price-fixing and marketing agreements. Under pain of being cut-rated, or harried in other ways, most of the genuinely independent concerns were forced to fall into line with prices established by the Association. A so-called "Fundamental Agreement" of 1889 divided the United States into seven districts and embraced companies controlling ninety-five per cent of the rifle powder and ninety per cent of the blasting powder output in the country.

Now and then a spunky independent got up on his hind legs and howled a protest. Occasional letters to the papers or complaints to Congressmen coupled the Association and its members with other corporate monopolies then attracting unfavorable attention.

Henry du Pont brushed aside such criticism. He *knew*

that his business methods were right. One of his last communications was a sizzling reply to an agent in Texas who warned him that the people and law-making bodies were growing highly critical of corporations.

"We are a partnership," he wrote, "a firm composed of individuals. We are not an incorporated company, nor have we ever been a corporation. We have always been a firm and never had but one firm name. We manage our own business in every particular, and allow no trusts or combinations to rule or dictate what we shall do or what we shall not do. We make our own powder, and we make our own prices at which it shall be sold, here, there and everywhere in the world where it is for sale. We are every day dictating to our agents as to prices, terms and conditions to govern them; but we do not allow anybody to dictate to us as to what prices, terms and conditions we shall dictate. We do our own dictating.

"If we choose we can as quickly as wires can carry the orders change the price at each and every point in the world where Du Pont powder is for sale. And no trust, no combination, no set of people nor persons can interfere. We have not changed our mode of selling. Our mode today is the same as it has been since our firm was established very nearly a hundred years ago and we expect to continue a hundred years more in the same way."

"We do our own dictating!" The words serve well as *l'envoie* for Henry du Pont, individualist, benevolent autocrat, fifty-five years a powder maker, who died August 8, 1889, on his seventy-seventh birthday.

Chapter Three

THE REIGN OF EUGENE

EUGENE DU PONT, eldest son of Alexis, representing the third generation of the "powder"
Du Ponts, became senior partner and chieftain
of the clan upon the death of General Henry.

After graduating from the University of Pennsylvania,
Eugene had spent the next thirty years of his life in the
company, both in factory management and in the laboratory. He was now fifty and well prepared for his new
responsibilities. Though lacking his predecessor's driv-
ing force and peppery personality, he was thorough,
methodical and a typical Du Pont plodder.

Like many of his generation, he had married a cousin.
She was Amelia Elizabeth du Pont, of the Victor line.

In the reorganization that followed, three new partners were taken into the firm. They were: Alexis I. 2nd,
younger brother of Eugene, who had taken a medical
degree at Pennsylvania but never practiced; Charles I.,
great-grandson of Victor; and Alfred I., eldest son of
the eldest son of the eldest son of the founder. The middle initial of all three names stood, of course, for Irénée.

Francis G., also a brother of Eugene, remained in the
company's laboratory, working out chemical engineer-

THE REIGN OF EUGENE
1889–1902

ELEUTHÈRE IRÉNÉE

ALFRED   HENRY   ALEXIS

LAMMOT   HENRY A.   WILLIAM   EUGENE   FRANCIS G.

IRÉNÉE 2ND   ALEXIS 2ND

ALFRED I.

VICTOR — CHARLES I.

VICTOR — CHARLES I.

ing problems. The late General Henry's two sons were still connected with the company: Henry Algernon, wearying of the heavy rôle his father had destined for him, as a part time partner; and William as President of the Repauno works.

William du Pont had also married a cousin. She was May Lammot du Pont, daughter of Victor, grandson of the original Victor. Her brother, Charles I., was now a junior partner in the company and her sister, Ethel, had married Hamilton MacFarland Barksdale, one of the rising officials in the Repauno company.

It was no secret that William and May du Pont were not happily mated. But the family was thrown into consternation in 1892 when William went to North Dakota, established residence and divorced his wife. It was the first public discord in a family that had prided itself upon its impregnable unity. Furthermore, for a husband to divorce a wife in that era was a matter of universal social condemnation.

Eugene du Pont, as head of the family, handled the scandal in his own way. Few knew what went on behind the scenes but action was short and swift. William "retired" from active business, his duties being largely taken over by Hamilton Barksdale. William sailed for Europe. In London he married Mrs. Annie Rogers Zinn, divorced wife of George Zinn, of Wilmington.

May du Pont was represented in the divorce proceedings by Willard Saulsbury, a young attorney and Democratic politician of Wilmington, who had practiced law with her father. On December 5, 1893, they were married.

With occasional explosions, some more destructive

than others—and a series of mystifying fires which broke out periodically over a four-year span, causing much damage to the company's barns and buildings—E. I. du Pont de Nemours & Company continued its steady expansion under Eugene.

In Europe, smokeless powder was developing rapidly. American manufacturers had two choices: either to purchase the foreign patents, paying heavy royalties, or to puzzle out a feasible composition of their own by methods of trial and error. The Du Ponts decided upon the latter course.

Since guncotton, the chief ingredient of smokeless powder, was a menace in gunpowder mills, the company bought a large tract at Carney's Point, New Jersey, across the Delaware River from Wilmington, and built a wharf there in April, 1891, as well as experimental laboratories. Francis G. du Pont moved a cot into the laboratory and dedicated himself to the task of developing a distinctive "Du Pont Smokeless" both for sporting and military purposes. He took with him as his assistant Pierre Samuel du Pont, the oldest son of his late cousin, Lammot.

There was nothing turbulent about this Pierre Samuel. Of medium height, with placid, blue eyes and a slightly hooked nose, the only indication of his Hebrew strain, he was a mild, studious, reticent young man. There was, however, a dignity about him which made him seem older than his twenty-one years. Since his father's death, Pierre Samuel had taken very seriously his responsibility as eldest son in a family of eleven children. Since receiving his B. S. degree in chemistry the year before at Massachusetts Institute of Technology, he had been helping around the mills. He reveled in physics and mathematical formulae. Francis G. found him useful.

There followed at Carney's Point several years of the most intense research in smokeless powder. From time to time other youngsters of the family were called in to help: Eugene du Pont sent his son, Alexis I. 3rd; while Francis G. enlisted his own sons, Francis I., and A. Felix, as soon as they were old enough.

In the summer of 1893, the experimenters sent out a few small cans of smokeless to friends for opinions. Thereafter, every few months, came a further bulletin of progress. Thus—May 4, 1894: "Radically changed the method of manufacture since last fall; put in new machinery and buildings. We are now making a very fine grade of powder—in every way better than the first. It is not yet on the market, because we desire to have a stock on hand before we distribute it." And a little later: "Our new smokeless powder is ready for the market, as yet only for shot guns; we have not yet adapted it for rifles or revolvers."

Because of its nitro-cellulose base, the new smokeless readily responded to natural dyes. The Du Ponts got "fancy."

"We can dye the Smokeless almost any color desired," Eugene du Pont wrote to an agent, in June, 1896. "We send you a box of thirteen smokeless powders—all of these are on the market and you can judge of the colors. They are Giant; Walsrode; Robin Hood, made in Canada; E. C. Powder; W. A.; Laflin & Rand; Schultz; Austin; S. S. Hazard; Gold Dust, made in California; King; Du Pont; Troisdorf. We also send you some small bottles of Du Pont powder dyed various colors. Some are very pretty. If you do not like any of them we can send others as we have a multitude of shades."

Despite the chromatic appeal, the development of smokeless for large guns lagged. Hudson Maxim, however, had all but solved the problem with his patented process and die for pressing smokeless powder into multi-perforated grains. Maxim, hard put for funds, sold the Du Ponts exclusive use of his formulae and inventions at a royalty of $500 a month for seventeen years. The Carney's Point experimenters quickly set about devising new machines for fabricating Maxim's multiperforated grains.

These were not developed in time for the Spanish-American War, which was fought chiefly with the old brown powder. To suit the guns of the *New Orleans* and other cruisers which had been purchased in Europe, the Government was forced to import English smokeless cordite powder. The situation was not at all pleasing to the Navy which, after the war, erected a smokeless powder plant at Indian Head, Maryland, and went to work in earnest on its own formulae. The Army was not far behind in building a plant at Picatinny, New Jersey.

This action by the Government spurred the private manufacturers. The Du Ponts arranged for interchange of information with the Army and Navy experts, and set up a laboratory for the Government's use at Carney's Point. The work was interrupted one sparkling April day, in 1899, when Captain Sidney Stuart, U. S. A., and five workmen were blown to pieces while compressing wet guncotton in a 13 inch shell.

"No one had any idea the operation would be attended

with danger," wrote Eugene du Pont, in describing the accident. "The operation was as follows: the cavity of the shell, about 8 in. in diameter was lined with thin copper. The conical head was filled with guncotton sawed from blocks to fit it. Two compressed blocks, full size of the cavity, were placed upon the guncotton sawed to fit the conical point. After that, loosely compressed guncotton containing seventy per cent of water was inserted in the end of the shell and forced home by hydraulic pressure. The pressure was ten thousand pounds per square inch and enough to reduce the soft blocks of guncotton to about two inches. The water flowed incessantly from the end of the shell as the guncotton was compressed. When the guncotton was fully compressed it contained at the least eighteen per cent of water. One shell had been loaded in the forenoon of Saturday, and the work on the second shell (which exploded) had proceeded until about twenty pounds of guncotton had been placed therein under pressure. We have pressed very large quantities of guncotton in the regular shapes and never had any accident of any kind. All the guncotton did not explode. We found quite a large amount of this guncotton and no doubt some of it was scattered; the shell and casing were broken into very many fragments, some of them larger than others; the men standing around were badly cut to pieces."

Whatever the tragedies and triumphs of the laboratory, the outer business structure of the company expanded rapidly. Through methods reminiscent of the Standard Oil in its ugliest years, the Du Ponts, Laflin & Rand and their associates in the Gunpowder Trade Association destroyed or absorbed independent companies. Explosives were sold below cost in the territories of the independents until the latter were either forced to go out of business or to sell out to the Association. The pool maintained an elaborate spy system, obtaining business secrets from crooked employees and bribed railroad agents. There were inexplicable "accidents" in the rival mills.

By 1896, the Gunpowder Trade Association embraced seventeen companies. Blandly ignoring the Sherman Anti-trust Act, a law since 1890, the combination governed itself through a secret agreement known as the "Understanding." A syllabus, or abstract copy of the "Understanding" was given to each member, with a key. Letters of the alphabet were used to designate the members.

The Association's methods of eliminating competition were monotonously simple. The moment a new mill in any part of the country seemed to be catching on, it would be visited by a very polite gentleman who would suggest the advantage of a tie-up with the Association through sale of an interest to a member company, generally Du Pont or Laflin & Rand. If the owner remained stubborn, other agents of the Association, not so polite, dropped in on his pet customers and offered them powder, bearing quality trade-marks, at prices considerably lower than those of the independent. As the new mill lowered its prices, the powder pool automatically followed suit. Few independents could stand the gaff. Generally, the fight was over in a few months.

In rapid succession, during Eugene du Pont's régime, the company bought into the Enterprise, Marcellus, Chattanooga, Phoenix, Southern, Equitable, Indiana and Northwestern Powder Companies; also the Dittmar Powder & Chemical Company, Chamberlin Cartridge & Target Company, American Ordnance Company, of Washington, and the Peyton Chemical Works. Some were owned outright, others with Laflin & Rand. The two groups moved also toward control of the high explosives trade. In 1895, they jointly formed the Eastern Dynamite Company, a $2,000,000 coalition of the Repauno Chemical Company, the Hercules Powder Company and the Atlantic Dynamite Company. Eastern soon acquired the New York Powder Company, U. S. Dynamite Company, Clinton Dynamite Company, Mount Wolf Dynamite Company, American Forcite Powder Manufacturing Company and several other concerns.

The American powder barons no sooner had the domestic situation well in hand than they were threatened, suddenly, by a more formidable competition— nothing less than the invasion of European manufacturers, headed by the Nobel Explosives Company of England, and the Rhenish Westphalian Company of Cologne, Germany.

The Nobels were incensed because the Aetna Powder Company, a member of the Gunpowder Trade Association, had sent a cargo of dynamite to South Africa which they, the Nobels, considered exclusively British territory. In retaliation they purchased five hundred acres near Jamesburg, New Jersey, and started to put up a dynamite plant. At the same time the Germans bought an even larger tract near New Brunswick, New Jersey, and planned a chain of mills for every variety of explosives.

Manufacture of metallic blasting caps had actually begun at Jamesburg when there was a hasty calling together of the Gunpowder Trade Association. They decided to offer the Europeans a traffic agreement and division of territory on dynamite sales. Two representatives of the Association—Barksdale, of the Repauno Chemical Company, and Fay, of the Aetna Company—sailed for Europe May 19, 1897.

No fatted calves were slaughtered for them, according to a report relayed by Eugene du Pont to Henry Belin, his relative by marriage, who now managed the Du Ponts' interests in Pennsylvania, with headquarters in Scranton.

"After reaching Europe," Eugene du Pont informed Belin, "Messrs. Fay and Barksdale had many interviews with the Europeans, and found that the latter were determined not only to manufacture blasting caps, but to extend their operations to all explosives; black powder, rifle and blasting, dynamite and smokeless powder. The Europeans were especially desirous of entering into the manufacture of rifle and blasting powder, because smokeless powder in Europe had made great inroads on their sporting powder business; and the flameless explosives had practically driven the blasting powder out of the European markets. Their machinery was standing idle. They intended to put up blasting mills in this country wherever the prices and delivery were such that they could run their mills at a profit."

The foreign companies agreed to remain on their side of the water and to give the American manufacturers a clear field in the Western Hemisphere, North and South America and the West Indies—for a price. That price, they demanded, should be computed on a basis of the American and European output of smokeless military powder, a matter of rather complicated mathematics.

The Nobels were chary of accepting the signatures of Messrs. Fay and Barksdale, so in July Eugene du Pont made a hurried trip to England. The result was a formal pact, called variously the Jamesburg, the London, or the International Agreement, binding American and European manufacturers not to invade each other's territories for ten years. The Americans would be required to pay the foreigners each year a varying sum representing possible losses the Europeans would suffer by keeping out of the American market. But, as Eugene du Pont explained to Henry Belin, the American manufacturers were compelled to accept "the situation as they found it," and "the payments will remove the danger of this competition."

Eugene du Pont was also concerned with another matter, nearer home and of more moment to himself and the family group. As the end of the century neared, it became increasingly difficult to conduct such a complicated business under a simple form of partnership. Though the office force had grown only from General Henry's four men and a boy to seven clerks and stenographers, the business had spread out, fan-wise, with the growth of the country. Profits, for years, had not fallen below one million dollars annually. The volume of the firm's transactions, particularly in connection with controlled companies in other states, required a more flexible form of organization.

Colonel Henry Algernon du Pont suggested that the firm be incorporated. There were many long and serious conferences. Finally, October 23, 1899, E. I. du Pont de Nemours & Company, a corporation, was chartered under the laws of Delaware. The officers were: president, Eugene du Pont; vice presidents, his two brothers, Francis G., and Alexis I. 2nd, and Colonel Henry du Pont; secretary and treasurer, Charles I. du Pont.

The first four each owned twenty per cent of the stock, while Charles I. owned ten per cent, and a similar amount was placed in the name of Alfred I. There was some opposition to this change of business structure among the younger men, who saw themselves shut out of an opportunity to become partners.

Young Pierre S. du Pont was particularly disgruntled that his nine years in the mills had won merely the scant recognition of a small salary and sparse royalty interests in a couple of smokeless powder patents upon which he had worked. When an outside business opportunity was offered to him in Ohio, he accepted gladly, resigning from the company in the midst of the long negotiations and compromises that preceded the formation of the corporation.

In January, 1902, Eugene du Pont was stricken with pneumonia and died on the 28th, after a brief illness.

Eugene's sudden passing at sixty-one was more than a shock to his associates. It was a blighting calamity. For the first time in Du Pont annals, there was no one to take his place. His brothers, Francis G., and Alexis I., vice presidents, were in declining health, as was Charles I., secretary and treasurer. Nor was there hope in Colonel Henry. The doughty warrior had been lured into politics and had his heart set upon donning the dignified toga of a United States Senator. Alfred I. was young, erratic, and totally without business experience.

The dismayed and panic-stricken partners consulted the able Hamilton Barksdale. He refused to consider the presidency "until," as he said, "they had exhausted all efforts to secure a man of the name to take the helm."

A rudderless fortnight ensued. The older Du Ponts bustled about looking strained and worried. Alfred I.'s advice was not asked but he expostulated to his superior, Francis G., one morning: "If you can't run the business, get someone who can." In fact, everyone was so upset that they didn't notice when Alfred spruced up a bit by changing his grimy work clothes to city garb and disappeared out of town for a few days.

The only way to solve the problem apparently was to sell the works, holdings and all, to Laflin & Rand, the only other combination that could possibly swing so large a deal. Finally a meeting was called and those that were left of the reigning tribe foregathered and passed a hesitant resolution empowering Barksdale to negotiate with Laflin & Rand.

At this point, Alfred I., eldest son of the eldest son of the eldest son of the founder, spoke up. "Why not sell to the highest bidder?" he demanded. One of the gloomy group impatiently asked who, besides Laflin & Rand, could possibly raise any such sum as $12,000,000, the tentative valuation placed upon the business.

"I can," replied Alfred I., and one could have heard a pin drop in the somber council chamber. "Gentlemen, I'll take the company."

The young man convinced his skeptical elders that he was not joking. He revealed that he had canvassed the dozen or more young men of his generation and had selected as his associates his two first cousins, Pierre Samuel and Thomas Coleman du Pont; that the three were convinced they could swing the deal. Would the older men give them a chance?

Colonel Henry Algernon, for one, would. His warm words of encouragement won the day.

On March 1, 1902, while the financial details were still being worked out, the three cousins, Alfred, Coleman and Pierre, moved informally into Eugene du Pont's former office. They were like race horses, waiting for the springing of the barrier—Alfred, lanky, careless in dress and manner; Coleman, a mountainous individual with the build of a heavyweight boxer; Pierre, small, slender, neatly-garbed. Their one point of physical similarity was the tell-tale cleft in the chin.

With glowing imaginations but cool heads, the new partners had mapped their plans, not only for saving the company but for guiding it to new heights of glory and power. They would bring it in tune with Twentieth Century Industry—and make it lead the orchestra. Coleman, an experienced organizer and business executive, would be president; Pierre, cautious and prudent, would be treasurer; fiery, incisive Alfred, a powder maker and a good one, would be vice president, in command of the mills.

The following July Fourth, a gala fête marked the one-hundredth anniversary of the settlement of the Du Ponts on the Brandywine. There were fireworks, music, dancing. Du Pont men, women and children mingled with Du Pont workmen and their families. In this gaiety there was pathos. Notices were already posted that the executive offices of the company were to be moved to Wilmington. No longer would the members of the firm labor side by side with their workmen. Intimate ties of three generations would be broken.

A few days later, a gnarled old veteran of the powder line, Pierre Gentieu, heading a committee of the workmen, stood near the desk used by old General Henry and haltingly paid tribute to the new order.

On one side stood the Du Pont men of the old firm, tired, aging, ill; on the other, the three young cousins, in the full flush of mental and physical vigor, in whose hands the future of the clan lay.

Part Four

EXPANSION VERTICAL

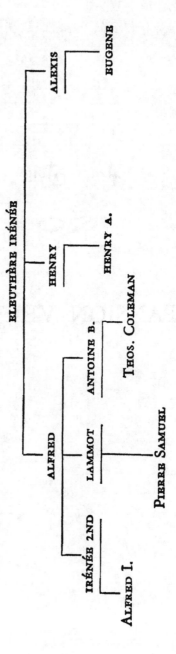

THE REIGN OF THREE COUSINS
1902–1915

ALFRED   ELEUTHÈRE IRÉNÉE   HENRY   ALEXIS

IRÉNÉE 2ND   LAMMOT   ANTOINE B.   HENRY A.   EUGENE

ALFRED I.   PIERRE SAMUEL   THOS. COLEMAN

Chapter One

ENTER A ROBBER BARON

W HEN they took over the family business,
Coleman and Alfred I. du Pont were thirty-
eight, Pierre just turned thirty-two. They
were grandsons of Alfred Victor, oldest son of the
founder.

Coleman, Alfred and Pierre. And the greatest of these
was Coleman!

A huge, crude, colorful, earthy, Rabelaisian individual, Coleman du Pont burst upon the powder industry
like a force of nature. Within three years he and his
cousins were masters of an impregnable monopoly.

Coleman sprang from a branch of the family that had
nothing to do with the powder business. His father,
Antoine Bidermann du Pont, youngest son of Alfred
Victor, had yearned for adventure. Rebelling against
what seemed to him a monotonous occupation, he quar-
reled with his father and went West to seek his fortune.
This was in the rough and rowdy decade preceding the
Civil War. He finally settled in Louisville, Kentucky,
where he married Ellen Susan Coleman. It was there that
his first son, Thomas Coleman, was born, December 11,
1863. Antoine Bidermann du Pont had his average share

[155]

of ups and downs, finally acquiring an interest in a paper mill, street railroads and coal mines in western Kentucky.

Coleman grew into a physical giant. At nineteen he stood six feet four inches and weighed 210 pounds. At Urbana (Ohio) University, he went in for every form of athletics—he was stroke of the crew, baseball and football captain, once ran 100 yards in 10 seconds flat, could swim, shoot and ride, was anchor man in tug of war competitions, and held his own in the boxing and wrestling rings. But he couldn't learn to spell, and flunked in many studies.

From Urbana, Coleman went to the Massachusetts Institute of Technology for a course in mining engineering. Here he came into contact with his cousin, Alfred I., who was studying chemistry. At "Tech," Coleman found a student had to work or quit. He worked.

When he got out, at twenty-two, his father sent him to Central City, Kentucky, to learn coal mining, from underground up. The term "City" was a decided euphemism. Central City was a crude, sprawling mining village with but one general store and a few dozen unpainted, clapboard shacks.

Coleman shouldered a pick and dug coal, drove mules, shod horses in the blacksmith's shop, ran an engine and tackled what engineering problems there were. He mixed with the miners, attended their weddings and funerals and became the most popular man on the property. His grimy mates loved his rough and ready horseplay, practical jokes and sleight of hand tricks with cards, eggs and other objects, at which he was adept. Saturday nights Coleman presided over roaring Falstaffian feasts of beer and kraut and the miners elected him a member of the Knights of Labor, the union of that day.

He rose to be superintendent and was largely instrumental in developing the Central Coal and Iron Company into an extensive enterprise. Central City grew into a prosperous industrial town of 7,500 inhabitants, and long rows of model dwellings. Superintendent du Pont liked to build and he knew that men comfortably housed and fed would mine more coal.

The Kentucky du Ponts never lost contact with their Brandywine relatives. Coleman acted as agent for the du Pont Company in western Kentucky and passed more than one vacation in Delaware. During his Central City days, he married his cousin, Alice du Pont, sister of Charles I., of the Victor line, and of May, divorced wife of William.

In 1893, at thirty, Coleman du Pont pulled up stakes and left the Kentucky coal mines, to explore wider fields.

"The best man in the western Kentucky coal region," he subsequently explained, "the president of the biggest coal company there, was getting only $4,000 a year. Shucks, that was no money. I made up my mind to break into the biggest industry in the country—steel.

"Arthur J. Moxham, the steel man of Johnstown, Pa., and Tom L. Johnson, afterward Mayor of Cleveland, had started to work for my father at fifty cents a day, so I got a job as general manager with their concern in Johnstown."

What was then the Johnson Company afterward became the Lorain Steel Company, now a subsidiary of the United States Steel Corporation.

"Old Man" Moxham, as everyone called the Johnson

Company's chief stockholder, was an old-fashioned, homely type of capitalist, who carried an umbrella on sunny days, and put his money to a hundred uses. He liked Coleman and saw to it that the young man learned not only the art of steel making but the intricacies of finance and of promotion. Coleman was an apt pupil. Soon he felt ready to branch out on his own. He took a flier in a button factory that failed before it made a button, then turned his attention to street railways. He bought the car line in Johnstown and made it pay. Then he resigned from the Johnson Company and formed an organization to build street railways all over the country.

As Coleman passed from the Johnson Company to more lucrative pastures, another Du Pont came in. This was young Pierre Samuel, who, as we have noted, had grown weary of the long hours, small pay and scant recognition of his labors in the smokeless powder laboratory at Carney's Point. In 1899, Coleman got Pierre a job liquidating realty holdings of the Johnson Company in Lorain, Ohio. Pierre liked the new connection so well that he invested $50,000, which his father had bequeathed him, in the Johnson Company and became its president. "Old Man" Moxham was kind enough, also, to guide Pierre's education in the ways of finance.

For the next three years Coleman roamed the country, successfully promoting street car lines in New York State, New Jersey, Alabama and elsewhere, while Pierre stuck to his desk. It was at this stage of their respective careers that Cousin Alfred I. called upon them to take the helm with him and keep the du Pont Company in the family.

ENTER A ROBBER BARON

Coleman was not particularly enthusiastic at first. He loathed the ordinary routine of conventional business and, besides, was rapidly making his pile as a promoter, and planning to retire at forty. He was happiest roaming the hunting field with gun and dog or snaring trout in a mountain stream. Alfred I. persuaded him, however, that there was bigger game, and just as much fun, at that particular time, in the powder business. So Coleman swung into line and joined Alfred and Pierre at the old Waldorf-Astoria Hotel in New York. Here, over choice food and wines, a new du Pont Company was born.

Pierre brought with him from Ohio a short, stocky young man of twenty-three, with darting brown eyes and a steel trap mouth, as shy and retiring in manner as Pierre himself. This was John Jacob Raskob, whom Pierre had taken from a $45 a month stenographer's job in a Lockport, New York, pump concern, and made his secretary. Son of an Irish mother and an Alsatian cigar maker, long dead, young Raskob and his boss had become inseparable. The association was to make Raskob a pivotal figure in the rejuvenated du Pont Company.

When the time came to discuss the practical details of the purchase with the members of the old firm, Coleman did the talking. Without batting an eye, he made an extraordinary proposal: he, Alfred and Pierre would pay $12,000,000 for the company, not in cash, but in four per cent notes. If this offer was satisfactory, a bonus of twenty-five per cent, or $3,000,000, in stock of the new corporation would be distributed among the stockholders of the old company.

"Gentlemen, we are going to keep the company in the family and we are going to make it pay!" exclaimed

Coleman, emphatically. "But you wouldn't want to cripple our plans by tying up all our cash, would you? This is a fair proposition. Will you accept it?"

Alexis I. looked at Francis G., and Francis G. looked at Henry A. They all looked at Coleman, at the bulk of him, at the muscles that almost burst the seams of his coat, at the flashing conqueror's eyes, the big, hawk-like nose, and the jutting chin with the family cleft. This frontier giant was a new type of Du Pont. They were overwhelmed, and rather proud of being overwhelmed.

Finally Colonel Henry said: "I accept, if the others do."

And Francis G., and frail Alexis and Charles I. said, one by one: "I accept."

And so it was arranged.

The only cash the cousins had to raise was $3,000— the sum needed to incorporate a new company, which they capitalized at $20,000,000, for the purpose of purchasing the 1899 corporation. The new partners took more than $8,000,000 of the new stock as promoters' profits, Coleman getting the larger share, Alfred and Pierre equal amounts. Of course, all this stock was pledged as security for the $12,000,000 purchase money notes.

Surveying the explosives industry, Coleman du Pont saw to his satisfaction that the materials for a Powder Trust were at hand. It was an era of combination. Holding companies were beginning to flower, beautifully and effectively. Businesses were beginning to merge, through vertical financial control, from the top down. Later, these groups were to coalesce, in turn, into the huge combinations of our day.

The du Pont Company, in slow, conservative fashion,

had forged to unquestioned leadership in its industry. Now, in the new management, men and opportunity met. Alfred and Pierre were practical powder makers. Coleman had imagination, a mind that thought systematically and in great arcs, a lust for conquest—and a ruthless determination to accomplish whatever he set out to do. A resolute and resourceful fighter, he believed in hewing his way through opposition, like a scythe decimating a wheat field.

To build his trust, Coleman now conceived a plan magnificent in its simplicity:

Through a few operating corporations, the fewer the better, he would take over all the companies affiliated with the Gunpowder Trade Association; dissolve them; run their plants through his operating corporations; and, finally, bind these operating corporations in one great holding company. This super-company would be able to fix prices and prescribe policies with a great deal more certainty than a trade association.

This human dynamo at Du Pont's head swung into action with a series of financial maneuvers that soon had the trade dizzy. He formed and manipulated companies and subsidiary companies, and sub-subsidiaries, and sub-sub-subs, with the agility of a circus juggler.

In 1902, the Du Ponts had minority holdings in fifteen explosives companies; majority in one; fifty per cent in one; and the entire capital stock of the Hazard Powder Company, which had minority holdings in six other companies. Du Pont took precedence over Laflin & Rand, which held minority stock in thirteen companies; fifty per cent in two companies; majority interests in two.

Coleman realized that, if Du Pont could absorb Laflin

& Rand, it would be well on its way toward monopoly. With the aid of his keen treasurer, Pierre, and the latter's alert man, Raskob, he opened negotiations with ten men who held 5,524 shares of the 10,000 Laflin & Rand total. They finally agreed upon the price as $4,000,000. The Delaware Securities Company was organized for the purpose of purchasing and holding the Laflin & Rand stock.

There was a string, however, to the agreement. The ten Laflin & Rand men demanded that Du Pont also buy 950 shares they held in the Moosic Powder Company of Pennsylvania. This didn't please Coleman particularly. But he promptly organized another subsidiary company for the purpose of purchasing for $2,000,000 the entire Moosic stock.

Both purchases were made with bonds of the Du Pont subsidiaries. The subsidiaries at once transferred the majority of their stock to the du Pont Company. The Du Ponts now had voting control of Laflin & Rand and of Moosic—without having extracted a single dollar from their treasury.

In rapid succession, other powder concerns were likewise bought up, with stock or bonds of Du Pont subsidiaries. By the close of 1902, Du Pont had obtained practically complete control of all companies in the powder and explosives business that once had been members of the Gunpowder Trade Association.

Over his desk, in Wilmington's Equitable Building, Coleman kept a chart, upon which he gleefully checked each new acquisition. Those who called upon the Du Pont president generally found him in his shirt sleeves, a cigarette between his lips. Sometimes he entertained them with feats of legerdemain. Or he would wind up a mechanical frog and set it hopping about the room. It delighted him to "catch" a caller with an exploding cigar or a stick of "candy" made of metal.

Such pleasantries, however, diverted but did not deflect his mind from more serious business. He had an aversion for details. One of his pet expressions was: "Let me have the round figures, not the pennies."

He and his partners were thinking in figures both round and large by the spring of 1903, a year after the trust-building campaign had been launched. On May 13th, of that year, Coleman, Pierre and Alfred formed in New Jersey the super-holding company—E. I. du Pont de Nemours Powder Company of New Jersey—which Coleman had planned as the towering apex of his financial structure. It was capitalized in the impressive amount of $50,000,000, equally divided into common and preferred stock. A majority of this stock, $15,000,000 preferred and $13,600,000 common, was issued to the du Pont corporation in Delaware. In return the Delaware corporation transferred to the New Jersey holding company all equities in the numerous companies that had fallen into Coleman's bag.

Now the Du Ponts really *were* Big Business and Coleman had the instrument he wanted in his march toward monopoly.

That fall Moosic Powder was merged with three other companies into a Pennsylvania subsidiary—E. I. du Pont de Nemours Company of Pennsylvania. This new Du Pont arm monopolized blasting and explosives sales in the coal regions.

The Du Pont offices, from a small suite, soon flowed

over an entire floor in the Equitable Building. Close tab
was kept over each mill and group of mills through a
"Trade Record Bureau." Each pound of powder or
cartridge of dynamite sold by a subsidiary had to be
reported, in duplicate, to this bureau. Each mill was
told to whom and in what territory it could sell, and
the price. Incidentally, prices had been steadily rising
since the acquisition of Laflin & Rand. Profits rose with
equal steadiness. Net returns in 1904 were $4,000,000.

In that year a $10,000,000 subsidiary—the du Pont
International Powder Company—was organized in Delaware to take over the International Smokeless Powder &
Chemical Company. This was a brilliant move, for
International sold large quantities of ordnance powder
to the Army and Navy, and its president, Colonel Edmund G. Buckner, was famous as a salesman. He was a
salty gentleman, with a sense of humor as acrid as his
powder. Coleman du Pont enticed him into the organization and made him sales manager. He was Du Pont's ace
salesman until his death in 1920.

Du Pont now controlled all the plants in the country
that made military powder.

By 1906, the company was selling seventy per cent of
all the powder and explosives consumed in the United
States. Stocks of more than one hundred corporations
had been acquired, and sixty-four of them had been dissolved. Coleman continued slashing right and left,
cutting away the deadwood, and aiming at a single
huge and unique industrial combination.

At this juncture, there came an interruption, not
wholly unexpected. Robert Stuart Waddell, a former
Du Pont agent, who had tried to become an independent

manufacturer, began to fill the press and the mail of Congressmen with circulars assailing the Du Ponts and their Powder Trust. He was armed with impressive facts and figures. Smokeless powder, he asserted, that cost 31 cents to manufacture, was sold to the U. S. Government at 75 cents a pound. The Government, therefore, according to Waddell was being rooked out of $2,000,000 a year on current purchases.

The embattled Mr. Waddell also called the attention of Congress to a recent statement of the Secretary of War that the Government should have a reserve supply of powder for the Army alone of 30,000,000 pounds. The cost, if made by the Du Ponts at 75 cents a pound, would be $22,500,000. If made in Government factories, the cost would be but $10,500,000, a saving of $12,000,000.

Colonel Henry A. du Pont had been elected United States Senator from Delaware and Mr. Waddell made caustic reference to the political influence of the Du Ponts and to reports that they had contributed $70,000 to the 1904 Republican Presidential campaign fund, adding:

"If a $70,000 campaign contribution is sufficient to obligate the executive and legislative departments of the Government to take $12,000,000 from the taxpayers of the country and give it to the millionaires of this gigantic powder monopoly, the independent powder companies and the voters of the country want to know it now."

The Waddell strictures fell as seed in fertile ground. President Theodore Roosevelt's trust-busting crusade was in full cry. On July 30, 1907, the U. S. Government filed suit in the United States Circuit Court for the District of Delaware against the Du Ponts for violation of the Sherman Anti-trust Act.

A paragraph in the petition bore testimony to the efficiency of Coleman's work: "The defendants already have a complete monopoly of the production and distribution of smokeless ordnance powder and have a monopoly of 95 per cent of the production and distribution of gunpowder and high explosives other than smokeless ordnance powder."

The great, screaming newspaper headlines worried Pierre, fascinated Raskob, annoyed Alfred, but did not faze Coleman. His only regret was that the Government had stepped in before his monopoly was one hundred per cent. Coleman liked "round figures."

VICTORY IN DEFEAT

THE suit of the United States Government versus Du Pont—and its aftermath—is one of the outstanding farces of American judicial history.

The Government charged—and proved—that for two generations the Du Ponts had schemed to control the explosives industry, regardless of law, and that under T. Coleman du Pont this scheme had been realized.

Flanked by a host of the country's most imposing and expensive legal luminaries, Coleman du Pont sat in the court room, scowling in the boredom of his inactivity, and listened to himself vividly portrayed by the Government prosecutors as a power-thirsty butcher pole-axing rival companies one by one, while his cousins Pierre and Alfred I. dragged out the carcasses.

The suit lagged. Thousands of pages of depositions and testimony, affidavits, hearings before special masters, records and historical background data on the Gunpowder Trade Association bear witness to the involved unwinding of Coleman's devious trial. But in the welter of all this testimony, the name of Pierre's able, tight-lipped little emir, John Jacob Raskob, was not mentioned. Yet the shadowy Raskob had been as active in consolidating, reorganizing and filling his pockets as any of the three Du Ponts under fire.

Meanwhile, in Washington, the powder monopoly was vigorously attacked. T. Roosevelt was still in the saddle. One naval appropriations bill had been passed only after its sponsors in the House and the Senate had been forced to amend it by prohibiting the purchase of powder by the United States Navy from "any trust or combination in restraint of trade" or from any corporation having a monopoly in the manufacture of gunpowder "except in the event of an extraordinary emergency."

Still the suit dragged, covering in all a period of over three years. Finally, June 12, 1911, the Circuit Court of the United States in the District of Delaware found Du Pont guilty of violation of the Sherman Act. The court's opinion read in part:

The record of the case now before us shows that from 1872 to 1902, the purpose of the trade associations had been to dominate the powder and explosive trade in the United States by fixing prices according to the will of the managers. . . . Although the associations were not always strong enough to control absolutely the price of explosives, their purpose to do so was never abandoned. Under the last of the Trade Association agreements, the one dated July 1, 1896, and which was in force until June 30, 1904, control of the combination was firmer than it had before been.

Succeeding the death of Eugene du Pont in January, 1902 and the advent of Thomas Coleman du Pont and Pierre S. du Pont, the attempt was made to continue restraint upon interstate commerce and the monopoly then existing by vesting, in a few corporations, title to the assets of all corporations affiliated with the Trade Association, then dissolving the corporations whose assets had been so acquired, and binding the few corporations owning the operating plants in one holding company, which should be able to prescribe policies and control the business of all the subsidiaries without the uncertainties attending upon a combination in the nature of a trade association. That attempt resulted in complete success. . . .

It is a significant fact that the Trade Association organized under the agreement of July 1, 1896 was not dissolved until June 30, 1904. It had been utilized until that date by Thomas Coleman du Pont, Pierre S. du Pont and Alfred I. du Pont in suppressing competition and thereby building up a monopoly. Between February, 1902, and June, 1904, the combination had been so completely transmuted into a corporate form that the Trade Association was no longer necessary.

Consequently the Trade Association was dissolved and the process of dissolving the corporations whose capital stocks had been acquired, and concentrating the physical assets in one great corporation was begun. Before the plan was fully carried out this suit was begun. The proofs satisfy us that the present form of combination is no less obnoxious to the law than was the combination under the Trade Association agreement which was dissolved on June 30, 1904. . . .

The dissolution of more than sixty corporations since the advent of the new management in 1902, and the consequent *impossibility of restoring original conditions in the explosive trade, narrows the field of operation of any decree we may make.* It should not make the decree any the less effective however.

The court's admission that original conditions in the powder trade could not be restored was indeed a high tribute to the thoroughness of Coleman's censured work.

Baffled by such unprecedented circumstances, the court sought to solve the predicament by handing down an interlocutory decree, permitting the Government and Du Pont, jointly, to present a plan for the dissolution and reorganization of the company. In other words, the culprit could suggest his own punishment!

Whereupon, the three wise, acquisitive Du Pont cousins went into a huddle. They decided, above everything else, that they *must* retain their monopoly of military powder. The fact that they had just been proved guilty of monopoly did not in the least swerve them from their purpose, though it did dictate caution.

Realizing that suggestions from the United States Government would of course be more potent with the court than their own, Coleman du Pont headed for Washington. He was no novice in the delicate art of propaganda and the beneficial uses of practical politics. He had manipulated his kinsman, Colonel Henry A. du Pont, into the United States Senate—an episode we shall deal with later; contributed handsomely to Republican campaign funds; had been himself elected a Republican National committeeman from Delaware; and by honorary appointment from the Governor of Delaware had now the title of "General" of the National Guard.

From the Du Pont point of view, the situation in Washington was improved. The fiery T. R. had been succeeded in the White House by the stout, amiable and complaisant Taft, who, unlike his predecessor, obviously had no thirst for the blood of corporations.

Coleman concentrated on Taft. Wrapping his ledgers in the flag, he contended that it was a patriotic necessity for Du Pont to retain its monopoly of military powder. The President consulted with his Cabinet; the Secretaries of War and of the Navy consulted with their chiefs of ordnance.

The result was that an impressive array of military

men—Admiral Knight, President of the Joint Army and Navy Board on Smokeless Powder; Admiral Twining, Chief of the Navy Ordnance Bureau; Admiral Mason, of the Navy; General Crozier, Chief of Ordnance of the Army; and others, filed before the Circuit Court of Delaware and testified emphatically in favor of leaving Du Pont's smokeless powder organization intact. Said Rear Admiral Knight: "I think there is every reason to say that smokeless powder is the one substance in the world which naval officers and everybody else who have to sleep over it for months and years at a time do not want to get into competition."

The final decree was handed down June 13, 1912. It called for distribution of Du Pont's assets among three companies: Du Pont and two new companies which were to be named the Atlas Powder Company and the Hercules Powder Company. Hercules was given a plant for the manufacture of smokeless sporting powder and assigned Laflin & Rand brand names. Both Hercules and Atlas got plants for the manufacture of general explosives. *But*, Du Pont was instructed to keep the *entire* military smokeless powder business on the ground that a division of this branch of manufacture "would tend to destroy the practical and scientific coöperation now pursued between the Government and the defendant company, and to impair the certainty and efficiency of the results thus attained."

On paper, Coleman's trust was busted. In reality, as it turned out, the Government gave back to Du Pont far more than that which for three years it had tried to take away. The decision paved the way for further Du Pont development, more fantastic than any the company had

[171]

yet known. The Great War of 1914 was but two years away. Even in 1912 the divorce of two small companies meant little. Du Pont remained the pace setter. It would be a rash rival who would attempt to ignore its leadership in the matter of prices and policies.

In the first decade of Coleman's leadership, Du Pont's net earnings totaled over $50,000,000—more than four times the price he, Pierre and Alfred had paid for the company in 1902.

By 1912 the company's clerical employes numbered over a thousand. The eight-story Equitable Building in Wilmington was inadequate. One day Coleman called in an architect and told him the company had bought most of the two blocks bounded by Tenth, Eleventh, Market and Orange streets. "We want to put up an office building, a real big one," he said. "I don't want to bother with too many complicated plans. How do you think this would do?"

With his quick, competent engineer's hands, he rapidly sketched out a rough plan for a big, square structure built about a court.

From that rough pencil sketch developed the huge Du Pont Building, with its 2,000 rooms, a hotel containing 300 rooms at one end, stores along the street fronts, and a theater in its court. The hotel chambers were so designed that they could be turned into offices overnight, when needed.

The theater was John Raskob's idea. The up and coming assistant treasurer had married Helena Springer Green, a school teacher, of an old and distinguished Maryland Catholic family. Raskob's cultural tastes were expanding noticeably. They did not detract him, however, from promptly putting in a bid for the cigar counter privilege in the lobby of the proposed building. He was not one to overlook a little side flier.

The fourteen-story Du Pont Building, when finished, stuck out in Wilmington like a giraffe in a barnyard. Outwardly it marked the final Du Pont permeation of what had once been a peaceful little Quaker town. From the Du Pont point of view their Delaware headquarters proved an excellent boon, giving them a dynasty wholly their own and a duchy vastly more imposing than that "Pontiania" dreamed of by old Du Pont de Nemours. Now each executive looked from his office window into the peace of the countryside. But below, the citizens of Wilmington, clinging to their lovely old red brick houses, felt themselves constantly in the shadow of Du Pont.

Coleman du Pont, too, was in ferment. This Du Pont's restless, frontiersman spirit could not be cabined. Following the Government suit and the building of the new skyscraper, he felt that he had reached a climactic point in his career with the family business. A mighty urge to move along stirred in him. He was fond of quoting a maxim of the elder J. P. Morgan: "If you want to launch a big ship, you've got to go where there is plenty of water."

New York had long been his playground, a place where he could throw off restraint. He loved the city's color and action, its shifting panorama, its beautiful women. It was said that Coleman could see a slit skirt a mile away. As a younger man he had been familiar with the old Waldorf-Astoria and the famous figures who frequented it—the Moore brothers, Leeds the Tinplate King, Daniel G. Read, John W. (Bet-a-million) Gates, Diamond Jim Brady, John A. Drake and many others. These amiable and awesome personages had been succeeded by a more subtle school of commercial gamblers, less picturesque individually but equally venturesome.

Now New York beckoned imperatively. Coleman du Pont plunged in among the new buccaneers of modern business. He came as a peer and these great playful cuttlefish welcomed Coleman to their circle. There was a bigness and a breadth about him and, at the same time, a disarming ingenuousness of manner and bearing that led some men, and many women, to look upon this powder magnate as a rather simple soul. Those that did soon discovered their mistake. The big man, with the moppy moustache, partly bald head and cleft chin, uptown or down was as shrewd as an Iowa horse trader.

"The General," as everyone soon began calling Coleman, occupied a splendid suite on the twenty-first floor of the Hotel McAlpin, which, as member of a syndicate, he had helped to build. Here he proved a genial and generous host. Nothing pleased him more than to have friends drop in for dinner or after-theater supper. When he ordered places for twenty, the maitre d'hotel would automatically provide food and vintage for at least twice that many.

About his banquet board, while the champagne flowed, the General was in his element, and he took an unholy glee in perpetrating his practical jokes. A dainty plaster of paris cake, a leg of chicken made of succulent hard rubber, mice that squeaked, snakes that hissed, flowers that gave forth the sweet odor of garlic, might be encountered at any moment! And the genial host's feats of magic and card tricks became more adroit than ever.

There was nothing of the clown, though, about Coleman's commercial legerdemain. His preternatural energy bounced him out of bed at sunrise. By the time the city roared into life, he had ripped through his correspondence and drawn up an agenda of the day's activities for his secretary and confidential man, Lewis L. Dunham. The relationship of Coleman du Pont and Dunham was peculiarly close. Lew Dunham was the son of the general storekeeper in the small settlement of Moxham, near Johnstown, Pennsylvania. In 1894, when he was eighteen, he had been selected by Coleman du Pont from the employes of the Johnson Company as his personal clerk. They had been together since, in ever widening fields. Dunham kept his finger on the pulse of a dozen speculative activities in which his principal was interested.

Coleman kept his hawk's eye on the powder business, though the more irksome details of direction were left to Pierre, who became executive vice president, passing his treasurer's job over to Raskob. Neither Pierre nor Alfred relished the idea of a part time president but there was nothing they could do about it. Coleman held the largest portion of the company's stock.

By temperament and training Coleman was a builder. He became utterly fascinated with the idea of erecting the biggest skyscraper office building in the world. In 1913, he selected a site on lower Broadway and began putting up the Equitable Building, a giant which for years had no equal. His plan called for a structure of 40

[175]

stories, with 2,300 offices accommodating 15,000 people, a veritable city in itself. The cost reached $30,000,000.

While Du Pont dynamite was blasting through the rocks for the foundations of this mammoth building, its owner was forced to undergo an emergency operation, in Philadelphia, for an intestinal obstruction. The wound did not heal properly. For months after the ordeal, Coleman was subjected to spasms of piercing pain. X-rays were taken. "Adhesions" reported the doctors and advised him to go to the hospital of the noted Mayo brothers, in Rochester, Minnesota, for a corrective operation.

Before he left, realizing that he would need more money for his gigantic skyscraper, Coleman decided to offer a fairly sizable block of his common stock to the powder company to sell or distribute among its younger executives. Through a curious chain of events, the offer, quite innocent in itself, brought to a head the most bitter public feud the clan Du Pont has ever known.

The rift spread, embroiling the business as well as the family. It disrupted the partnership of the cousins, after thirteen years; launched long and vicious litigation; and aired a scandalous situation the Du Ponts had striven to settle privately by their own stern tribal methods. That situation—bubbling, boiling, simmering for a decade—contained all the elements of a Greek tragedy.

Chapter Three

A HOUSE DIVIDED

OF THE triumvirate that ruled Du Pont, Alfred I. was the most difficult to decipher.

A practical powder maker who read poetry and composed music, a person of culture who was happiest with the workmen and rather scorned intellectual companionship, this member of the tribe tantalizingly eludes classification. Alfred was a born non-conformist, concealing brilliant gifts under a sardonic manner and a barbed tongue. He pulled poorly in harness. At times he was irked by Coleman's lusty back-slappings, Gargantuan energy, and steamrolling commercial tactics. Then he would lash out with biting sarcasms. Nor could he be appeased by Pierre's silken diplomacy.

For their part, Coleman and Pierre considered Alfred erratic and lacking in business judgment. Though they always consulted him upon matters of importance, they seldom based vital decisions upon his suggestions. Indeed, with Coleman slashing ahead on new methods and projects, and the agile Pierre close in his wake computing percentages, Alfred felt himself a little out of the picture. To cover his hurt he assumed an arrogant, devil-may-care air, lounging into his office at all hours, carelessly attired and apparently unconcerned with business. However, overshadowed as he might be, he never forgot that he was the eldest son of the eldest son of the eldest son of the founder.

Some of Alfred's jars and discontents flowed into the old brick mansion in Brech's Lane, near the mills, where he lived with his wife, Bessie Gardner du Pont, and their four children.

Bessie Gardner's father was a scholar, a deep student of history. She had been reared in the atmosphere of a cultivated New England home. She was exceedingly fond of social activities, conducted with decorum and as much ceremony as the occasion demanded. Such affairs ruffled Alfred's unruly, rebellious nature. Eventually he kicked over the traces, and in a manner so spectacular that the conservative clan of Du Pont was rocked to its very foundations.

In the nearby countryside, off the Kennett Pike, was the home of Judge Edward Bradford. His half-sister, Elizabeth Canby Bradford, had married Alexis I. du Pont and he, himself, had married Alexis I.'s sister, Eleuthèra Paulina du Pont. Their daughter was Mary Alicia Heyward Bradford.

Alicia Bradford, then in her twenties, was the sort of girl men describe as a "stunner." She had hair black and glossy as a raven's wing and dark gray eyes. Clean-limbed, athletic, she was fearless on horseback or in the hunting field. And she was fearless, to the point of reck-lessness, in other matters. Uncurbed, full of spirit, imperious of will and temper, she usually got what she wanted.

Soon little arrows of gossip winged within the family circle about Alfred du Pont and Alicia Bradford. The cousins had been seen far out in the country, holding intimate horseback tête-à-têtes. They had wandered into the woods with a hamper of luncheon. They had . . . buzz, buzz, buzz.

At that time the heads of the family, male and female, were Colonel Henry A. du Pont and Alicia's twofold aunt, the widowed Mrs. Alexis I. As the gossip widened, they took counsel. Then Mrs. Alexis I. spoke to her half-brother, Judge Bradford, who, in turn, talked long and solemnly with his daughter. No one knows what transpired in these interviews but, within a few weeks, Alicia quietly married George Amory Maddox, a poor and personable young man, who was Alfred du Pont's secretary; and with her husband moved into a commodious house across the Brandywine owned by Alfred. The couple's most constant visitor was their landlord.

In due course Alicia gave birth to a daughter. The infant, named for her mother, had the latter's dark hair and eyes and decisive chin. Few Du Ponts, however, sent gifts to the child, for, by now, the driblets of gossip had become a raging flood.

Finally, in 1906, Alfred and Alicia took matters into their own hands. Alfred went to South Dakota, established residence, and divorced his wife, giving her custody of their children and a financial settlement that was far from liberal. Alicia Maddox, at the same time, left her husband and set up an establishment in Carlisle, Pennsylvania. At the proper time Maddox appeared, accepted papers in a divorce action, and then quietly faded out of the picture.

A fortnight after Alicia's divorce, she and Alfred met in New York and were married. Returning to Wilmington, they settled on a small estate called Rock Manor and awaited tribal approval, now that their romance had been sanctified by bell, book and candle. Little was forthcoming. The Du Ponts had split into two opposing factions, the greater number taking the side of Bessie Gardner du Pont, who had gone through her ordeal with inflexible dignity.

Conspicuous among those who ignored Rock Manor were Coleman and Pierre and the latter's industrious younger brothers, Irénée and Lammot, who were now with the company and rising rapidly under Pierre's tutelage.

The social ostracism sank deep into Alfred's soul. The lines of his mouth and chin, once so sensitive, hardened into bitterness. His appearance became actually saturnine following a hunting accident when the sight of one eye was destroyed by birdshot, fired in the dusk by William Scott, a plant superintendent.

However, there was no timid streak in the makeup of Alfred and Alicia du Pont. As the feud grew in bitterness, they fought back viciously, and so effectively that they became the Terrors of the clan. When Baby Alicia Maddox was formally adopted by her stepfather, there was a fresh outburst of gossip and snubbing. Alfred put his foot down most efficiently by bringing suit for slander against his wife's aunt, Mrs. Alexis I., and the latter's friend, Mrs. Mary Thompson, Wilmington social leader. There were several such actions in 1909 and 1910. Alfred kept these slander suits hanging over gossipy heads for a while and then dropped them.

Similarly, he sought to force a bill through the Delaware Legislature changing the name of his only son,

Alfred Victor. He said he did not wish the son by his first wife to bear his name. Young Alfred, a schoolboy at Groton, wrote a note of protest. The bill, however, slipped past one branch of the Legislature before the rest of the Du Pont tribe awakened and threw their influence against it. The measure was killed.

Alfred's eldest daughter, Madeline, was the only one of his children who was ever seen with their father. He broke even with her when she eloped with John Bancroft, a Princeton sophomore. Three weeks after Madeline bore a child, Bancroft filed suit for divorce, charging that on their wedding trip to Germany she had become intimate with a young student. Alfred announced virtuously that he would have nothing to do with his daughter. But his wife, Alicia, surprisingly flew to Madeline's defense. She stated in so many words that if young Bancroft pressed his charges against Madeline, her stepdaughter, she, Alicia, would rip the hinges from many Delaware closets, Du Pont cabinets among them.

Whether she could do it, no one ever had the courage to find out. Bancroft withdrew his suit and got a divorce on the conventional grounds of desertion.

Alicia du Pont, like Alfred, became embittered, terming her Du Pont kin "hypocritical pussycats." But she was always tender with her little daughter, whom she trained in music and foreign languages. She gave the child a playhouse all her own, "Wren's Nest." It had three rooms and an electrically equipped kitchen. Little Alicia gravely presided over tea parties for her dolls.

For his wife, Alfred built a larger playhouse near Rock Manor: a magnificent chateau of one hundred rooms, set in a park of two hundred acres on an estate of more than five square miles. Nemours, as the place was named, was one of the most luxurious homes in America, far surpassing anything Delaware had ever known. Two great grilled gateways of bronze flanked this limestone palace: one, from old Wimbledon Manor in England; the other, from the palace of Catherine of Russia. An ancient Spanish gun guarded the front porch.

The entire estate was encircled by a stout wall ten feet high and studded with broken glass. The purpose of the wall, people said, was to bar the Du Ponts. Behind this frowning shelter, Alfred and Alicia lived, contemptuous of their clan.

So far as known, only two Du Ponts—Francis I. and William—ever crossed the threshold at Nemours. Francis I., of the Alexis line, was a gifted chemist and inventor, employed by the company. William had returned to Wilmington after long exile following his divorce in 1892 from May Lammot du Pont. He was now a shaggy man in late middle life, with gold-rimmed glasses and a walrus moustache. In 1900 he had purchased the former home of President Madison, near Orange, Virginia, and established a breeding farm for hackney horses and blooded cattle. His hackneys won many blue ribbons at horse shows. He and Alfred, who had both come under tribal condemnation, found much in common. William was now a member of the Finance Committee of the company. In addition to the interest he had inherited from his father, old General Henry, he was custodian of the stock of his brother, Colonel Henry A. When Colonel Henry went to the United States Senate, he had transferred his holdings to William as a matter of political expediency.

Alfred was particularly wroth with Pierre, who took
Bessie Gardner du Pont under his wing and encouraged
her ambition to write. She became the historian of the
family. Under her modest signature, B. G. du Pont, have
appeared many volumes, some for private circulation
only. Still beautiful, still charming, risen above her
tragedy, she lives now, amid her books, a few miles from
Wilmington, in Chevannes, a lovely retreat modeled
after the original chateau of Pierre Samuel du Pont, near
Nemours, France.

Nursing his bitterness to keep it warm, Alfred du Pont
awaited only opportunity to avenge himself upon his
foemen within the family. That opportunity came late
in 1914 when Coleman decided to dispose of a slice of
his powder stock.

Coleman needed large sums to complete his gigantic
Equitable Building. The outbreak of the Great War had
thrown the New York money market into a chaotic
condition. Everywhere, bankers and business men were
trimming sail. Although war orders from the Allies
began to roll in upon Du Pont in gratifying volume, and
though *any* war promised a golden harvest to the powder
company, the General figured he'd better trim sail too.
A lot of fellows who seemed to know what they were
talking about were filling the papers with predictions
that the war in Europe could not possibly last very long.
Whether it did or it didn't, it seemed to the General
that now was the time for a prudent man to assemble a
comfortable cash reserve.

Coleman's was the largest individual interest in the
du Pont Company—63,314 shares out of 294,272 common shares outstanding and 14,599 shares of preferred

out of some 160,000 outstanding. Alfred was second with 37,000 odd shares of common; Pierre a close third. The preferred stock, more than the common, was concentrated among the older members of the family.

On December 7, 1914, Coleman wrote to Pierre, then executive vice president:

As you know I have always felt those in responsible positions in our company should be encouraged to become importantly interested in the common stock and I have, as you know, always thought well of the common stock and put a higher figure on it than you have. I think it well worth 185 today and think it will go to 190 to 200 before the year 1915 is many months old. This ownership of common stock by the leading men is of so much importance to the company that as a member of the Finance Committee (the company having cash beyond its requirements) I would recommend the funds needed to carry the stock for these men be advanced by the treasury.

I am willing to sell for the purpose twenty thousand (20,000) shares at $160 per share ex-dividend payable in say thirty or sixty days.

To guide me I should like to have a suggestion from the Finance Committee or a committee appointed by them, as to how it should be distributed.

Inasmuch as important men associated with us have asked me to sell them some stock I should like to have a prompt answer from the Finance Committee to enable me to reply.

If the important stockholders in Hercules Powder Co. think well of the plan make a similar offer to president of Hercules Powder Co., except the number of shares will be much smaller say 4,000, and I think and hope you gentlemen feel the important stockholders in that company should recommend to the directors of that company that the Hercules Co. advance the cash needed as the company can spare it to enable the directors (and those they suggest) to secure this stock.

The same with much reduced number of shares, 700 or 800, to the president of the Atlas Co.

At this juncture, Coleman's physicians peremptorily ordered him to the Mayo Clinic for the intestinal operation to which we have referred. A week later he wrote further to Pierre:

I have given a great deal of thought to my letter of Dec. 7th as to distribution of this stock, and my judgment is that each member of the Executive Committee be allowed 1500 shares. That the men whose salary is $500 a month and over will be allowed to subscribe for three times the amount of their salaries. This makes a total, according to the memorandum you left with me, of 20,700 shares. I am willing to furnish the other 700, or the company can do this as in your judgment seems advisable.

I suggest you make this announcement some time prior to the 23rd of this month as I think it has some advantage.

As I am going away today and do not know how long I will be gone, I have left the matter in Mr. L. L. Dunham's hands. He can come to Wilmington and see you upon receipt of telegram from you.

Pierre took the offer up privately with Alfred, who considered the price, $160 a share, too high. He pointed out that 160, at the current dividend rate, would be purchasing the stock on a five per cent basis, adding in a memorandum to Pierre:

"This is too low a rate for the company to invest its spare funds, and furthermore, if it were offered to any of our employes, it would not be sufficiently attractive at that price. I see no objection to the company's purchasing this stock, but the question of price is one of grave importance, owing to the large investment. I would suggest that no decision as to the actual price be given the present owner until the Finance Committee has had ample time to think the matter over and discuss it together."

On December 23rd—the very day, by coincidence, upon which Coleman went under the knife in Minnesota —Pierre called a special meeting of the Finance Committee, of which he was chairman, and Coleman, Alfred and William du Pont were the other members.

Pierre favored paying Coleman's price, $160 a share. Alfred and William disagreed and voted into the minutes a resolution instructing Pierre to inform Coleman that "we do not feel justified in paying more than $125 per share for this stock." Alfred and William subsequently insisted that this resolution ended with a qualifying clause "at this time" or "at the present time"; and that they had orally directed Pierre at this meeting to continue negotiations with Coleman. Pierre disagreed with them on both points. However this may be, there is no record that Pierre ever sought more favorable terms from Coleman.

For the next few weeks, Pierre and Coleman carried on a revealing correspondence. This correspondence gives, also, a fascinating close-up of the reigning Du Ponts, their business philosophy, and their activities in the initial stages of the Great War.

Chapter Four

A SHEAF OF LETTERS

T. C. DU PONT, PRESIDENT,
ROCHESTER, MINNESOTA.

DEAR COLEMAN:

I have been intending to write you about the reception of your proposition by the Finance Committee. Unfortunately, Alfred, who had approved the plan before you went away, got somewhat crosswise in the meeting and I think it wise to let the matter rest for the moment; preferably until I can see you, before taking any other step. I am sorry and provoked that the proposition did not go through, for I feel that your offer was a generous one and should have had more considerate treatment; but like many other things, the final result cannot be obtained quickly.

The Hercules plan was accepted in very good spirit. It is held up temporarily because their attorneys have told them their company cannot loan the money to the directors. Technically, this may be correct: but I do not think they should hesitate to put the thing through, nor do I think they will. The Atlas people, acting under the same laws [of Delaware] have accepted the proposition and I understand from Lew Dunham today have taken over the stock. Undoubtedly the Hercules will come to the same conclusion.

Colonel Buckner still continues busy. The Nobel and Russian contracts are to be closed today or tomorrow and we have other similar items in view. The actual sales amount to about thirty-five million. Construction work is reported well along.

On New Year's Day I was surprised to find Moxham[1] ill in bed. By this time you have probably heard that he was threatened with pneumonia, but I believe all danger has now passed. He seemed quite himself and willing to talk. I understand that his company is determined to go ahead on smokeless powder and guncotton. It seems a great mistake, but not for us to dictate.

Lew Dunham gives me the good news that you have been up from bed already. It seems almost too good to be true and shows your reserve strength. Altogether your operation, severe as it was, seems to have promise of very good results. All here are interested in hearing from you. I have daily inquiries.

YOUR AFFECTIONATE COUSIN,
PIERRE S. DU PONT,
Vice-President.

ST. MARY'S HOSPITAL.
JANY. 6TH, 1915.

DEAR PIERRE:

This is my first letter a note yesterday to the Kids was somewhat shaky as is this but I hope you can read it.

I am sorry that Alfred had taken the position you indicate and too that it has passed the 1st of Jany. as to have made the announcement at Xmas seems to me would have been much more value to us from the human nature stand point.

After talking to you I told some New York Bankers that I

[1] Arthur J Moxham, formerly of the Johnson Company, who had followed Coleman into the powder business.

[188]

would not need the money that I had arranged to get from them, as I had made a more permanent arrangement, but can I feel sure fix this when I get back, perhaps it would be well for me to withdraw the proposition, if you think so do it. I of course know Alfred has some ulterior motive in mind, as he has tried to do what he could agin me at every opportunity, but this we both know and I always take it into consideration.

Yes it is a mistake for Arthur to go into military smokeless powder for the present foreign needs as they will be over by the time he can do anything.

What are the chances of a bill going thro. Congress against shipments of powder from U.S. and if good would it be well for us to get ready to mnfg. in Canada, at least take option on site and get Engr. work out of the way, except if that time comes we couldn't well wait for Engineering work but would have to build & make the goods then do the Engineering. . . . I am thinner by 15 or 20 pounds than the day I came to Rochester but lost ½ of it before coming to the hospital, you know I was here a week before the operation during which they either starved me or gave me a meal & pumped it out again, if however they have really removed the cause a few months will do the rest.

Without promising the Dr. says I can go to the sanitarium Hotel in 10 days or two weeks from now and will have to be there perhaps a month, so you can guess as nearly as I can when I will get home.

I think Lew Dunham will be able to look after everything in the way of Equitable Finances until I get back, even with the changed conditions; if not he will let me know and I will write you.

I guess this scrawl will keep you busy some time so I had better stop don't tell anyone I am writing yet as I am not supposed to but got one letter passed by Board of censorship.

Glad to know 35,000,000 is safe this is 10,000,000 increase

since I left and I think if we get started we will be able to ship more or faster than was figured out at first, it's a pity we can't make the McCarty powder that drys in 24 hours for the 13″ guns, and this is when I felt McCarty greatest value would be.

Dictate a letter or two to me advising how things are going. Love to family.

YOUR AFF. COUSIN,
(*Sgd.*) COLEMAN.

JANUARY 9TH, 1915.

COLEMAN DU PONT, PRESIDENT,
ROCHESTER, MINNESOTA.

MY DEAR COLEMAN:—

I was very happy to receive your letter of January the 6th, particularly as it was in your own handwriting, indicating that you are feeling much better. I could hardly believe that you would be about so quickly after all that you have gone through in the past few weeks. It all indicates to me that the fifteen pounds you have lost was mostly in useless parts that have given you a lot of trouble, but are now in position where they cannot do so.

I feel you must be much disappointed in the question of the stock subscription. I used my best judgment in not trying to force the situation. Possibly I could have put it through by insisting, but at great risk of having the other side pitted against me; that might have complicated the whole plan for good and all. As it remains now, I feel that the proposition is open for reconsideration at your option, of course. Willie[1] is away at present, but will be back in a couple of weeks; at which time I will take up the work again, unless I have word from you to the contrary my judgment is that the deal will go through this time.

The march of the smokeless powder business is going on

---

[1] William du Pont.

uninterrupted. In order to take care of deliveries for the latter part of this year we have now increased our manufacturing capacity to 6,000,000 pounds guncotton per month. The powder manufacturing capacity is not quite equal to this, but a new negotiation will probably make it necessary to round out the 72,000,000 guncotton capacity per annum to a similar amount of powder. The actual sales of the latter now amount to 35,000,000 pounds, of which 2,000,000 are for the British Government and, though not signed up (*signed to-day*)[2] everything is in readiness for final action; also the Russian order for 6,000,000 pounds is still unsigned, but everything is arranged and there is no doubt that the first payment will be made within the next week. This may seem like an old story, but each day we get closer to the goal. In addition to the above order we have sold 3,000,000 pounds of guncotton and 5,684,-375 pounds of trinitrotoluol. In all these contracts the prices have been maintained. We are now negotiating a second order of 4,300,000 pounds with Nobels and 2,000,000 pounds with Bethlehem Steel. Day before yesterday in New York, Colonel Buckner and I met the financial representative of the Russian Empire, whose mission in the States is to place Russian securities in New York. He spoke quite frankly about their endeavors to establish credit and of the advantage to his country if a large block of 4 per cent. bonds could be placed with us. The discussion led to a proposition by us to furnish 30,000,000 pounds of powder over 1916, payable one-half cash; $1.00 per pound, subject to discount of $2\frac{1}{2}$ per cent. at time of final payment. We also made an alternative proposition for 50,000,000 pounds under similar conditions of payment, but delivery extending three months in 1917, with the additional provision that our company was to purchase at the signing of the contract, $5,000,000 in the Russian 4 per cent. bonds. This feature was added on account of the recommendation of the Russian

[2] Marginal note on letter.

representative that a subscription to the bonds at this time would have very good effect on the Russian financial situation. Of course, the final result will be equivalent to accepting 40 per cent. in cash and 60 per cent. in bonds. As the cash payment will let us out with some profit, it seems unlikely that the net result will be anything but very satisfactory. Russian 4 per cent. bonds before the war sold in the 90's; to-day they are about 82. The total bond indebtedness of the Russian Empire amounts to $4,600,000,000; population, 1912, 170,-000,000. This compares with the indebtedness of others in this way:

France	$6,300,000,000
German States and Empire	4,900,000,000
United Kingdom and Colonies	3,700,000,000
United States	1,000,000,000

Considering the vast and enormous resources of the Russian Empire, it would seem their bonds are the safest of all the warring nations. The Russian representative, Gregory Wilenkin, received our proposition as though he thought something might come of this and purposed cabling Petrograd immediately. As we gave him ten days for reply, we will probably know shortly how far our proposition interests them. I am prepared to have a reply suggesting full payment in bonds. If such an offer should come to us I would incline to its acceptance.

We have given a great deal of consideration to the proposed law prohibiting shipments of powder, which law seems unlikely of passage; as its terms would seem to seriously infringe upon International Law. Moreover, from our point of view we are not concerned, as all of our contracts are for deliveries in the United States and have no relation to the question of shipment of material. In the last contract entered into by us with Nobel (for account of Vickers, London) 4,300,000, they took the precaution to make the contract for delivery to their Spanish house, which would be entirely apart from the proposed legislation, which deals with belligerent nations only. I suppose that a similar change could be made in other contracts if it was found necessary. Altogether, this legislation seems to be of small moment to us at the present time.

We are using every endeavor to properly watch our plants, but we all realize that this is difficult of accomplishment and we are prepared for some trouble in this line. So far nothing has happened to cause undue alarm. There was an explosion in the Lesmoke dryhouse on the Brandywine a few nights ago (about 3.00 A.M.). No machinery of any kind in the house, which was heated by steam; the latter having proved hardly sufficient for proper heating, there seems little likelihood of accidental overheating. No cause has been assigned the explosion, but it seems unlikely that the trouble should have been of incendiary origin, as the point of attack could have nothing, absolutely, to do with war conditions. The best theory is that the guncotton dust on the powder worked back into the heating-coil which was sufficiently heated to cause spontaneous decomposition. No one was hurt in the accident, but quite a little damage, such as broken windows, etc., occurred in the neighborhood.

The Engineering Department have responded splendidly to the heavy calls made upon them. The first extensions have come in ahead of time and we are now working at what would have seemed an enormous output a few months ago; though it is not nearly half of what we expect to do. The whole force, from one end to the other, seems working enthusiastically and in harmony toward obtaining the best results in the present emergency. There seems to be no trouble in diverting men from one department to another, or for getting hearty co-operation in carrying out any work that needs attention.

Commercial business is extremely sad. December was the

worst month for a long time. I do not think the prospects particularly bright, though it would seem very unlikely that business will decline further; any change should be the other way. It is much to our advantage that the commercial end should not demand too much attention at this time, although we could stand a large increase without much extra effort.

The Moxham-Aetna Explosives Company's entrance into the guncotton and possibly smokeless field gives me some concern, not that I believe they will materially interfere with our business at this time, though I do believe they will give us a lot of trouble in the future. However, this part of the problem is small compared with the risk that I believe Moxham is running in branching out into a new field, when he has not yet started to straighten out what he now owns. I should be very sorry to see him get into further financial difficulties, but I believe that he is in great danger of doing that very thing.

Now here is a very long letter; but it gives you a look into our business minds to-day. It is a large and rapidly developing situation of great interest, but one where many unexpected difficulties may arise before we are through with these large orders.

Looking for your continued and rapid improvements, I remain,

YOUR AFFECTIONATE COUSIN,

PIERRE S. DU PONT,

Vice-President.

THE KAHLER

ROCHESTER, MINN.

J. H. KAHLER, MANAGING DIRECTOR.

A. L. ROBERTS, MANAGER.

ROCHESTER, MINN, 1-11-15.

DEAR PIERRE

I have just written Buss about a room, and it occurs to me the new working force may want more of the rooms I occupy, if so they ought to have them and let me go some other place in the building, it is not important now that I am in the middle of things but I would like quarters somewhere near you. Keep this in mind and if you see it an advantage to the Co. let me know.

Your letter just received and I was very glad to get it.

As you see we moved back to Hotel today rather sudden but this Hotel is $\frac{1}{2}$ Hospital & I think they needed the rooms. Else & I had at Hospital 2 rooms & one patient probably was not business.

As to stock subscription I believed it was a good thing for the Co. when I made the offer and made a price that I thought low, but I conceed that I have always placed a higher value on the stock than others, I did it for the good of the new committee but am not anxious from a selfish standpoint to carry it out, except for the good of the Co. and that is more important than personal reasons.

If you feel it a good thing *for the Co.* talk to Willie and do it if not don't. It may make some diff in my Equitable Finances but I think not that is I think I can make same arrangment when I get back that I cancelled before leaving so use your own judgment.

Glad to note British govt had signed. I don't follow the Russian Bond cash payment argument you say 30,000,000 payable $\frac{1}{2}$ Bds 80/85 $\frac{1}{2}$ cash at 1.00 per pound disc $2\frac{1}{2}\%$ final payment or alternate 50,000,000 $\frac{1}{2}$ per cent at 85. and that a substantial sub at this time would help them. Why not take the $\frac{1}{2}$ cash now & the $\frac{1}{2}$ bonds too now that would be a sale of 25,000,000 bonds & give them receipt for interest until Powder was at their disposal certainly a sub of 25,000,000 would help them more than 5,000,000.

I don't think selling to Agt for an Allie would let us out of the law *if it passes* but shipment to Spain, Norway or Sweden would.

If we accept all Bds at 80/85 for 50,000,000 it means

20,000,000 cash to make powder so we would have to spend the 20 or sell bds at whatever they would bring and at 50/60 per bond would leave a profit. I cannot imagine the Russian Govt Bonds being that low while the figures you give

Say U.S. 1,000,000,000 pop 90,000,000
Rusn 4,600,000,000 '' 170,000,000

look favorable the Russians are not as well off as people of U.S. I think taxes are much higher on same reason for 4% Govt bds on 80/85 our 4% are usually 1.01 . 1.02 if these bonds are safest why this difference. I would certainly get 50% cash if possible and gamble with our profits.

Before knowing from you that Moxham was going into smokeless I wrote him urging he did not branch out until he was well under way & had things safe, since you have advised me of this I will write again explaining that I didn't know of the smokeless &c. or would not have written as he may put false meaning on it but progress & extravagance *combined* have been cause of his failure twice & will be again.

I enjoyed & appreciated every word of your letter if you have time send another one in a week or two.

Love to all

YOUR AFF. COUSIN
(*Sgd.*) COLEMAN.

JANUARY 14, 1915.

MR. T. C. DU PONT,
ROCHESTER, MINNESOTA.

MY DEAR COLEMAN:

It was very good to hear from you again and at such length, showing improvement you are feeling. . . .

Things are still moving rapidly with the company. At last all the contracts in negotiation when you left here are signed and the first payments made—an aggregate of 35,000,000 pounds of powder, 3,100,000 pounds of guncotton and 5,116,-

ooo pounds of trinitrotoluol. Meantime other important negotiations are in progress. I think I wrote you that Nobels want
4,300,000 pounds and Bethlehem Steel 2,600,000 pounds of
powder and Nobels 3,500,000 pounds of guncotton. In addition to this we have the large Russian negotiation part
payable in bonds, but in looking over your letter I find I have
not clearly explained the proposition.

You are correct in understanding there are two alternatives;
one of thirty millions pounds, another fifty. In case the price
of one dollar per pound payable one-half in cash and half in
bonds (the latter valued between 80 and 85). At the end of the
contract and upon final payment, a two and one-half per cent.
discount, in cash, is to be allowed on the one dollar price.
However, our offer to purchase $5,000,000 Russian bonds on
the larger proposition would be the equivalent to the taking
of thirty million bonds and twenty million cash. I hope this is
now made clear to you. You understand of course that this
order would be filled out of existing plants, so that no depre-
ciation would have to be charged off. The cash would be very
ample for taking care of manufacture. If, however, we should
accept all bonds, we would have to put up on the larger
proposition, say, twelve and a half million, which I think we
could easily arrange through sale of bonds, or our other
resources. With such large business as this, such an item is
quite safe. Apparently the proposition has been well received
by the Russian representative in this country. We hope to hear
from Petrograd this week. Of course anything final can hardly
be expected, but we should at least have an indication of their
interest. Buckner has made a similar proposition to the
French representative and cables have been sent to France
on this subject. It seems possible that two large orders could
be secured in this way, thus establishing our 1916 business.
I believe in my last letter I wrote you these orders would
necessitate our increasing, this year, our guncotton capacity
from the figure I gave you (70,000,000 lbs.) to about 100,-

ooo,ooo lbs. Powder capacity must be raised from sixty to ninety million pounds. This means we will have to increase our appropriations to $8,300,000. A total of $5,700,000 is the figure already authorized.

To-day the Finance Committee authorized the purchase of $3,000,000 short term notes and bonds, in order to make some return on our large cash balances. I do not think it the right time to invest any funds in a permanent way, particularly if we are to take securities in payment for future powder orders.

Our raw material arrangements seem in satisfactory shape. Very large quantities of cotton have been covered at a low price, as well as sufficient nitrate of soda; the latter, however, is in storage in Chile. We are now working on a plan to have in this country sufficient nitrate to produce all the powder already sold, as a matter of insurance. Diphenylamine, over which we had some concern, is now being manufactured by us; the plant having been started, but it has not operated sufficiently long to establish what we can do. The General Chemical Company have also succeeded with their factory, so I think it unlikely that we shall fall short of a supply. Sulphuric acid is to be supplied largely by the General Chemical Company, but in addition we are to erect a comparatively small plant at Hopewell, Virginia. Nitric acid we will of course supply ourselves in the usual way. I do not see how we can "fall down" in any way as far as raw materials for existing contracts are concerned.

It is reported that Francis I. is negotiating with Moxham in regard to guncotton and smokeless powder manufacture. I understand that Peyton announced he was going into the smokeless powder business on his own account if the Aetna Explosives Company did not join him; hence their determination to go ahead, in which they are, I believe, much in error. Francis will have to decide soon whether he is to go with them or not. He should not be working on both sides of the question.

The demand for offices is not sufficient to necessitate any change in the rooms occupied by you. I think that everything is straightened out at present, though the building is pretty well filled.

As to the stock offer: In Willie's absence I shall do nothing. He will be here in a week and I will try to get some action. If this is not possible it will mean that the question of value of the stock was not uppermost in their minds. If not finally accepted would you approve making an offer direct to the men? I should think that a financing suitable to you might be arranged. I am quite sure that they would like to take the stock, but do not feel in position to say anything while you are negotiating with the company. No one but the Executive Committee and directors know of the offer as far as I know. The board of course knew it through the minutes of the Finance Committee.

Getting back to the large orders we are negotiating: I will let you know as soon as anything develops, as they are of great importance. Colonel Buckner, who has been in New York the last few days, returns tomorrow and there may possibly be something to report.

YOUR AFFECTIONATE COUSIN,

(*Sgd.*) PIERRE S. Du PONT.

TELEGRAM.

JAN. 17TH, 1915.

ROCHESTER, MINN.

P. S. DU PONT, WILMNG.

Letter of fourteen received. If you are not committed withdraw my offer. Will write.

COLEMAN DU PONT.

JANUARY 18TH, 1915.

MR. T. C. DU PONT,
KAHLER HOTEL,
ROCHESTER, MINNESOTA.

MY DEAR COLEMAN:

. . . . I have not talked with Willie alone, as he has been absent a couple of weeks and will not return for another week. However, as he supported Alfred in the stock proposal, I feel that I have obtained his opinion; but I had hoped that they would both swing around at our next meeting. There is, of course, no commitment; but I think there will be some disappointment, as I believe that the members of the Executive Committee were anxious to take the stock. Of course no others than the Executive Committee and the board know of the offer, but I am sure that all the men would like to make the subscription if the offer was made to them. I will of course do nothing further until I am authorized by you.

Nothing new has turned up since the last writing. We have not yet heard from the large order for Russia; though tomorrow is the last day. I will write you later what we hear.

YOUR AFFECTIONATE COUSIN,

(*Sgd*) PIERRE S. DU PONT.

ROCHESTER, MINNESOTA,
JAN. 19, 1915.

MR. P. S. DU PONT,
WILMINGTON, DEL.

DEAR PIERRE:

Upon receipt of your letter of the 14th, I telegraph you, "letter fourteenth received. If you are not committed withdraw my offer. Will write," which is now confirmed.

Inasmuch as Christmas and January first are past I don't think two or three more months will make any difference, and in my mind it would be such a good thing for the young men to have a stock interest that I am sure we can arrange for them to take it without being purchased by the company, through one of the New York banks, probably the Bankers Trust Company, but I believe if this is left until I get home we can work it out better.

I note by the Wilmington papers of a few days ago that common stock was selling at 1.55 to 1.60. With the outlook and the orders ahead I can't understand why the prediction in my letter to you that the stock would be 1.80 even 2.00 during the first few months of 1915, is not being fulfilled.

I note that the total orders are something over $40,000,000 with $10,000,000 more in prospect, not counting the two partially payable in bonds. These should certainly make the dividend 50 per cent. on 1915 and 1916 and 17, which should make the stock easily worth 200. At any rate, I feel sure we can work out some plan that will be beneficial to the important men in the company and, therefore, beneficial to the company, just as soon as I get back home.

Speaking from memory, you or someone told me that Alfred considered the common stock worth 300; therefore the price was not the reason for his changing his mind after I left Delaware.

Your letters are all fully appreciated, but, of . . .[1] there is nothing going on at this end of the line . . . give me the opportunity of writing much in reply.

> Your affectionate cousin,
> (sgt) COLEMAN Du PONT.

> Rochester, Minn.,
> Jany. 20/15

Dear Pierre:

Yours 18th received this a. m. and I am sure we can work out some plan on my return that will accomplish what we

[1] Corner of letter torn off.

[201]

want. I cannot understand why the other two should not have taken advantage of the offer and let the Co. help the men on who the success must depend.

Am always glad to get your letters and only sorry nothing of interest at this end to write you about.

Peyton will not be much of a competitor his handling of the acid business showed that, and I hope Moxham will not start until he finds where he's at, as it is not possible for him to have a balance sheet he can swear by yet. This the Belins will agree with me I think, though $1.00 50% cash would seem to be a game at which they could not lose.

Would be glad to know how the Russian order came out ($\frac{1}{2}$ or all bonds) and what Francis I. decision was or is going to be.

Regards to all.

YOUR AFF. COUSIN,

(Sgt) COLEMAN.

JANUARY 25, 1915.

MR. T. COLEMAN DU PONT,

ROCHESTER, MINNESOTA.

MY DEAR COLEMAN:

On my return from New York, where I have been for a couple of days, I find your letter and am glad to hear from you again. I am sure that some plan of advantage can be worked out when we next meet. A couple of days ago Alfred suggested to me that the Finance Committee take up the question of selling Treasury-stock to our important men. What would you think of such a plan? I do not know what he has in mind, but suppose something similar to your offer, excepting at a lower price I do not think it need interfere with your arrangement if you desire to put it through also.

Since my last letter, the Nobel Company has closed for 6,500,000 more pounds of powder and guncotton on account of the British Government. This order comprised three different lots which had been negotiated for the Belgians and Vickers' Sons originally, but the British Government stepped in and took them; so that Mr. Purvis, the Nobel representative here in the States, has asked for deliveries on duplicate orders for the original buyers. I feel confident that this duplicate will also be closed. We have heard from the Russians that they cannot consider our offer further; I judge on account of the difficulty to issue bonds. However, Colonel Buckner has taken up the question of supplying powder for the British Government with J. P. Morgan & Company who have been appointed financial agents for the purchase of supplies. He has offered them substantially the same amounts as offered Russia, namely:

7,000,000 lbs. for delivery this year,

3,000,000 lbs. per month over next year.

These offerings together with what we have closed take up practically all that we have for delivery between now and March 1916; though we have increased our capacity, as I wrote you, 103,000,000 lbs. guncotton (94,000,000 lbs. powder) starting with September and October deliveries.

My New York visit was to meet Mr. Kraftmeier, who, with his wife and daughter, arrived on the LUSITANIA Saturday. He had cabled he wished to meet Irénée and me immediately on his arrival. I supposed that his mission was to place additional orders so we took Colonel Buckner along and were much surprised to find that Mr. Kraftmeier made no mention of orders. Finally, after he succeeded in drawing me aside, he told me that they had had a report that Kuhn, Loeb & Company of New York (who are pro-German firm) had gained control of our company through the embarrassment of one of our large stockholders and that they on that account had fears concerning the orders placed with us. I, of course, assured him that nothing of the kind had happened, or would happen; that all orders would be filled according to contract without any shadow of a doubt. He seemed somewhat relieved to hear this and said this was one of the important things that brought him over. From his conversation I judge that it was THE important thing, for no other part of our discussion seemed to be of moment. I imagine that the orders placed with our company are of serious concern to the Allies and a rumor such as Kraftmeier outlined might well be worth a visit of investigation to the United States.

Kraftmeier inquired for you and was glad to learn of your improved condition. He expects to be here about a month, though I understand he will go to Palm Beach for part of his stay.

I am recommending to the Finance Committee the equalization of Executive Committee salaries. Do you not think this a good plan?

Owing to the congestion of our Brandywine Machine Shop, we have been obliged to lease the shop of J. Morton Poole, in Wilmington. Here we will do work on special pieces of apparatus such as powder presses. We do not contract outside, owing to the necessity of keeping secret our designs. Pusey & Jones Company have undertaken to manufacture guncotton wringers for the Aetna Explosives Company on designs which are substantially ours, though we have no legal claims. This shows the importance of keeping our own designs to ourselves.

Your predictions as to the common stock have been nearly realized. John Raskob tells me this morning that the price has reached $188/190.

It is difficult to judge of the effect of earnings by the extraordinary business. In the neighborhood of 100 per cent. seems a fair guess. That amount re-invested, say, on a 10 per cent. basis would mean a permanent increase of 10 per cent. on the earnings. Eventually this can be accomplished, so I think it would be fairer to count on 5 or 6 per cent. for the first couple of years. My judgment is that we will be warranted in resuming a 12 per cent. dividend basis for this year. I have another reason for advocating this,—that I am quite thoroughly persuaded it will be a mistake to publish our quarterly statements this year. Perhaps the connection of the two ideas is not obvious! As to the discontinuance of the statement: I think it would not benefit the company and probably do material harm to publish the effect of the extraordinary business any sooner than is necessary, which I judge will be the end of the year 1915. We could hardly be criticised for withholding information, excepting that stockholders might accuse us in the future of having withheld the report of profits in order to buy in the stock. To safeguard ourselves against this accusation and to be quite fair with the stockholders, I propose to increase the dividend, which, together with rumors of large orders, should certainly place any stockholders on guard against selling. Increase of dividend alone should be a warning that withholding of statements is due to prosperity and not reverses. Those who notice the absence of a quarterly statement and write to us about it can receive a reply that will satisfy them that statements are not withheld because of their poor showing. I should like to have your thought on this question. I have not talked it over to any extent—with John and Irénée only, I think. I confess that they do not respond very readily to the idea, but we have plenty of time to think it over, as the first quarterly statement is not published until May. The annual statement for 1914, which reflects little of the extraordinary business will be published in due season.

You probably do not realize how much this extraordinary military business has diverted attention from the routine of the company's business. We must be careful that our point of view is not entirely warped out of line by this temporary situation. It will take very careful thought and maneuvering to return to former conditions. The Engineering Department has expanded beyond our wildest dream. Those in the Smokeless Operating Department have seized men from the other departments in order to quickly meet demands. The other departments have responded splendidly and have done their utmost to adjust themselves to the new conditions. As far as I can see there is but one purpose throughout the entire force; that is to "make good" on these large contracts and to do it quickly. It is a situation of which we may well be proud and satisfied. There is of course a danger of overloading, but apparently no danger of anybody "falling down" through lack of willingness to work and co-operate.

The following are the figures on total sales, to date:

	QUANTITY POUNDS.
Cannon	33 291 000
Rifle	7 952 200
Guncotton	8 772 000
Triton	5 984 375
Total	55 999 575

In addition to the above we have offers for 14 027 500 lbs.

YOUR AFFECTIONATE COUSIN,

(*Sgd.*) PIERRE S. Du PONT.

At a meeting of the Finance Committee, on February 10, 1915, Alfred du Pont asked Pierre what progress he had made in negotiating for the Coleman stock.

"Why, none," replied Pierre. "The negotiations are off. You and Willie turned the offer down."

"We most assuredly did not," returned Alfred emphatically. William nodded in agreement. "The only question was one of price."

There were more words and Pierre agreed to furnish Alfred and William copies of his correspondence with Coleman. Alfred waited in vain for a few days, then exchanged the following letters with Coleman in Minnesota:

A SHEAF OF LETTERS

MR. T. C. DU PONT,
ROCHESTER, MINN.,

DEAR SIR:

At a meeting of the Finance Committee, held some time in December, Mr. P. S. du Pont brought to the attention of the committee your wish to dispose of twenty thousand shares of common stock of the Powder Company at $160.00 per share with the suggestion that same be re-distributed upon some liberal basis among the more important of the company's employees.

The committee were in accord with your general idea: viz., the purchase from you of 20,000 shares of stock, and I believe were also a unit on the point of a re-distribution of at least a portion of this stock to the company's employees, upon some plan to be subsequently defined.

The one point, on which there seemed to be a difference of opinion, was the question of price. The position which I took on this point, and which I believe was similar to the one maintained by Mr. William du Pont, was that in purchasing this stock at the price suggested by you, which would involve the expenditure of $3,200,000 of the stockholders' funds, an investment of this size by the Finance Committee could not be defended on a return of less than approximately $6\frac{1}{2}\%$ or at least better than 6% and for this reason, the price of $125.00 or an investment on a basis of, roughly, $6\frac{1}{2}\%$ was suggested.

Again, in offering this stock for subscription to our employees, it should be made on an attractive basis, which, in my opinion, should not be less than $6\frac{1}{2}\%$, and, as the company cannot afford to lose on a transaction of this kind, it was manifestly impossible for it to purchase stock at one figure and offer it to its employees at a lower one.

I believe it an excellent time to make an offer of this

character to the employees at as low a figure as is consistent with the company's interests, in order that the employees may benefit by any increment in value, which the present conditions would seem to indicate as quite probable.

I am setting my position before you clearly, for the reason that I have lately ascertained from Mr. P. S. du Pont that he did not understand my position as I had intended to present it, and for this reason, I feared that he had unintentionally conveyed to you a wrong impression as to my reasons for advocating the Finance Committee's decision in the matter.

Yours truly,

(*Signed*) ALFRED I. Du PONT,

Vice-President.

Rochester, Minn. Feb. 19th, 1915.

Mr. Alfred du Pont,
Wilmington, Del.

Dear Alfred:

I am in receipt of your letter of February 16th, and have read it several times. I cannot, however, make out why you wrote it.

To reiterate, the offer I made in December to sell 20,000 shares at $160.00 was made, as Pierre will tell you, at what I then considered, *and now know*, was a sacrifice to myself.

In that proposition, I stated the stock would go to $200.00 early in 1915. Having made up my mind that it was wise to get the young men of the company interested, I took the question up with Pierre, who agreed with me that it was a good thing for the younger men of the company, and, therefore, a good thing for the company. Pierre told me that you too had agreed it was a good thing. That it was a good thing, subsequent events have proven.

A few days after my operation, Pierre advised me there was some misunderstanding in regard to this proposition, and that you were not prepared to accept it, while I had fully understood before leaving Wilmington that you would accept it.

I immediately wired Pierre to withdraw the proposition, unless he was, in some way, committed.

In the third paragraph of your letter you say, "The one point on which there seemed to be a difference of opinion was the question of price."

If you will have the date of my proposition to the Finance Committee looked up, you will find that the then accepted orders, and the money in our hands, was sufficient to make the stock have a book value beyond the price at which I offered it, and the earnings, by reason of the accepted orders, would make the $6\frac{1}{2}\%$ you mention in your letter, look like "a drink of water."

On the second page of your letter, you say—"I believe it an excellent time to make an offer of this character to the employees at as low a figure, etc.—"

To guide me, won't you please advise how much of your common stock you are willing to let go at this time to the important employees, at price suggested by you, $125 per share. Probably I can join with you in an offer.

The position that you take, that it is wiser to buy outstanding stock than to issue new stock, is, I think, a correct one.

I am really sorry, but, to be perfectly frank with you, I cannot understand the purpose of your letter to me.

YOURS SINCERELY,
(Signed) COLEMAN Du PONT.

A week after receiving Coleman's blistering reply, Alfred read in the newspapers an announcement that Pierre and five associates had purchased *all* of Coleman's stock for $14,000,000—$200 a share for the common, $85 for the preferred. The stroke gave Pierre complete working control of the company.

Alfred's fury broke loose. He knew how to hate.

Chapter Five

DU PONT VS. DU PONT

MONDAY, March 1, 1915. Alfred and Pierre du Pont faced each other in the former's office in the massive new Du Pont Building. It was thirteen years to the day since the cousins had taken over the company.

"Is the report true that you have acquired all of Coleman's stock?" demanded Alfred, without preamble. His voice was loud, for deafness was gradually coming upon him.

"Yes, it's true," replied Pierre, speaking with a slight dental whistle that emphasized his sibilants.

"How did it come about?"

Pierre supplied some of the details. It seems that out of a clear sky Lew Dunham, Coleman's confidential man, had come to Wilmington on February 17th and informed Pierre that Coleman would consider selling his *entire* stock holdings in the powder company. Then Pierre had talked the matter over with his brothers, Irénée and Lammot, his brother-in-law, Robert Ruliph Morgan (Ruly) Carpenter, his second cousin, A. Felix du Pont, and John Raskob—all directors or officials of the company. They had decided to form a syndicate and buy Coleman's stock.

Raskob had gone to New York to see if a loan sufficiently large to swing the deal could be arranged through the firm of J. P. Morgan & Co. Treasurer John, by now, knew his way about the sanctum sanctorum of High Finance at 23 Wall Street. He came to the Morgans as a friend. Just a day or two before, in fact, he had gained the du Pont Finance Committee's approval of a naïve little note: "Gentlemen—As a matter of diplomacy I think it would be well to maintain very substantial balances, say from $700,000 to $1,000,000, with J. P. Morgan & Co., while we have large cash balances, and I will arrange to do this if it meets with the approval of the Finance Committee. J. J. Raskob."

Morgan & Co. very kindly had agreed to finance the purchase, explained Pierre. Whereupon, the syndicate had been formed and the deal put through. That was all there was to it.

"What do you intend to do with the stock?" asked Alfred.

"Our syndicate is forming a company to hold it," replied Pierre. "The company will be known as the du Pont Securities Company. Bill Hilles, the lawyer, is drawing up the papers."

Pierre added that he would own about fifty per cent of the Securities Company stock, each of his brothers about sixteen per cent, and the others smaller amounts. He would be the president.

As to the amount borrowed through Morgan & Co., Pierre was cagily evasive. The loan, it later developed, was $8,500,000.

"Did Morgan lend you the entire sum?" pressed Alfred.

[211]

"No, the loan was redistributed among certain other banks."

"What other banks?"

"I can't tell you the names."

Alfred's anger mounted.

"You propose to distribute Coleman's stock solely among yourselves?" he asked.

"Certainly," replied Pierre, "in proportion to our various interests in the Securities Company."

Alfred leaned forward and his voice became rasping.

"Pierre du Pont, don't do this. It is wrong."

Pierre remained calm.

"Why is it wrong?" he asked. "It is purely a personal transaction."

"Oh, no, it isn't," shot back Alfred. "Whatever the amount was, do you think Morgan would have arranged that loan for you as an individual? Oh, no, my cousin, you got that credit because you are vice president in the du Pont Company! That stock belongs to the company and I ask you to turn it over to the company."

"I am sorry but I don't agree with you," returned Pierre with finality, to indicate their interview was terminated.

Alfred rose, approached his cousin until their faces almost met.

"Pierre, your father and my father were brothers. Neither of these men, I am confident, would have approved what you have done. For their sake, as well as your own, put that stock in the company's treasury. Don't injure your business reputation."

Both men were silent. Almost at their feet, far below, the broad Delaware River darkened as the late afternoon sun faded.

"Pierre, I ask you."

Pierre appeared to ponder a little, but said: "No. the matter is closed."

"It is not closed," shouted Alfred, as Pierre headed for the door.

Indeed, the matter *was* far from closed.

Next day Finance Committeeman William du Pont wired Pierre from Georgia: "Paper states you have purchased Coleman's stock. I presume for the company. Any other action I should consider a breach of faith."

William hurried back to Wilmington and he and Alfred called a family consultation for the evening of March 4th. Seven Du Ponts responded. Colonel Henry Algernon, caliph of the clan, wasn't there but his son Harry (Henry Francis) was. Harry was a tall, thin young man, firmly convinced that a special place in Paradise was reserved for those born Du Pont. He went in for Society and, although a director, never worked in the company. And there were also Francis I., impractical but brilliant scientist, who was negotiating for employment with an outside company, and the current Alexis I., son of that Eugene whose death in 1902 precipitated the change in management. This Alexis I., a bachelor, sat up late at night with his books but, as secretary of the company, always opened the office promptly at eight o'clock.

There were also the brothers, Philip Francis and Eugene E., sons of Mrs. Alexis I., the widow whom Alfred had sued for slander. Philip was eccentric. He liked to wander in the woods writing poetry and shooting birds. An earlier penchant for chasing fire engines won him the nickname of "Fireman Phil." Trim Eugene E. was a director in the company, but preferred racing sail boats or trap-shooting. He was adept at both sports.

Although not invited, Pierre du Pont and his bristling, aggressive brother, Irénée, attended. All in all, nine Du Ponts, of three generations.

For one good long hour, these Du Ponts sat like fidgety, tongue-tied schoolboys, shifting in their seats, smoking, looking everywhere except at one another. The reason for this "wait" was that the interloper, Pierre, who was calmest of them all, had determined to remain silent until the question of the stock transaction was opened by the other side, and the other side was playing the same game as Pierre. Finally, Pierre could stand the atmosphere no longer and he quietly asked William du Pont what he had meant by his telegram accusing him of bad faith.

The floodgates opened.

William replied that he meant just what he had wired: that Pierre, from his own individual wealth, could not possibly have made the purchase; therefore, directly or indirectly, either the company's credit or Pierre's official position must have been used. The transaction was in bad faith to other stockholders of the company. Alfred and Francis I. spoke out in similar vein. Pierre's husky young brother, Irénée, who, at thirty-nine, still called Pierre "Dad," shouted: "Poppycock, the company had its chance and turned it down!"

"Pierre, I again ask you whether you will sell that stock to the company?" demanded Alfred, when the others had quieted.

"No, I will not," again answered Pierre, and on that note the meeting closed.

The next day Pierre executed a surprising about-face. He wrote a letter to the Board of Directors offering to entertain an offer from the company. In part the letter follows:

I am accused of having used my position to enable me to obtain credit in New York that as an individual I could not have obtained. Messrs. Alfred I. and William du Pont, who have expressed this opinion most strongly, admit that they know neither the amount of the loan, the nature of the collateral used, nor the terms of the transaction. I have given them the following information.

That a loan was placed through J. P. Morgan & Company, with whom our Company first had relations by opening an account on December 9th, 1914. Messrs. J. P. Morgan & Company undertook to place this loan in their usual manner, namely for a commission: they selected a number of banks and distributed the loan among them. After the transaction was completed, we were made acquainted with the names of the banks, who took the loan; the latter was about fifty per cent oversubscribed and it was so far distributed that Morgan & Company had not retained more than 10 per cent., i.e. the allotments to banks amounted to more than 90 per cent.

I declare that neither I nor my associates, have used or attempted to use the Company's name in this transaction. I have been greatly surprised that Messrs. Alfred and William du Pont consider that the Company has in any sense the right to take this stock, and still more surprised that some others of our directors have at least entertained such a feeling, if they do not now possess it. The object of this letter is to endeavor to settle satisfactorily in everybody's mind the question of propriety by inquiring whether the Directors wish to purchase the stock for account of the Company.

For your guidance I give the following:—

1st. As our transaction was made in the form of an offer to

T. C. du Pont, I give the Company similar opportunity to make an offer to me and my associates.

2nd. I withdraw a statement made on the evening of March 4th, that I will not sell the stock. I am now open to consider a proposition. I have not formed a final opinion, nor have I and my associates discussed the acceptance of a proposition. The question is absolutely open as far as we are concerned.

Pierre's syndicate, the du Pont Securities Company, which was capitalized for 75,000 shares of $100 each, held not only the Coleman stock but much company stock owned individually by the six members of the syndicate. Coleman was paid $8,000,000 in cash and $6,000,000 in a note carrying 36,900 shares of the powder company common stock as collateral. Pledged as collateral on the Morgan loan of $8,500,000 was 14,599 shares of powder company preferred stock and 54,591 shares of common, as well as individual guarantees of syndicate members. The Morgan loan agreement carried a rigid proviso that all dividends on the collateral stock should be paid directly to the Bankers Trust Company—the Morgan agent in the deal. If the loan had been defaulted, outsiders—namely the Morgans—would have had a substantial interest and say in the du Pont Company.

The Board of Directors met in special session on March 6th to decide upon the purchase by the company of Coleman's stock and, since Coleman had, with the sale of his holdings, resigned as president, to choose his successor. Of the eighteen men present, exactly half were Du Ponts. There were also Pierre's uncle, Henry Belin, Jr., president of the Pennsylvania subsidiary; his brother-in-law, "Ruly" Carpenter, who directed the Develop-

1ent Department; his protégé, Treasurer Raskob; and
eteran department heads who had served Du Pont long
nd well: Harry G. Haskell, High Explosives; William
Coyne, General Sales; Harry Fletcher Brown, Smoke-
ess Powder; Colonel E. G. Buckner, Military Sales, and
others.

Pierre presided as acting president. He at once asked
hat the charge of his alleged breach of faith be cleared.
quabbling began.

"I made that accusation," said William du Pont, of
he walrus moustache. "I do not think any officer con-
ected with this company ought to use his position for
is personal aggrandizement."

Chimed in Francis I.: "I believe that Morgan and
Company loaned the money with a full expectation that
n case these notes were not paid they could force the
ayment from the company's treasury by some financial
cheme. Morgan could get control of the company if the
otes are not paid."

"There is no question as to that," announced Alfred I.
The notes and obligations eventually must be met by
he powder company unless I am misinformed. As the
yndicate controls approximately $37\frac{1}{2}$ per cent of the vot-
ng control of the company, they will be entitled to that
ercentage of dividend return and to satisfy that obliga-
ion the powder company would have to make extra-
rdinary dividend disbursements."

Irénée du Pont took up the discussion.

"Mr. Alfred du Pont has made a strong presentation
n a misleading argument," he insisted. "The powder
ompany won't be forced to pay the loans. The stock has
old at from 211 to 215. It's worth $200. Profits on the

[217]

extraordinary business alone would amount to a value of $110 a share."

"We could have gotten our loan for 4 per cent, not 6, if we had used the company's credit," remarked John Raskob. "The bankers told me so. Mr. P. S. du Pont never saw any of them. Besides a wide margin of collateral, the notes are personally guaranteed by individuals. It was necessary to put up that guarantee. These charges are outrageous. I feel them keenly."

Finally, Pierre, who had been sitting pale and tense, said: "If I have not the confidence of the Board, I don't care to remain with the company."

At once there was a hubbub. The veteran Coyne, distress, bewilderment, pain burgeoning his countenance, chokingly moved for a vote of confidence in Pierre and Raskob. The spectacle of his adored bosses quarreling was too much for him. Francis I. vetoed such a resolution because, he said, it might have a "legal significance." Irénée du Pont pounced upon the phrase, demanding an explanation. "I am not enough of a lawyer to tell you," Francis I. retorted. "I think Pierre is mistaken but I don't want to vote lack of confidence in him."

"There is no one about this table who doubts you," F. L. Connable, another Du Pont veteran, assured Pierre in moist tones. Whereupon H. F. Brown suggested that all present sign an *informal* letter of confidence. "That puts us in as foolish a position as the other," snorted Francis I. "I would not sign such a letter to my own brother."

"The company's credit has been used," Alfred I. suddenly boomed, returning to the attack. "We'd have to put out over $40,000,000 for the du Pont Securities Company to meet its obligations" . . , etc.

Pierre stood his ground by firmly demanding a formal expression of confidence, which was finally voted. Alfred left the room during the voting and Francis l. refused to vote. The Board further expressed their confidence by electing Pierre to the presidency and re-electing him chairman of the Finance Committee. Brother Irénée also came in for an inning. Coleman's former post on the Finance Committee was given to Irénée. Pierre's control was now obvious.

When the question of the company's purchase of Coleman's stock came up, Pierre staged his master move. He artlessly suggested that John P. Laffey, the company's counsel, be consulted. As if delivered by genie, the rubicund Mr. Laffey appeared, with marked copies of law books under his arm. Mr. Laffey read from the books in a sonorous voice; then gravely gave his opinion that the company could not legally purchase the Pierre-Coleman stock except out of its surplus funds. These, he said, were insufficient.

The gentlemen decided to refer the matter to the Finance Committee, which was instructed to report back to the board on March 10th.

The Finance Committee now was composed of Alfred, William and the new member, Irénée. Pierre was chairman.

Alfred and William du Pont, despite Laffey's opinion, voted in favor of the purchase. Irénée voted against it. Pierre, himself, did not cast a ballot. His refusal to place himself on record defeated the proposal, since the by-laws required a majority vote for affirmative action.

[219]

At the March 10th meeting of the board, seeking to end the dispute once and for all, Treasurer Raskob introduced a resolution that the company make an offer to purchase the Coleman stock from Pierre's syndicate, at the price paid by the syndicate. Alfred, William and Francis I. du Pont voted for the resolution. Fifteen directors voted against the purchase, *including Raskob*, Pierre and the four other members of the du Pont Securities Company.

At this meeting, Lawyer Laffey, who so effectively had advocated non-purchase by the company, was elected a director and later given an interest in the syndicate, as were five other pro-Pierre directors—H. F. and Eugene E. du Pont and Messrs. Harry Haskell, William Coyne and Harry Fletcher Brown.

While the Du Ponts battled among themselves, the most terrible war the world had ever known created a clamor for Du Pont powder.

It soon became evident that the Great War was developing into a protracted struggle. Daily the Allies revised upward their estimates of the munitions required to beat back the Central Powers. Orders for powder and other explosives, in fantastic amounts, poured into Wilmington. By June, 1915, Du Pont had booked more than $100,000,000 in war orders; by fall another $120,000,000. The profits kept pace—running about 1,000 per cent ahead of 1914.

Coleman du Pont's prediction that $160 as a valuation for Du Pont common stock would look like a "drink of water" was amply realized, though too late for Coleman. The company was again reorganized in September,

1915. A new $120,000,000 corporation was chartered in Delaware, which issued two shares of stock for every share in the old (New Jersey) company. This new Du Pont common went up to $300, $400, $500 a share.

There was no question now of du Pont Securities Company's ability to meet its obligations. Within eight months of its founding, it cancelled its notes both to the bankers and Coleman, issuing in their stead $10,000,000 in low interest debenture notes.

Meanwhile, the right of Pierre to the Coleman stock was still burning Alfred I.

In December, 1915, Philip Francis du Pont filed suit in the Federal Court at Wilmington against Pierre and his associates. The Court was asked to compel Pierre et al. to turn the Coleman stock over to the du Pont Company. Philip, it will be recalled, was the erratic son of the widowed Mrs. Alexis I., who had attended the protest meeting in Alfred's office the evening of March 4th. Though he had inherited a few hundred shares of Du Pont stock, it was not long before rumors that Alfred was behind the suit were confirmed.

Alfred joined Philip as plaintiff, as did four brothers and a sister of Felix du Pont, who was one of Pierre's staunchest supporters. They were Francis I., Ernest, Archibald and Paul du Pont, and Mrs. Eleanor du Pont Perot. Another sister, Sophie, the wife of Irénée du Pont, did not sue.

Inasmuch as Felix and Irénée were both defendants, the split in the family grew wider than ever. Indeed, some of those who now joined Alfred had been bitter critics of his marital shindigs. Pocketbooks, as well as politics, sometimes make relations even stranger.

William du Pont did not join the suit but gave notice that he would testify for the plaintiffs. He was promptly ousted from the company, as were Alfred and Francis I.

Alfred exploded. He bought Wilmington's only morning newspaper, the *News*, and lustily flayed his enemies. He lambasted the political policies of Senator Henry Algernon du Pont; printed a photograph showing Coleman disporting himself on the sands at Palm Beach between two scantily-clad, glossy-toed sirens, and, of course, lashed at Pierre at every opportunity.

The suit of Du Pont vs. Du Pont came to trial before Federal Judge J. Whitaker Thompson, June 28, 1916.

By this time, the Coleman stock had a market value of $60,000,000, some $45,000,000 more than Pierre & Co. had paid for it. Dividends in the form of cash or stock totaled 183 per cent.

It developed that the fifteen banks and trust companies which loaned Pierre the $8,500,000 were the company's depositories. Du Pont deposits in eleven of these fifteen banks trebled the day after the loan was made. This was the basis for Alfred's claim that company credit had been used in financing the purchase. Pierre and Raskob insisted that this was merely a coincidence; that Morgan & Co. had apportioned the loan without informing them of the identity of the banks. They denied, too, that knowledge of lucrative contracts had been concealed from Alfred and William.

A parade of famous bankers took the witness stand to testify for Pierre. Albert H. Wiggin, president of the Chase National, mopped his perspiring brow and yawned as he swore that he had taken $500,000 of the loan on the word of Morgan & Co., and understood the powder company had nothing to do with the transaction. Seward Prosser, of the Bankers Trust Company, testified that Pierre had told him that the individual wealth of the six men in the syndicate totaled $10,000,-000. Henry P. Davison, of Morgan & Co., said the loan had been made to Pierre and the others as individuals, not as Du Pont officials.

"I scarcely knew the men," explained Mr. Davison. "My partner, William H. Porter, had done business with them when he was president of the Chemical National Bank."

Q. Do you know that in this case Lammot du Pont and Irénée du Pont made no statement whatever of their individual property, and yet took a million and odd in this loan upon their personal holdings?

A. I did not know that. I did not discuss that with Mr. Porter.

Q. That would have been unusual, would it not?

A. The whole transaction was unusual.

Q. The dealings, so far as this concern had dealings, were dealings by the company with your firm up to this date, were they not?

A. Entirely.

Q. Your firm, in its official connection with the Allies, had had the distribution of very large contracts and these people had been the recipients of very large contracts for the benefit of the Allies, had they not?

A. That is true.

Q. And very naturally, growing out of that relation, you would have very kindly feelings toward the people?

A. As a rule, yes.

Q. And when they came to you making loans, they came with the advantage which attached to the fact that as officials of the company you had had very large pecuniary transactions with them, which had been satisfactorily conducted?

A. Yes.

Q. And they did not come to you with that scrutiny that you would give to strangers who came to you and wanted to borrow $8,500,000?

A. We never loaned $8,500,000 to a stranger.

Alfred was on the stand for three days, Pierre the better part of four. Under the bludgeoning cross-examination of John B. Johnson, the shaggy chief of counsel for the plaintiffs, Pierre admitted he had gotten Lawyer Laffey's adverse legal opinion on the purchase before he offered to consider a bid from the directors. "But if they had all voted in favor of it, and it could legally be done," insisted Pierre, "I am convinced that I would have turned over those shares."

Q. Alfred du Pont had been vice president of the company since its organization, had he not? A. Yes.

Q. And director? A. Yes.

Q. And William du Pont had been director for many years? A. Yes.

Q. Tell us what sin they committed that you thought justified you in turning them out of their positions. A. Justification, did you say?

Q. Yes, give it as full as you can formulate it.

Pierre's calmness dropped from him. His eyes gleamed behind his glasses. He leaned forward with every eye upon him, the court room suddenly had grown silent, then he replied with more vehemence than anyone had ever heard him use:

"I had felt from about the summer or the autumn of 1914 that the company was not getting coöperation from either Mr. Alfred I. du Pont or William du Pont; in the case of Alfred I. du Pont it dated prior to that, I believe —I know. The question of the purchase of this stock raised grave suspicions in my mind. The plan of campaign was not one which was open and above board, not one which a director honestly interested in the company's affairs would have taken. The news of this purchase was published in the papers, but no action was taken with reference to bringing the matter before the Board of Directors or in any official way until I myself acted. After that whole question had been settled by the board, I learned indirectly that Mr. Alfred du Pont was not acting openly and above board. I was told by one of the directors of the company that he had made serious charges against the principal men in the company which I knew were not true. Mr. Alfred I. du Pont, some time prior to that, had made serious charges against Mr. T. C. du Pont. Later he tried to interest the Department of Justice in Washington to keep this trouble going; at least the Department of Justice had been solicited by somebody, and they refused to state whether or not it was Mr. Alfred I. du Pont, but I had every reason to believe that it was."

Q. You do not know anything about it but you had every reason to believe that it was?

A. I asked him the question and he refused to state yes or no. Later on, when this suit came up—no, when this Department of Justice matter was being agitated, I went to Alfred I. du Pont and William du Pont and told them that if they were still acting against the company's interest, it was about time that I knew it; that the company had the largest work on hand it had ever had before; and that it was necessary for every man to attend to his duty and do it well; and trouble makers must either mend their ways or get out. Later, when Mr. Philip F. du Pont brought his suit, I again went to Mr. Alfred I. du Pont and Mr. William du Pont and asked them if

[225]

they had anything to do with it. They said no. I asked them both as officers of the company to discuss the matter and they both refused. They did not coöperate. So, at the meeting of the directors, I, as a stockholder, advocated that they should not be re-elected and they were not put off the board, but they were not re-elected.

Q. What had they done but oppose you in the acquisition of this stock for your personal benefit?

A. They tried to stir up trouble, making charges that were unwarranted; Mr. Alfred I. du Pont did, against some of the principal men of the company.

Q. Charges against you, I suppose?

A. As reported to me, charges against me and against the treasurer, Mr. Raskob; against Mr. Irénée du Pont and earlier against Mr. T. C. du Pont. Charges that I was totally incompetent, extravagant and wasteful, and that I would probably wreck the company within three years. Charges that the others were incompetent and held office only through my influence.

Coleman du Pont was called but permitted to testify only that he had never offered more than 20,700 shares of his stock to the company, that his entire holdings were offered only to Pierre.

Public testimony ended July 18, 1916. Judge Thompson's decision, in April, 1917, castigated Pierre unmercifully as a double dealer and a faithless officer of the company.

Pierre's side had asked the Court to rule that the complainants had ratified the refusal of the Board of Directors to buy the disputed stock by voting for the re-election of the Board at the 1915 annual stockholders meeting. Judge Thompson said: "I decline to so find because at the meeting held on March 15, 1915, the plaintiffs and all of the stockholders, with the exception of those interested in the acquisition of Coleman's stock, were fraudulently kept in ignorance of Pierre's breach of trust and that of his associates and therefore the action of the stockholders meeting was obtained by fraud and concealment which renders it null and void."

So far, so good—for Alfred. But the one thing that Alfred most desired, an order to turn the disputed stock back to the company, Judge Thompson refused. Instead, he appointed Daniel O. Hastings as special master to hold an election at which all the stockholders should decide the issue by majority vote. The former Coleman shares—which now amounted to 126,628 shares in the new company—were barred from voting. The Alfred and Pierre groups each controlled approximately one-third of the remaining 461,432 shares. The balance was widely scattered among small stockholders, some 2,000 of whom were employes of the company. These minority holders would determine the winner. The plebiscite was set for October 10, 1917.

Now began the wild scramble for proxies. Each side sent agents over the country to round up holders of even a single share of stock. Alfred's *Wilmington Morning News* berated Pierre and his group as though they were pickpockets. Pierre established a publicity bureau and fought back through the *Journal*, a Wilmington afternoon newspaper. Most people in Wilmington grew thoroughly sick of the name Du Pont.

Coleman du Pont published a letter upholding Pierre and advising stockholders that "if for any reason the sale to Mr. Pierre S. du Pont was not effective, then title to the stock is properly mine." Three prominent officials of the company, Hamilton M. Barksdale, J. A. Haskell, and C. L. Patterson, wrote the stockholders that *serious business consequences* might follow a vote adverse to Pierre, emphasizing the astonishing current earnings under Pierre's management.

It was this thought that probably decided the election in Pierre's favor by a vote of 312,587 to 140,842.

Judge Thompson thereupon dismissed the suit and left Pierre, his brothers, Raskob and their group in control of the company.

But Alfred, once he had started hating, couldn't stop. He fought on, and thereby committed a tactical blunder. Though on the outside looking in, he was still the largest shareholder next to Pierre; and sharing the company's Aladdin-like earnings, which were ample for his battle. Though friends advised him to drop the case, he insisted upon carrying it to the Circuit Court of Appeals, in an effort to upset Judge Thompson's order of dismissal.

In March, 1919, the Circuit Court of Appeals handed down an opinion that was a complete reversal of Judge Thompson's original findings. It held that Pierre's purchase was *not*, in itself, a breach of trust; that he and his associates had *not* used the powder company's credit in the Morgan financing; and it reaffirmed the lower court's order dismissing the suit.

Tweedledum, tweedledee.

Alfred tried to carry the case further. But the Supreme Court of the United States refused him a hearing. His bitterness, thereafter, turned in upon itself.

Meanwhile Du Pont powder, largely, was fighting the Great War. And the profits thereof, almost overnight, transformed the staid and ancient tribe of Du Pont into a dynasty of overwhelming wealth and power.

Part Five

THE GOLDEN FLOOD

Chapter One

MARS AND THE CASH REGISTER

I T IS not often, in the course of human events, that there is such a stupendous, golden mating of men and opportunity as that which was realized by the Du Ponts in the World War of 1914.

It would seem as if everything that had transpired in the century and a decade since the first Irénée du Pont arrived on the Brandywine with his dogs and his sheep, his children and his hopes, had been only in preparation for the harvest now reaped by his descendants. Their wealth and power rose to heights that would be unbelievable if not demonstrable by cold facts.

During the four-year war period, Du Pont's capacity for powder manufacturing expanded from 8,000,000 to almost 500,000,000 pounds a year. Du Pont produced for the United States and the Allied nations 1,466,761,219 pounds of military explosives—smokeless powder, T. N. T., guncotton, dynamite and the like. It sold 125,000,000 special rounds of ammunition for airplanes, 50,000,000 caps, 206,000,000 black-powder pellets for loading in shells. Its plants handled 2,660,000 bales of cotton; produced 1,930,000,000 pounds of nitric acid; 2,500,000,000 pounds of sulphuric acid; 216,500,000 gallons of alcohol.

The factory personnel increased from 5,300 to 47,914, the engineering department from 800 to 45,000 men. Construction work, costing $220,000,000, resulted in 14 square miles of factories, covering 9,000 fenced-in acres; 10,790 individual dwellings for the war workers, as well as hotels, boarding houses, women's dormitories and bunks capable of accommodating 65,000 persons. Capacity of pumping stations at the plants was 305,000,000 gallons a day, more than the combined daily water supply of Philadelphia and Boston. Refrigerating apparatus generated 9,000,000 pounds of ice a day, equal to the consumption of the city of Chicago. Railroad classification yards handled 1,600 freight cars at one time.

Du Pont supplied forty per cent of the explosives used by the Allies. It made ninety varieties of powder for the United States.

Financially, too, the war changed the company from a comparative pigmy into a giant. Gross income reached $1,000,000,000. Capital employed in the business increased from $83,000,000 to $308,000,000. And net profits, for the four years 1915–1918 inclusive, after numerous deductions for depreciation and other bookkeeping devices, *were $237,000,000*. The net earnings, for one year alone, 1916, reached an all-time high of $82,000,000. The company distributed to its stockholders $140,983,000 in dividends. These dividends amounted to *458 per cent* on the par value of the stock.

Reverberations from these inordinate war profits still rumble in and out of the halls of Congress. Du Pont's colossal returns are cited today, with terrific effect, by those who favor nationalization of munitions making. Nor is the criticism lessened by the rather startling absence of Du Ponts from the roster of those who served their country in the World War. Of the younger Du Ponts in the company, only Alfred Victor, who, in spite of his father, Alfred I., retained the name of Du Pont, saw active combat.

The largest gross sales of all commodities, commercial as well as military, in any one year before the war, aggregated a little over $36,000,000. On this basis the war orders provided nearly 26 years' business. Compared with military business only, the most lucrative year before the war witnessed sales of $3,600,000. The war sales, therefore, represented 276 years' military business. These computations were made by Colonel E. G. Buckner, Du Pont's super-salesman, who executed the largest powder contracts in history.

"We guessed right but we were not taking any chances of the war ending in six months," said Colonel Buckner, subsequently. "We asked the Allies $1 a pound for our powder. They accepted but wanted to secure us by depositing in banks, named by them, twenty-five per cent of the face value of the contract, which twenty-five per cent was to be deducted from the lots of powder as delivered by us. Our demand was a cash payment of fifty per cent to be made to us without any conditions or restrictions attached—and the balance was to be paid as each lot was delivered. Our demand was finally agreed to. It was the wisest thing the Allies did. To it alone is due the credit of the huge job we did. It put our organization both in funds and in confidence. All limits were off. We were ready to accept any proposition involving any amount, which contained the fifty per cent cash payment clause. Contracts followed and were accepted so

[233]

fast we were forced to start a new plant nearly every day. Sure, we made tremendous profits, but it wasn't extortion, under the circumstances. If we had lost millions, we'd have been called idiots and fools."

One day in 1916, J. P. Morgan beckoned Colonel Buckner from the swarming crowd of salesmen and manufacturers that milled through the Morgan corridors and took the Du Pont man into his office. "Buckner," remarked the King of Wall Street, "I thought you might be interested in something I heard at dinner last night from Mr. De Lancey Nicoll who is just back from London, where he talked with Lord Moulton, head of the British Munitions Board. Lord Moulton said the British and French armies wouldn't have held out last year except for the efforts of three American concerns: Morgan & Co. in purchasing munitions, Du Pont in supplying powder, and Bethlehem Steel in making guns and shells."

The vast Du Pont Building in Wilmington was, of course, a hive of war activity, yet a cathedral calm pervaded the ninth floor suite of President Pierre du Pont. Callers found him at a desk that appeared always miraculously clean, irreproachably attired in modest dark clothing, looking as fresh as though he had just stepped from a scented bath. With Coleman out and Alfred in open rebellion, the burden of the prodigious war expansion fell chiefly upon Pierre. Always working smoothly, with never the slightest trace of haste, he handled the tremendous volume of business with an almost machine-like efficiency, developing talents for finance and for organization that amazed even those on the inside who had watched his progress with the company from the beginning.

Ever near Pierre was the company's treasurer, John Raskob. They were a wonder team. Realizing that the fountain of human enterprise is closely identified with self-interest, they passed out the word, at the very beginning of the war, that the company would share its prosperity with those who worked for Du Pont. Pierre released small but rich blocks of stock in his du Pont Securities Company to half a dozen of the more important executives. Company stock was sold on liberal terms to others, while bonuses were dangled before practically every workman's eyes.

Pierre also created an all-powerful executive committee, which met almost daily and kept in continuous touch with the various department heads. This executive committee, nine in number, was the main staff of Pierre's organization. After the Armistice, he singled out its members, along with seven department heads, as principally responsible for the company's war achievements. The roster: Executive Committee—Irénée du Pont, chairman; H. Fletcher Brown, smokeless powder operations; R. R. M. Carpenter, development work; Frank L. Connable, special purchasing; William Coyne, sales; Lammot du Pont, miscellaneous manufacturing operations; Harry G. Haskell, explosives manufacturing operations; John J. Raskob, finance; Frank G. Tallman, purchasing. Department heads—Colonel Edmund G. Buckner, military sales; Major William G. Ramsay, who died in 1916, and his successor, Harry M. Pierce, engineering; Dr. Charles L. Reese, laboratories and research; Daniel Cauffiel, real estate; William A. Simonton, traffic; and John P. Laffey, chief counsel.

From the Wilmington center, their net-work extended into far-reaching fields. Newer and deadlier explosives, including poison gas, were developed in Europe, which had to be matched by Du Pont. Dr. Charles Lee Reese, who had been a professor of chemistry at Johns Hopkins University in Baltimore until enticed into Du Pont service as Chemical Director, was in charge of the research laboratories. His staff of chemists was enlarged five fold to 987 men.

Into the Du Pont plants, with their smoking stacks, strange-looking buildings and guarded gates, swarmed a horde of men, women and boys lured by wages of $12 and $15 a day. Behind these wages, however, lurked the hazards of mixing the hell's brew of death-dealing material. At Deepwater Point, New Jersey, across the Delaware River from Wilmington, toluene for T. N. T. was produced from coal-tar derivatives and gas house oils; and tetryl, picric acid and ammonium picrate, explosives used by the Allies for filling artillery projectiles; and chlorine and phosgene and the lethal-benzol series, which turns blue the bodies of its victims.

At Penns Grove, New Jersey, where picric acid was made, the workers were called "canaries" because of the brilliant yellow their skins turned from the picric. The fumes of picric acid—the result of nitric acid on phenol, or carbolic acid—irritate the mucous membranes of the respiratory tract, attack the intestinal tract, and infect the kidneys and nerve centers when breathed into the system. Fulminate of mercury, another war product, subjected the workers to risks both from nitrons and mercury fume poisoning. When the British Government studied the hazards in the production of fulminate of mercury, it found forty per cent of the employes in English factories suffering from mercury poisoning. The fumes, too, of nitroglycerine can cause permanent injuries to lungs and heart.

In the manufacture of smokeless powder and dynamite, Du Pont had plenty of accidents under normal conditions. Now, with new, inexperienced workers, dangers were multiplied. Those who so blithely rushed into the munitions plants for their $1 or $1.50 an hour often encountered perils more deadly than those overseas. Though the Du Pont records report only 347 workmen killed, there is no estimate of the "wounded" or "maimed for life."

There was another hazard: sabotage. After powder, apparently perfect, had been packed into air-tight boxes, samples would be withdrawn for the inspectors of foreign countries. Occasionally they found nails driven into the boxes to cause leakage; or foreign matter, such as dirt, old lunches and rags, in the powder itself. Many thousands of pounds were thus rejected. There were also explosions that defied explanation.

To combat the sabotage, the company created a force of 1,400 guards and planted hundreds of secret agents among the workers. No one knew whether the man in the next bunk or the woman at the next bin was a company informer. Amid drama and tragedy, the great war machine hummed on.

While Du Pont sped steadily on to power, the man at its head remained unruffled. Pierre du Pont himself is as fascinating a study as any of the events which swirled about him. His brother-in-law, "Ruly" Carpenter, in charge of the company's espionage system, assigned a bodyguard to him but Pierre slipped away whenever he could. For diversion he learned to play the piano. Often he went with John Raskob to Claymont, Delaware, where his bustling little ex-secretary had built a fifty-room Italian Renaissance mansion in token of his new prosperity. Here Raskob had an electrically lighted tennis court, upon which he was fighting off a tendency to fleshiness; an organ, upon which he picked with one finger such tunes as "There'll Be a Hot Time In the Old Town Tonight"; and ample nurseries for the numerous little Raskobs who were arriving as rapidly as nature permitted.

Pierre himself had bought an extensive property near Kennett Square, Pennsylvania, seventeen miles from Wilmington, which he christened "Longwood." The place, locally known as "Pierre's Park," contained hundreds of magnificent trees—a hobby of its former owner—and when Pierre moved into the modest brick mansion, he decided to launch into some arboreal experiments of his own. Eventually he made Longwood one of the horticultural wonders of America. He began by transplanting some rare azaleas, which he bought from a Belgian fancier. This owner, it seems, fled from Brussels when the Germans invaded Belgium, taking his beloved plants with him. As the German push was extended, the Belgian retreated further and further, still hugging his azaleas. Finally he landed in Antwerp, where, penniless, he begged agents to find a purchaser for his plants, preferably an American. Pierre bought them.

Pierre's constant companion, during those crowded days, was a strikingly handsome young Delaware farm boy, Lewes Mason, who served him as chauffeur but wore no uniform, dined with his employer when they were away from Wilmington, and lived at Longwood. This lad, named for the town in which his family had lived for generations, entered Pierre's service in 1913. He was then seventeen, gentle, modest, faithful. Soon he so endeared himself to Pierre that the latter adopted him almost as a son. Pierre, though a bachelor, had raised his brothers and had a tremendous paternal instinct.

However, the marital urge finally caught up with Pierre. As business brought him to New York with increasing frequency, he leased an apartment at 400 Park Avenue. Here, very quietly, on October 6, 1915, he married his first cousin, Alice Belin, daughter of his mother's brother, Henry Belin, of Scranton, Pennsylvania. Pierre was forty-five; his bride, an attractive, energetic woman, some years younger.

The Belins and the Du Ponts had been associated for more than a century. The first Belin, Augustus, a Frenchman, was the original Irénée du Pont's first bookkeeper and was succeeded by his son, Henry H. Belin. This son's daughter, Mary Belin, married Lammot, Pierre's father, and his granddaughter married Pierre. Indeed a Du Pont-Belin alliance!

Pierre's bride loved flowers and music. She entered enthusiastically into his horticultural experiments, and soon grew as fond as her husband was of his young chauffeur-protégé, Lewes Mason. In the influenza epidemic of October, 1918, the youth became desperately

[239]

ill. Pierre and his wife dropped all other interests to nurse him. No son of their own could have received more devoted attention. In fact Pierre's mother was a little outraged when she learned that an eider-down comforter she had sent her son had been given to the patient. The boy became worse and, despite the efforts of specialists from Philadelphia and Baltimore, died. Pierre and his wife were desolate. Several years later, Pierre laid the cornerstone of the $1,200,000 memorial Lewes A. Mason Hospital erected by him at West Chester, Pennsylvania, near Longwood, and murmured chokingly that, if he had a son, the dead youth would be the type he most desired.

For many years prior to the war Du Pont had an agreement for the interchange of patents and processes with the Nobel Company of Great Britain and its affiliate, the German Nobel Company. From the latter they had learned the immensely valuable use of diphenylamine as a stabilizer for smokeless powder; and had obtained sufficient technical leads to enable them to manufacture diphenylamine in huge quantities upon America's entrance into the war.

The foreign alliances were to be abrogated in the event either of war or the objection of any of their three governments.

Since 1908, Du Pont had jealously guarded its trade secrets from the U. S. Government. No government representative was admitted into a Du Pont plant unless he signed an agreement pledging himself not to reveal the company's manufacturing processes. In 1909, when Congress voted to increase the capacity of the government powder plants at Indian Head and Picatinny, Du Pont considered the Government as a competitor and further protected itself by issuing rigid instructions that no information was to be given to anyone without specific authority from Du Pont headquarters.

After 1914, the secrecy pledges were tightened and the Government felt itself hampered. The Secretary of War wrote Du Pont a blunt letter in which he held that information obtained from Du Pont was well known and could not be considered as coming within the category of secret processes; further that the War Department would willingly consent to the abrogation of agreements in order that the Government might benefit thereby. The Du Pont reply was caustic. "The latter hypothesis," it asserted, "we reject as unworthy of our consideration or belief, and accept, with much reluctance, the former."

In this letter the company added:

We deem it advisable, under the extraordinary conditions of the present time, to limit inspection at our factories to the selection of samples for tests and such other observations as may be agreed upon as necessary to insure the production of a satisfactory article without in any way disclosing the methods by which the results are obtained by us and the character of the machinery and appliances used at our plants . . . it is our desire to protect ourselves in the use of the many details of manufacture which we claim are of value and not readily obtainable, but which the Department in its new policy believes open to the world.

Two months after the entrance of the United States into the World War, the Government asked Du Pont—now operating on a cost plus basis—to exchange detailed information with other manufacturers of war materials

[241]

because of the necessities of national defense. Du Pont refused, again pointing out that its trade secrets were valuable assets, and that it would not yield them without compensation, but would "continue to coöperate by giving information when specific cases arose."

The following spring, in response to a similar request from the War Department, Du Pont's Executive Committee decided that it "should not divulge secret processes when Du Pont has ample capacity to meet the requirements." The Committee adopted a resolution amplifying this policy:

"When necessary to divulge secret processes, it should be done with the understanding that said processes should be licensed for use only upon explosives supplied the Government of the United States or its Allies, and during the war period; that protection of some kind should be given us against the use of our secret processes by competitors when we return to normal conditions."

The first test of the new policy came when the Army asked for complete data on Du Pont's T. N. T. plant, including detailed information on the power and quantity of raw materials per unit of the finished product. The company replied that it was ready to manufacture whatever quantity of T. N. T. the Army required and more than that could not be expected of it.

Secretary of War Baker took up the gage. Du Pont backed down, agreeing to supply the information if the War Department would issue a formal order.

Time and again, the Secretary of War, a fighting pacifist, became exasperated over his dealings with the Wilmington company.

The day came when the U. S. Government decided

that neither the Government nor Du Pont had the "ample capacity" which the war required and proposed to build a government plant near Nashville, Tennessee—incomparably the largest smokeless powder factory in the world. In this gigantic undertaking, the Government was forced to turn to Du Pont. No one else had the men. the facilities or the experience.

This mammoth plant, "Old Hickory," launched a controversy between the Government and Du Pont in the fall of 1917 that has continued to this day. Old Hickory cost the Government more than $85,000,000 and was salvaged for less than $4,000,000.

The Du Pont demand, in the first weeks of the negotiations, was for ten per cent commission on the construction and fifteen per cent on the operation returns of the plant. Robert S. Brookings, of the War Industries Board, reported to Secretary of War Baker that the proposed contract would net Du Pont $13,500,000 for constructing the plant and $30,000,000 additional for one year's operation. Baker blocked the contract. Daniel Willard, chairman of the War Industries Board, intervened.

A few weeks later Mr. Willard advised Secretary Baker that the board had reached the point where it was unable to agree with the Du Ponts in the matter of compensation and suggested that Mr. Baker call the heads of the Wilmington company to Washington for a conference and "say to them that the emergency nature of the government needs is such that you must insist upon their taking hold of the project without delay, as the agents of the Government, to construct, organize and operate the plants in the shortest possible time."

[243]

The War Industries Board proposed an advance payment of $1,000,000 as compensation to the Du Ponts over and above cost of construction and operation; and, if, when the plant was completed, the du Pont Company and Mr. Baker were unable to agree as to the amount of additional compensation, the question should be submitted to arbitration. This proposal was rejected by the Du Ponts.

Pierre du Pont later told the Nye Senatorial Munitions Committee, on December 14, 1934, that Secretary of War Baker plainly indicated to him, in November, 1917, that he considered the Du Ponts "a species of outlaws" because of the terms Du Pont insisted upon. Pierre said he especially resented a remark made by Mr. Baker that "the time has come for the American people to demonstrate that they can do things for themselves."

At the same hearing Colonel T. C. Harris, of the Army Ordnance Bureau, told the Nye Committee that because of the Old Hickory wrangle "three months were lost during the middle of the war," adding: "It had a serious effect on our preparations. It didn't have a fatal effect, but it might have had."

Finally, a contract was signed under which Du Pont's gross profits were about $2,000,000.

When their percentages had been worked out to their satisfaction, Pierre and his men went full speed ahead. The du Pont Engineering Corporation, with a nominal capital of $5,000, was organized for the project. Nine units, each complete in itself, were to be built; each of these units to be approximately eight times the size of the largest smokeless powder plant in the United States prior to 1914. The entire plant was to be seventy times as large as the largest plant before the war. It would cover an area one and one-half miles wide by three miles long. To operate it at capacity for one day would require 1,500,000 pounds of nitrate of soda; 675,000 pounds of sulphur; 4,500 tons of coal, equivalent to 100 carloads, or two trainloads; 100,000,000 gallons of water, or as much as is used by a city of 1,000,000 inhabitants. The central power plant, largest in the world, would contain 68 boilers, each with a rating of 825 horsepower.

Complete architectural and structural layouts were rapidly made of factory buildings, offices, laboratories and shops; as were designs for process equipment, fire protection, heating, lighting and ventilating, together with layouts of power plants and distributing systems for steam, electricity, refrigeration, water and compressed air.

The Old Hickory job called for expenditures at a rate twice as great as the cost of the Panama Canal. While machinery for the plant was being built in the Du Pont shops, Chief Engineer Harry Pierce threw a force of 25,000 men into the field. The first task was construction of a seven-mile railroad between the plant site and Nashville.

If the swivel chair gentlemen at headquarters had been dilatory in figuring profits, there were no laggards among Pierce's boys. Ground was broken for the plant March 8, 1918.

The first unit, for the manufacture of sulphuric acid, was put into operation June 1, 1918—two months earlier than the contract called for. The first powder was made July 2nd. Successive units were each completed ahead of schedule up to the signing of the Armistice. At that time five units were producing at full capacity and the sixth was ready for operation. Construction was 96 days ahead of schedule time and 13,000,000 pounds of powder above contract requirements had been manufactured.

Furthermore, a city to house 30,000 employes had gone up in like magic—a city provided with light, water and sewerage system, incinerating plant, hospitals, churches, schools, hotels, eating houses, amusement places and Y. M. C. A. and Y. W. C. A. buildings.

In spite of the charges of fraud and waste which have cropped up at intervals since—at one time the Department of Justice had 103 auditors in Wilmington checking over the accounts—Old Hickory is a monument to Du Pont efficiency.

The complete story of Du Pont's war-time activities would require volumes. Using basic ingredients that go into the composition of explosives, the company also manufactured acids and chemicals for many other purposes: paint for camouflage, pyroxylin dopes for airplanes, fabrics for dugout curtains, clothing especially coated as a protection against fire and poisonous gases, pyralin for battery jars and gas-mask eye-pieces, etc.

At the top of the great Du Pont pyramid was Pierre, planning, organizing, coördinating, above all handling the finances with the same touch of wizardry with which he directed the mating of rare orchids under glass at Longwood.

Cousin Alfred I. played no part in the company's war activities, though still he battled over his own grievances. A block away from Pierre's office, he erected a structure as tall as the Du Pont Building to house the Delaware Trust Company, a bank which he founded to rival the Du Pont-dominated Wilmington Trust Company. Alfred was not an outstanding success as a banker. Eventually he sold the Delaware Trust to William du Pont. He continued to take pot shots at Pierre and the reigning Du Ponts through his *Wilmington Morning News*. And he continued, with sardonic pleasure, to draw his fat war dividends.

What of Coleman? The General's colossal skyscraper in New York, the Equitable Building, yielded him such fat rentals that he didn't mourn, at least loudly, over his lost Du Pont stock. The loss, on that little 1915 dicker with Pierre, ultimately totaled more than $200,000,000. But this did not feeze Coleman. Instead, he bought out his biggest tenant, the Equitable Life Assurance Society, with its $600,000,000 assets, mutualized it, and sold it back to its policyholders, incidentally with a loss of $2,000,000.

Coleman had many irons in the fire. He built a broad, hundred-mile, concrete highway from Wilmington to the border of Maryland and presented it to the state. To promote his interests, he greased and oiled a political machine and was Delaware's choice for the Republican presidential nomination in 1916. He got thirteen votes. Impressed by Lucius Boomer's management of the Hotel McAlpin, in New York, he backed the Boomer hotel chain and later Boomer's Savarin and Louis Sherry restaurants, without conspicuous success. The Boomer chain included the McAlpin, Waldorf-Astoria, Claridge and Martinique, in New York; Bellevue-Stratford, in Philadelphia; and Willard, in Washington.

Coleman bought Horn's Point, a picturesque estate,

with a huge ducking marsh nearby, on the banks of the
Choptank River, on Maryland's famed Eastern Shore.
Here he farmed, bred cattle, hunted, and entertained
lavishly. Nothing pleased him more than to don a
chef's apron and broil steaks or scramble eggs for a party
of fifty. He gave gorgeous parties, too, in New York and
on his speedy motor yachts, which were named succes-
sively *Tech* I, II and III in honor of his alma mater,
Massachusetts Institute of Technology.

Pierre and his industrious mates, despite the huge
dividends paid to themselves and other stockholders,
emerged from the war with some $90,000,000 surplus
funds in Du Pont's treasury. A lush little nest egg which
must be made to hatch.

Careful, canny John Raskob went scouting. General
Motors Corporation was the result.

Chapter Two

GENERAL MOTORS BONANZA

G ENERAL MOTORS was the first big merger
in the automobile industry, and the most
successful. It produced and distributed motor
cars on a huge scale.

The founder and presiding genius of General Motors
was William Crapo Durant. As a salesman and promoter, Durant was incomparable. As a financier, Durant
was such an agile money juggler that he had plunged far
through the pioneer pasturages before anyone caught up
with him to determine his status along this line.

Like the Du Ponts, Durant was of French extraction.
His forebears followed the sea as fishermen, sailors,
finally shipbuilders in the old New England port of
New Bedford, Massachusetts. His maternal grandfather,
Henry H. Crapo, moved to Michigan before the Civil
War, amassed a comfortable fortune in the lumber busi-
ness, and was elected war-time governor of the state.

In 1878, at seventeen, Billy Durant went to work in
his grandfather's lumber mill at Flint, a center of
Michigan's magnificent pine belt. The youth was small
and spare, with a big, blocky head set close upon his
shoulders, and a restless, impatient nature. He could

talk a parrot off its perch. At twenty, he branched out on his own as an insurance and realty broker. One day, while visiting Coldwater, Michigan, he met a mechanic who had patented a new road cart, with improved suspension. Durant bought the patent for $50 and decided to market the carts. He took into partnership a thrifty young hardware clerk of his acquaintance, Josiah Dallas Dort.

Durant walked in on William A. Paterson, Flint's pioneer carriage manufacturer, and asked him whether he could make 10,000 carts and at what price. Paterson had never received an order of such magnitude but he enlisted an emergency force and turned out the snappy little carts, at a wholesale rate of $8 apiece. Durant sold them like hot cakes—for $12.50 each. Flushed with this success, the elated young men formed the Durant-Dort Carriage Company, employed expert designers, and, within a few years, their "Blue Ribbon" carriages were acknowledged pace-setters in the vehicle industry, with an annual output of 50,000.

At forty, Durant was a millionaire. His success was the talk of Flint, and he was eager for more adventurous forays. Withdrawing from active participation in Durant-Dort, he went East and observed Wall Street and the Stock Exchange at close range. He returned to Flint in the summer of 1904, when a proposition came to him to buy an automobile company which built three cars a month in the plant of the Flint Wagon Works. This was the Buick Motor Company, which had gone through considerable financial vicissitudes under the management of its impractical though brilliant inventor, David Dunbar Buick, a manufacturer of plumbers' supplies, and the latter's successive backers.

Durant's imagination had already soared into the future possibilities of horseless-buggies. In New York he had seen Chauncey M. Depew, Lillian Russell and other celebrities whizzing along at twelve and fifteen miles an hour in their shining Oldsmobile roadsters, with the new curved dashboards.

He took a two-cylinder Buick and for weeks drove it over every conceivable road, up hill and down, through mud, sand and swamp. The car satisfied him. He bought the company and, as was his habit, at once went into quantity production. The new Buick swept into the motor industry like a tornado, increasing its tempo from a slow walk to a run. Within ten months, Durant had enlarged his capitalization from $75,000 to $1,500,000. In a single day he himself sold $500,000 worth of stock to the people of Flint.

Durant's men were turning out Buicks by the hundreds and he was selling them as fast as they could be put together. He built new plants, bought raw materials in huge quantities, opened retail agencies in the larger cities, and poured every dollar he could beg or borrow into the business. The search for capital was insatiable. Always his "vision ran far ahead of his treasury."

By 1908, Buick was making more than 8,000 cars a year. Flint had doubled its population. Dividends had been paid with clocklike regularity. Men halted Billy Durant on the street to catch his lightest word. The press referred to him as the "Little Giant" and dragged in the inevitable "Napoleon."

In the fall of 1908—the accepted birth date is September 16, 1908—Durant organized the General Motors Company of New Jersey, with an authorized capital of $12,500,000. This was a holding company. In two years of dizzy maneuvers, General Motors rapidly acquired control, through stock ownership, of the Buick, Cadillac, Oldsmobile, Oakland Motor Companies, Northway Motors Company, Weston Mott Company and fifteen other companies. Later General Motors became an operating company and most of the subsidiaries were dissolved.

Henry Ford just missed joining the combination. Durant wanted the Ford Motor Company, badly, and got his directors to authorize its purchase for $8,000,000 —$2,000,000 down and the balance in one and two years, "if arrangements can be made to finance." The gigantic little conjunction—"IF"—prevented Durant from absorbing what has since become one of the world's most valuable properties. T. F. MacManus, in *Men, Money, and Motors*, describes a fateful meeting in October, 1909:

> Henry Ford and James Couzens were at the Belmont Hotel, in New York City. They were together in their room and Ford, suffering from lumbago, was lying on the floor because there was no comfort for him in bed. The telephone bell jangled and Couzens, picking up the receiver, heard a voice:
> "This is Billy Durant. I'd like to see you."
> "What about?"
> "I can tell you when I see you."
> Returning upstairs within half an hour Couzens . . . said:
> "Billy Durant wants to buy the Ford Motor Company."
> "How much will he pay?"
> "Eight million dollars."
> "All right. But—gold on the table!" snapped Ford.
> "How do you mean that?"
> "I mean cash."
> Durant came back the following morning, and Couzens delivered Ford's message. The two men shook hands on the

proposition and Durant left to raise the necessary money. With him he had a résumé of the Ford business and its prospects. The capital stock of the Ford company was $2,000,000 and it had a surplus of $1,180,000, exclusive of goodwill and patents. Its earnings in 1908 were $2,684,000 on a business of $9,000,000 and it was planning to do a business of $15,000,000 in 1909 including an output of 21,000 automobiles. Durant had reached an agreement with Couzens to pay $2,000,000 in cash and the balance in one and two years.

On October 26, 1909, Durant received the sanction of his board of directors for the acquisition of the Ford business, went back to his bankers and was informed:

"We have changed our minds. The Ford business is not worth that much money."

Such episodes were comparatively common in those days.

Durant, in action, was a cyclone. "When he visited one of his plants," says an early associate, "he would lead his staff in, take off his coat, begin issuing orders, dictating letters and calling the ends of the continent on the telephone, talking in his rapid easy way to New York, Chicago, San Francisco. That sort of thing was less common than it is now: it put most of us in awe of him. Only the most phenomenal memory could keep his deals straight; he worked so fast that the records were always behind."

The Little Giant worked so fast, indeed, that in two years he lost control of his company. In 1910 he found himself with properties which, though earning $10,000,000 a year, were woefully short of working capital. He had to borrow $15,000,000. This was a difficult task. The motor industry was still in its infancy and considered risky. Durant's methods did not appeal to conserva-

tive bankers. Finally, to get the money, Durant had to
create a five-year voting trust under the laws of New
York, under which two banking firms—Lee, Higginson
& Company of Boston, and J. & W. Seligman of New
York—agreed to loan $15,000,000 for five years with
the understanding that they would have control of the
board of directors.

Durant's wings appeared to have been definitely
clipped. But not so. He promptly flew out and before
long was marketing a new, light, rakish, medium-priced
car designed by Louis Chevrolet, a Frenchman, whom he
had employed as a racing driver years before. The Chevrolet filled a need and scored a phenomenal success. It
furnished funds with which Durant determined to regain
control of General Motors. Furthermore, it brought
Durant for the first time into contact with the Du Ponts.
Hamilton Barksdale, a Du Pont in-law, took a flyer on
Chevrolet and appeared as director in the $20,000,000
Chevrolet Company organized by Durant in Delaware in
1915. About the same time, the du Pont Company invested some of its early war takings in 3,000 shares of
General Motors stock.

This was a small block, compared to the 160,000 shares
of General Motors outstanding; yet it became a deter-
mining factor, in the fall of 1915, when Durant's five-
year voting trust agreement expired and he went to the
mat with the bankers for control of General Motors.
The promoter and the bankers locked in a bitter wrangle.
The result was a compromise; the bankers elected seven
directors, Durant chose seven, *and* four Du Pont men
were agreed upon as neutral directors. The four were
Pierre S. du Pont, his wife's brother, Ferdinand Lam-

mot Belin, J. A. Haskell and John Jacob Raskob. Furthermore, Pierre was chosen chairman of the board, a position he was to hold for over thirteen years.

Now, verily, Du Pont was in General Motors and in a splendid position to sense its infinite possibilities.

Time soon demonstrated that Durant controlled the majority of stock and he took the presidency in June, 1916. In October, the New Jersey company was dissolved and General Motors Corporation, with authorized capital of $102,600,000, was incorporated in Delaware. Profits (net) for the fiscal year ending July 31, 1916, were $28,812,287.96.

"Members of the old board waited, in the expectation that the Durant-Du Pont alliance would not hold," observes Arthur Pound in his official history of General Motors, *The Turning Wheel*. "The Du Ponts were descendants of an elder American industrialism, and while intensely alert in technology and finance, had never taken their projects to the public as promotions. The birth pangs of General Motors, as presided over by Mr. Durant from 1908 to 1910, would have seemed almost incomprehensible to them if they had been watching closely that dynamic scattering of stock and accumulation of properties. Rather studied attempts were made to divide the two camps, but these came to nothing."

They came to nothing because the Du Ponts realized that daring promoters of the Durant type have their uses. And they had seen considerable scattering of stock and accumulation of properties during the hectic régime of their own kinsman, Coleman. They watched Durant's gyrations with keen, appraising eyes.

No matter how much money rolled in, Durant could

always use more. He incubated a thousand dreams and schemes, ranging from fully electrified farms with automatic refrigeration to huge transcontinental highways. These he talked over by the hour, with Raskob in particular. These two self-made men had much in common, though the tight-lipped little Du Pont treasurer always looked before he leaped—and first made sure the ground on the other side was soft. Durant made Raskob a member of the General Motors Finance Committee and Raskob became an active liaison-man between Pierre and Durant.

Two problems—in a sense they were twins—were heavy upon Pierre's mind: Du Pont's future after the war and the profitable investment of the company's tremendous war surplus. He knew that future prosperity could not be based upon munitions just as he knew the wholesale killings in Europe must some time cease.

At this juncture, Treasurer Raskob brought to Wilmington an invitation from William C. Durant for the Du Ponts to invest substantially in General Motors and share with him the management. Raskob proposed an initial investment of $25,000,000.

"The gross receipts of the General Motors-Chevrolet Motor Companies for the coming year will amount to between $350,000,000 and $400,000,000," Raskob reported to the Finance Committee, December 19, 1917. "General Motors occupies a unique position in the automobile industry and, with proper management, will show results in the future second to none in any American industry. Mr. Durant realizes this and wants us to assist him handle this wonderful business, particularly in a financial and executive way."

After fulsome expressions of confidence in the future of America, Raskob pointed out, with no doubt the Alfred I. unpleasantness still vividly in mind, that it would be preferable for the company itself to make the investment "rather than have a coterie of our directors taking advantage of this in a personal way."

Though naïvely worded, the Raskob report is historic —for it resulted in the greatest concentration of capital assets that ever came under one control. The treasurer pointed out that Du Pont would gain a good customer for the paints, varnishes, etc., it was already making and added:

Perhaps it is not made clear that the directorate of the motor companies will be chosen by du Pont and Durant. Mr. Durant should be continued as President of the Company, Mr. P. S. du Pont will be continued as Chairman of the Board, the Finance Committee will be ours, and we will have such representation on the Executive Committee as we desire, and it is the writer's belief that ultimately the du Pont Company will absolutely control and dominate the whole General Motors situation. . . .

During the past two years our Company has been doing big things. After the war it seems to me it will be absolutely impossible for us to drop back to being a little company again and to prevent that we must look for opportunities, know them when we see them and act with courage.

After thrashing over the entire proposition in joint session for two days, the Du Pont Finance and Executive Committees recommended the $25,000,000 investment. The deal was concluded in January, 1918. Later that year and in 1919, Du Pont put an additional $24,000,000 into General Motors.

Du Pont at once took charge of General Motors financing, with Raskob chairman of the Finance Committee. Durant was chairman of the Executive Committee and bossed operations. Wall Street wondered how long the alliance would endure. As long as the post-war boom, some observers guessed. They were right. In 1919 vast expansion moves were made. After the absorption of Chevrolet, capital was increased to the stupendous figure of $1,020,000,000; Fisher Body and other companies were acquired; a mammoth $20,000,000 office building and a huge Cadillac plant were erected in Detroit; profits reached a high of $60,000,000; employes numbered 86,000.

Du Pont cashed in at once on its $49,000,000 investment. Instead of immediately demobilizing its great engineering force of the Old Hickory project, Du Pont had its men do $60,000,000 worth of design and construction work for General Motors, including the Detroit Cadillac plant and 1,500 dwellings at Flint and Pontiac, Michigan. Durant's friends later claimed that the Du Ponts were largely responsible for the admittedly over-ambitious scale of the program. However that may be, the Du Pont chieftains and their hard-hitting subordinates swarmed in on Durant with a vim and vigor equalling his own.

Raskob was a rabid enthusiast on Motors, so much so in fact that he began grooming a successor for the Du Pont treasurership. He had tried to train his brother Bill, William F. Raskob, but Bill didn't quite make the grade. Now, Walter Samuel Carpenter, Jr., a young man in his department, appeared most promising. A native of Scranton, Pennsylvania, Walter was a younger brother of "Ruly" Carpenter, Pierre's brother-in-law. He had married Mary Louise Wootten, a governess in Irénée du Pont's family, which, altogether, made him almost a Du Pont. Mary Wootten was a vivacious girl, as lively as her husband was subdued. Walter took on more "go" after his marriage; and Raskob felt free to devote himself more fully to his fascinating job with General Motors.

The new Du Pont-Durant crew in General Motors were so surrounded with rainbow glows in the spring of 1920 that they could not perceive the quickening approach of the post-war liquidation. On March 1, 1920, Raskob engineered a ten-to-one stock split-up and the Corporation's authorized capitalization was increased to 56,100,000 shares divided as follows:

200,000 shares of 6 per cent preferred, par $100.

900,000 shares of 6 per cent debenture, par $100.

5,000,000 shares of 7 per cent debenture, par $100.

50,000,000 shares of common stock, no par value, of which upward of 20,000,000 were issued.

Then, like a summer storm, the post-war depression broke. Dealers turned back cars in droves. Production schedules were curtailed or canceled. Great mounds of raw materials, bought and paid for, lay idle. The Corporation needed money. Raskob went to his first financial god-father, J. P. Morgan & Co. The Morgans arranged for the distribution of 3,200,000 shares of the new General Motors common at $20 a share. Explosives Trade, Ltd., a great new chemical combination in England, was interested by the Du Ponts to the extent of 1,800,000 shares, the balance being underwritten by Morgan & Co.

While this deal was pending, and everyone was breathing easier, Durant got himself badly tangled in the stock market. He was an inveterate market gambler, always a bull on his own stocks. He tried to support a falling market in General Motors and other holdings and daily got in deeper, finally becoming involved to the extent of more than $30,000,000. A forced sale of Durant's securities would mean panic on the Exchange, perhaps even the collapse of General Motors.

Raskob and Pierre and the Morgans put their heads together. The result was a $35,000,000 bond issue, with which the du Pont Company bought Durant's General Motors stock, leaving him a few millions margin after he had paid his pressing bank loans. Du Pont now had over one-third interest in General Motors and Durant was through. The "absolute domination" predicted by Raskob had come to pass within two years.

Durant resigned the presidency on November 30, 1920, saying, as he left the great organization he had founded, for the second and last time: "Well, it's moving day."

A few days later he pulled up the window shade of a small office he had rented near the General Motors New York headquarters and exclaimed: "It's a new day!" But this time Durant's wings were clipped. His remaining fortune was eventually tied up in trust funds and, it is said, his family will not willingly permit him to employ a penny of this income in stock speculation. Durant's daughter, Marjorie, by the way, is a wizard in Wall Street.

"Durant always hoped for the best and never prepared for the worst in time to ward it off," observes Arthur Pound. "In his long business career, he wrestled many times with the business cycle without apparently becoming convinced of its periodicity. He could act boldly and daringly with money, and when circumstances favored the finance of courage he seemed a financier. But money is a two-edged sword, and when circumstances demanded the finance of caution, Mr. Durant was lost."

Under what he termed "a receivership of our own," Pierre du Pont took over the presidency of General Motors, in addition to his board chairmanship, and held it for two and a half years. He made a swing around the General Motors circuit, assuring agitated Chambers of Commerce and others that Du Pont had no intention of moving the manufacturing plants East, or making other revolutionary changes. With the aid of Alfred P. Sloan, Jr., vice president in charge of operations, he cut, pruned and arranged more workable inter-divisional coöperation, along Du Pont lines, in sales, purchasing, advertising, etc. He insisted upon controlled production and thawing out of frozen inventories. The independent buying power of individual plant managers was limited to the requirements of a four months' forecast.

It all sounds like rather dull, routine organizing work, but it got results. After experiencing its first and last deficit—$38,000,000—General Motors, in 1921, started again on its golden march. In May, 1923, Pierre turned the presidency over to Sloan, who had long been an important figure in General Motors and its various merged companies.

Though some Morgan representatives succeeded Durant directors, upon the invitation and the eager approval of Du Pont, the Wilmington men have had absolute control of General Motors since 1920.

In 1923, Du Pont induced eighty General Motors

senior and junior executives to go into debt to buy General Motors stock. The eighty—who became much-advertised "millionaires"—pledged themselves to buy $33,000,000 in stock, which was substantially the amount Du Pont had taken over from Durant. They put up $5,000,000 and borrowed $28,000,000. The stock appreciated phenomenally. During the last three years of the 1920's, when General Motors earnings averaged more than $250,000,000 a year, it might truthfully be said that every man who had put in $25,000 had become a millionaire. Raskob, especially, was fond of quoting these figures.

Each original $25,000 unit purchased, eventually gave the beneficiary 22,545 shares of $10 par value common stock. Even at the low price prevailing today, the value of an original unit is more than twenty times its original cost. Writes Mr. Pound:

It has been said that General Motors made many men independently rich through its Managers Securities plan. Of course, heaping up wealth for them so abundantly and swiftly was not contemplated when the proposal was made and the plan drawn. At that time, the prospect was that the managers, with good luck and the best of team-work, would reap perhaps a fraction of what they actually received. No one could anticipate the rosy future which was destined for the Corporation and the country at large during the six years that followed. To what extent the stimulation of managerial interest added to profits cannot be determined accurately, but this was probably a very considerable factor in the strides which the Corporation took. To some extent, the managers rewarded had created their own fortunes.

From the beginning, Du Pont's control of General Motors has been almost wholly financial. Actual operations have been left in the hands of men who fought their way to the top in the automobile industry, many of them hardboiled veterans of the Durant era.

Like their powder company, General Motors has been a training school for younger members of the Du Pont hierarchy. Pierre, present *pater familias* of the clan, often uses it as a practical laboratory to test the rising generation. For instance, a few years ago, when General Motors embarked extensively into aviation, both as manufacturer and operator of transport lines, Pierre's favorite nephew, Henry Belin du Pont, was placed in this department. After a slow start, young Henry got the hang of things and now handles the finances of the flying affiliates and subsidiaries of General Motors. Among other positions, he is chairman of Transcontinental and Western Air, Inc., of which Charles A. Lindbergh is technical adviser.

As a permanent investment, the du Pont Company retains some 10,000,000 shares of General Motors common, or twenty-three per cent of outstanding Motors stock. Another twelve to fifteen per cent, I am reliably informed, is owned by individual Du Ponts. The total is more than ample for ironbound control of the Corporation.

Upon its original investment of $49,000,000 in General Motors, the du Pont Company has received dividend returns of more than $250,000,000. Further, the great motor coalition is Du Pont's best customer. For, in its post-war renascence, Du Pont has included a vast, peace-time chemical empire.

Chapter Three

THE CHEMICAL EMPIRE

INDUSTRY, skill—and luck—all enter into the
story of Du Pont's emergence from America's
most favored war baby into the realm of biggest
peace-time Big Business.

Today, Du Pont, with eighty plants in thirty states,
is one of the three great world industrio-chemical combinations—the others are in England and in Germany.
With both, Du Pont has satisfactory relationship.

In many ways, Du Pont has been favored by the Gods.
At full tide it caught, and shaped, the surge of a new
industrial era, in which synthetic products replaced
those upon which man has been dependent. Some of
Du Pont's outstanding peace-time products are dye-
stuffs, rayon, cellophane, artificial leather and other
composition fabrics, new paints, lacquers and varnishes,
pyralin and plastics, synthetic ammonia, camphor and
rubber, shatterproof glass, photographic film, refrigerants and disinfectants. Altogether, it manufactures more
than 11,000 distinct and separate articles.

Directly and indirectly, these products enter the daily
life of every individual in the United States. And,
directly or indirectly, every one of us pays tribute to
the barons of the Brandywine.

Most of these products are chemically akin: all are based upon the ingredients of modern explosives. Indeed, Du Pont was extremely fortunate in the character of explosives with which the World War was waged. The old black powder of Spanish War days, with its simple mixture of sulphur, charcoal and saltpeter, would never have lent itself to the uses found for the celluloses and acids of modern warfare.

For instance, toluene, a coal-tar derivative, is the basis of trinitrotoluene (T. N. T.), and from coal-tar springs the entire synthetic-dye industry. At the beginning of the World War it looked as if America's only choice of raiment might be white, so complete was Germany's monopoly of synthetic dyes. In 1917, the United States Government confiscated the German-owned patents and sold them to Francis Patrick Garvan's Chemical Foundation, which licensed American manufacturers to use them at nominal fee. Du Pont, which had been experimenting in dyes for some years, was quick to snatch the bargain booty and set aside $12,500,000 of its war profits for plant investment and working capital in the new field.

After the war, German scientists were tempted with golden offers to flee post-war Germany and join the Wilmington dye-stuffs personnel. Today, Du Pont is the largest American producer of synthetic aniline dyes—with annual profits of about $2,500,000.

Cellulose is the primary ingredient in most of the other Du Pont products. This basic material of all plant life is found in its purest form in cotton and spruce wood.

John Hyatt, inventor of the roller bearing, opened a vast field in cellulose chemistry in 1868 with his invention of celluloid. He was seeking to win $10,000 offered by a billiard-ball maker for an ivory substitute. By treating cotton with nitric and sulphuric acid, he got a nitrocellulose mixture which, he discovered, became solvent in camphor. Heated, the camphorated cotton could be molded into any shape desired, and when cold it was hard and easily machined. The product was first used to take the place of rubber in dental plates for false teeth. Mr. Hyatt didn't win the $10,000 prize but he has taken his place in history as the father of nitrocellulose plastics. Their proper generic term is *pyroxylin*.

In 1917, Du Pont purchased the Arlington Company, of New Jersey, which made a celluloid-like pyroxylin plastic which it called *pyralin*. In 1925, it bought the Viscoloid Company, which made *viscoloid*, another pyroxylin material. Arlington, Viscoloid and a cluster of other plants were combined into a subsidiary, which was called, rather bewilderingly, du Pont Viscoloid, and its product *pyralin*. Du Pont Viscoloid turns out combs, hair ornaments, toilet sets, handles for toothbrushes, umbrellas and doors, brushes, mirrors, belt and shoe buckles, toys and napkin rings for children, advertising novelties and souvenirs and hundreds of other gadgets.

With the Pittsburgh Plate Glass Company, Du Pont, soon after the war, organized the Duplate Corporation to make shatterproof glass for automobiles. The glass was made by cementing a layer of pyroxylin plastic between two sheets of ordinary glass. In 1931, Du Pont sold out its interest in Duplate but continues to make the pyroxylin binder.

Similarly, in 1924, it formed an alliance with the Pathé Exchange Inc. to manufacture a special form of cellulose plastic for photographic film. The du Pont Film Manufacturing Corporation is owned fifty-one per cent by Du Pont and forty-nine per cent by Pathé; and supplies the motion picture industry with about two-fifths of its negative film and one-fifth of its positive film.

Plastics—Viscoloid, safety glass binders, photographic film, etc.—earn more than $1,000,000 a year for Du Pont.

Du Pont got into rayon and cellophane—its two biggest money makers—through purchase of French patents and processes. While America clung to nature's age-old textiles, silk, wool and cotton, Europe had been familiar with rayon since 1884. In that year, Hilaire de Chardonnet first produced a silk-like fiber by chemical means. De Chardonnet got his rayon by mixing cotton in nitric and sulphuric acids, dissolving it in alcohol and ether, forcing the resulting mixture through fine openings, and hardening the spray in hot air. This was directly in line with Du Pont's development work in cellulose chemistry. Later the so-called viscose process was developed in England, in which spruce wood pulp, instead of cotton, was used as the cellulose base; and caustic soda and carbon bi-sulphide in place of sulphuric and nitric acids.

In 1920, Du Pont took over the North American rights of the great Comptoir de Textiles Artificiels, which was making viscose rayon, and formed the du Pont Fibersilk (now Rayon) Company, of which it owned sixty per cent and the Comptoir forty per cent. Du Pont's first plant was erected at Buffalo, N. Y., with French technicians guiding the delicate transition of millions of pounds of wood pulp into millions of skeins of fiber-silk. Later three other rayon factories were added to the Du Pont string and the Frenchmen were bought out. Rayon brought about "the greatest textile revolution since the invention of the cotton gin." Though the silkworm continued to produce a superior fabric from mulberry leaves, rayon brought the luxury of beautiful, colorful fabrics that felt like silk and looked like silk to millions who could not afford silk. Early rayon had a tendency to return to its original state and there were many harsh comments upon the "vegetable silks" that disappeared down drains when washed. This tendency, of course, has been corrected. Today the United States uses almost four times as much rayon as silk—in hosiery, underwear, dresses, draperies, bedspreads and hundreds of other articles. Du Pont manufactures approximately one-sixth of the 200,000,000 pounds of rayon yarn made annually in the United States and earns around $5,000,000 a year in this field.

The story of cellophane—Du Pont's pet and biggest money winner—is a romance of the depression. This tough, sparkling, transparent wrapping material, which has become inescapable no matter what you purchase, is rayon in sheet instead of fiber form. Like rayon, La Cellophane—from *cello* ("cellulose") and *phane* ("window") —is a Du Pont stepchild, adopted from the French. It has gaily progressed from an experiment to a fad to a commercial triumph.

J. E. Brandenberger, a textile chemist in the Vosges district of France, stumbled upon cellophane in 1900 while seeking to coat cotton tablecloths with liquid viscose. By 1912 he had progressed from thick, brittle sheets to a film about as thin as the cellophane of today, had taken out patents, designed machines and interested the Comptoir de Textiles Artificiels, then as now the largest French rayon company. After the war, Alfred Bernheim, head of the Comptoir, demonstrated the new wrapping on perfume bottles and candy boxes in a shop on the bustling little rue de la Chaussée d'Antin in Paris. Cellophane caught the eye of Parisians and Du Pont's as well.

In 1923, Bernheim and Brandenberger journeyed to Wilmington and went into conference with some of Du Pont's brightest rayon minds, including W. C. Spruance, board chairman of Du Pont's rayon subsidiary; and Leonard A. Yerkes, rayon president, who was such an enthusiast of the artificial fiber that he always rolled up his trouser leg to let the sun and the eyes of callers catch the shimmer of his rayon socks. The result of the conference was a deal, hastened a bit by the fact that a certain Birn & Wachenheim, Inc. was already importing French cellophane into the United States. Pierre's lawyers tossed together a neat little affiliate (fifty-two per cent Du Pont, forty-eight per cent Comptoir); Du Pont was given sole North American rights, including exclusive use of the registered trade name "Cellophane"; inventor Brandenberger agreed to superintend first Du Pont manufacture; and the gentlemen shook hands with mutual expressions of esteem.

The following spring, 1924, at Buffalo, clean white sheets of spruce wood were shredded into a fluffy mass, the fibers dissolved into a sticky, amber liquid by means of carbon bi-sulphide, the liquid forced under pressure through narrow slits into a chemical shower, passed over a series of bleaching, washing, heating rolls—and *Voilà*—the first sheet of cellophane to be produced commercially in America appeared.

For some time thereafter Brandenberger and Comptoir engineers watchfully guided Du Pont's cellophane career. The Comptoir even sent over its ace salesman, M. Jacques Piani, who wafted through the marts of trade resplendent in spats and morning coat. Soon, though, Du Pont bought out the Comptoir and both selling and manufacturing were left in the hands of Messrs. Spruance and Yerkes and their canny, close-mouthed sales manager, Mr. Oliver Benz. The Americans opened their campaign with an advertising salvo. High-powered salesmen called upon manufacturers in practically all of the fields in which cellophane has since penetrated.

The campaign was a flop. At $2.65 a pound, cellophane was too expensive a wrapper for anything except the highest priced luxuries. For a time Whitman's candy was the only large account. Then Du Pont put its chemical efficiency engineers to work and was able to cut the cost to $1.75 a pound. At this rate cookies capitulated. Some cake manufacturers tried cellophane too, but, finding it less moisture-proof than waxed paper, soon canceled their orders.

A Canadian chain of stores wrapped bacon in the new cellophane, and sales began to soar. With this victory as a lure, the Du Pont salesmen brought the Chicago packers into line. Conquests grew with each reduction in cellophane's price, candies selling for a nickel and a dime falling into line when cellophane dropped to $1 a pound.

Meanwhile, William Hale Charch, a Du Pont chemist, after two thousand experiments, mixed a waxy, nitro-cellulose lacquer which, when applied to cellophane, made it moisture-proof. The new cellophane was at first a little murky; though not so appealing to the eye as the plain variety, it performed a more useful job. Charch soon cleared the cloudiness. The field widened. Mr. Clarence Birdseye festooned his frosted foods in mois-ture-proof cellophane and chirped with joy over his zooming sales figures. But the biggest triumphs were ahead. The era of foil-wrapped cigars was at its height. The new moisture-proof, transparent jackets began to supplant the foil. Cigarette companies accepted the in-evitable and followed the lead of the cigars. Camels, with sound and fury, arrived in the "humidor pack," Lucky Strikes in the "Lucky Tab." This was in 1931. The wily Du Pont men played one manufacturer against another. In 1932, cellophane began to do well by the bread industry. Bakers tried the moisture-proof wrapper on special breads which had had only limited sales, such varieties as rye, raisin, pumpernickel, cinnamon and cranberry. Sales mounted five, six, ten fold.

Soon cellophane was a craze. Everything was being wrapped in it from violins to spark plugs. New uses were constantly found, some of them trick ones. Novelty men began to make hats out of cellophane, artificial grass and water scenes for the stage, and costumes for choruses. People found they could make their own flypaper by smearing cellophane with glue and laying it over something flies like to eat. It's very effective. The flies don't see it until they're stuck on it. In Oregon a fishing guide discovered that a little piece torn off a cigarette package, when fastened on a hook, fools trout and salmon. It seems it looks like nothing at all to flies, but it looks like flies to fish. A man on a lonely road in Arkansas late one night pieced out a wire from the coil to the distributor with some cellophane, rolled tightly. It got him home. Cocktail wits discovered that, dropped in water, cellophane looked like ice, and that a cigarette, wrapped snuggly in cellophane, can be tied in a knot. Vaudeville comedians cracked cellophane jokes, cartoonists drew cellophane caricatures. Since the great bull market in Ford jokes, no commodity has known such popularity.

Du Pont has put up three new cellophane plants (guarded as though they contained the Kohinoor); scared out one or two would-be competitors through patent suits; and maintained its profit margin at twenty per cent—the fixed Du Pont rate. Last year the company made more than $5,000,000 on cellophane, at 52 cents a pound for the moisture-proof, 38 cents for the plain.

Moisture-proof cellophane's chemical godfather is Duco, the quick-drying nitrocellulose lacquer, which has speeded up automobile production enormously. Duco's development is a striking illustration of the highly profitable community of interests between General Motors and Du Pont.

For years that impatient and restless genius of General Motors research, Charles Franklin Kettering, along with other automobile men, had chaffed at having to wait a week or longer while motor cars were painted and dried. He turned the problem over to the plodding, painstaking Du Pont chemists. There was nothing new about quick-drying nitrocellulose lacquers but what the automobile men wanted was a lacquer durable enough to stand hard usage, yet sufficiently liquid to squirt through a paint gun. After hundreds upon hundreds of experiments, Edmund J. Flaherty, of the Du Pont research staff, succeeded in producing a mixture that contained forty ounces of cotton per gallon of solvent, yet was as fluid as previous lacquers that had only six ounces of cotton per gallon. This "low viscosity" lacquer was Duco. It saved fifteen per cent in labor and seven cents in material per automobile body. Mixed with color-giving pigments, it permits moderate priced cars to come to market today with chromatic effects once possible only at considerable cost in the custom shops.

Duco was first employed on General Motors' Oakland in the fall of 1923. Now this type of finish is being used on practically every make of pleasure car. Du Pont got patents on Duco as wide as the ocean and has sued competitors with such success that today Du Pont gets a six-cents-a-gallon royalty on *all* low-viscosity lacquers—a royalty that adds at least $500,000 a year to Duco's $2,000,000 annual earnings. Henry Ford is one of the few independents who have escaped paying tribute to Du Pont. He finishes his cars with a synthetic resin enamel, and seems satisfied. Duco, in brush form, is used widely outside of the motor industry.

Du Pont also sells its General Motors brother imitation leather upholstery (Fabrikoid) and the rubber-coated *Pontop* for the tops of closed cars. The imitation leather, dyed and embossed, has penetrated many fields once sacred to the hide of the cow—suitcases, handbags,

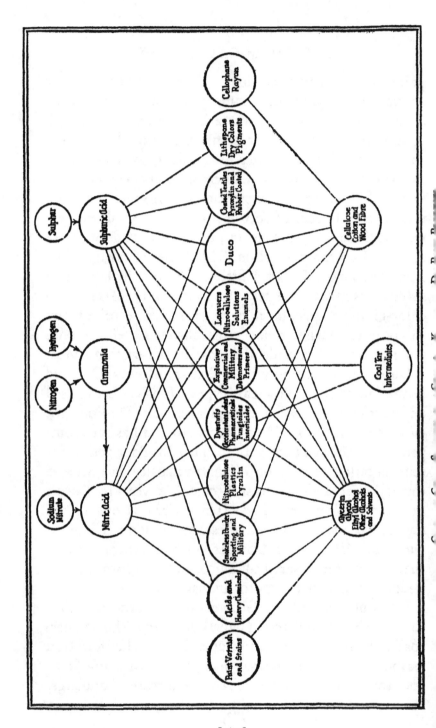

bookbindings, upholstery and novelty products. Fabri-koid is built of, and on, cotton through the familiar Du Pont pyroxylin composition. The pyroxylin "jelly" is colored with mineral pigments which have been finely ground in pure castor oil, making the finished product soft and pliable throughout its life. The colored jelly is applied to the base fabric by means of a "doctor knife," in a specially-designed coating machine, and the material is built up coat by coat until the desired weight or thickness is attained. Afterwards it is embossed and finished in grains which may simulate either natural hides or other special effects. Fabrikoid is waterproof, grease-proof, scuff-proof and washable. It is astonishingly resistant to wear and weather. This branch of the Du Pont business earns about $1,000,000 a year.

Tetraethyl lead for anti-knock Ethyl gasoline, which Du Pont makes in its huge Deepwater Point, N. J., plant, was a gift from General Motors.

One of the outstanding triumphs of automobile history was scored by Thomas Midgley, Jr., and his assistant, T. A. Boyd, of General Motors, when, after exhaustive labors, they discovered that a tiny quantity of an obscure and dangerous chemical—tetraethyl lead—added to ordinary gasoline would eliminate "knocking" in high compression motors. Their discovery paved the way for motors of greatly increased efficiency. With Standard Oil of New Jersey, General Motors formed Ethyl Gasoline Corporation (on a fifty-fifty basis) to market the new power fuel; and called upon Du Pont to supply the tetraethyl lead. This was in the summer of 1924.

The Du Ponts were jubilant. Ethyl gas seemed a *sure*

winner. Du Pont would profit doubly: through its General Motors dividends and its sales of "tet-lead." The elation was short-lived. In October five employes of New Jersey Standard, handling tetraethyl lead, ran amuck in Bayway, and died in raving delirium. They had contracted lead poisoning. Boards of health in many parts of the country banned further sales of Ethyl and the public shied from the "loony gas." A year before, the United States Bureau of Mines had investigated the danger of contracting lead poisoning from Ethyl and given it a clean bill of health. This investigation had been financed by General Motors. Now university scientists and others asserted the Bureau's inquiry had been inadequate. Criticism increased.

Surgeon General Cumming called a conference to meet in Washington May 20, 1925. A fortnight before the meeting, Ethyl Gasoline Corporation withdrew its product from the market. Up to that time 300,000,000 gallons of the "loony gas" had been distributed. The Washington conferees named an investigating committee which reported in January, 1926, that it "found no good reason for prohibiting the use of Ethyl gasoline . . . provided its distribution and use is controlled by proper regulation." Manufacture of Ethyl was labeled an occupational hazard but its use as a consumer fuel declared safe. Later regulations prohibited "use of more than three cubic centimeters of Ethyl fluid to the gallon of gasoline," specified that containers and pumps bear the words "contains lead," and that the gasoline be colored. Use of Ethyl in cleaning fluids and for other non-fuel purposes was banned.

Standard Oil of New Jersey, General Motors,—and

Du Pont—breathed easier. Now three-quarters of all gasoline sold contains "anti-knock," either the red Ethyl or a so-called Q fluid, licensed by the Rockefeller-Du Pont alliance. Du Pont, though, is the *only* chemical concern licensed to make tetraethyl lead, and clears on this alone an annual profit of about $3,500,000.

Whether any tragedies similar to that at Bayway have occurred in the "tet" plant at Deepwater Point is not known. For Deepwater is a gloomy citadel of silence, where visitors are discouraged, censorship more tightly drawn and processes even more jealously guarded than at other focal points of Du Pont activity.

Last year Du Pont opened a medical research laboratory, the Haskell Laboratory of Industrial Toxicology, the first of its kind in the United States. Here is studied the possible effect of the company's processes upon the health of its 40,000 employes, also the hazards of new products from a public health standpoint.

Haskell Laboratory is part of the elaborate equipment of the great Experimental Station built on the site of the original powder mills, long since dismantled. The Experimental Station and five other large research laboratories throughout the country were organized by Dr. Charles L. Reese and the latter's successor as Chemical director, Dr. Charles M. A. Stine. The Station, where scientific reports are received from the outlying laboratories, collated and studied, employs more than 1,000 chemists, and costs some $3,000,000 a year.

Though its research facilities, in number of men employed and money expended, rank among the first in the world, Du Pont's chief triumphs have been won through the cash box rather than the test tube. With the possible exception of Duco, Du Pont chemists have no major industrial invention to their credit. Yet they have been invaluable in satisfying the constant demand of the company financial overlords for lowered costs and increased production. In the main, the Du Pont lab man's principal task is a sort of coral insect's search for improvements and refinements of processes, no matter how minute.

To a remarkable extent, Du Pont is a self-sustaining organization. The words of old General Henry, back in 1875, still hold good: "We build our own machinery; draw our own plans; make our own patterns." Du Pont today does all its own designing, construction, repair work. The Wilmington machine shops are equipped to build every conceivable type of machinery. The Engineering Department employs operative and mechanical research engineers who study the company's various processes, familiarize themselves with details of all plant operations, improve old and develop new mechanical and power equipment, and coöperate with other technical departments in working out new manufacturing processes. If a site for a new plant is under consideration, studies are made involving elaborate analyses of freight rates on incoming raw materials and outgoing finished products, topography, labor conditions, water and power supply, climatic conditions, and so on.

Du Pont rounded out its chemical empire by absorbing companies making "chemists' chemicals," *i.e.*, chemicals used either by itself in manufacturing operations or sold to other manufacturers. In October, 1928, it bought the great Grasselli Chemical Company, of Cleveland, founded in 1839 by Eugene Ramiro Grasselli. The purchase was accomplished through interchange of stock—one share of Du Pont common for five shares of Grasselli common. The 150,000 shares of Du Pont figuring in the deal had then a stock market value of $64,500,000. In Grasselli, Du Pont got a rich source of sulphuric acid, also the services of the present Grasselli—the very capable T. S. Profits from this company run slightly over $3,000,000 a year.

In 1930, Du Pont bought another fine old company, Roessler & Hasslacher. It made metallic sodium, which du Pont needed in manufacturing tetraethyl lead, cyanides for hardening steel, and many other chemical products. R. & H., also, became a Du Pont division. It earns close to $2,000,000 a year.

To assure a domestic source of nitric acid, du Pont already had built a "fixed nitrogen" plant at Belle, West Virginia. Under this process, synthetic ammonia, from which nitric acid is derived, is made from the cheapest of all raw materials, water and air. Fixed nitrogen, also, was an outgrowth of the war. When the supply of natural Chilean nitrates was cut off, German chemists succeeded in producing synthetic ammonia by inducing one atom of nitrogen from the air to combine with three atoms of hydrogen under extremely high pressure and temperature. The process was so economical that, after the war, natural nitrates were driven from the market. Du Pont quickly duplicated the new method. Its ammonia earns about $750,000 a year.

Du Pont sells much of its excess ammonia to fertilizer makers. Du Pont has been tempted at times to manufacture its own fertilizers but the field is crowded and the farmers poor.

[279]

Household refrigerants, however, is a nag of another color. Du Pont supplies General Motors' Frigidaire with sulphur dioxide and with a non-toxic gas refrigerant, *dichlorodifluoromethane*, commonly known as *freon*. General Motors and Du Pont market freon through a forty-nine to fifty-one per cent company called Kinetic Chemicals, Inc.

Besides synthetic ammonia, Du Pont also produces synthetic camphor; and one of the labors of the Du Pont laboratories that holds tremendous future possibilities is the search for artificial rubber, a search that has gone on for two generations. In 1892, Professor Tilden, an English chemist, announced that, after years of standing, a derivative of turpentine known as isoprene clumped into what he took to be rubber. Since isoprene was known to be a constituent of rubber, cheap isoprene became a chemical will-o-the-wisp.

Twenty years later, in America, a scientific priest, Professor J. A. Nieuwland of Notre Dame, struck out on entirely new lines. Coal, limestone, salt and water were his elements. Heat the coal and limestone and calcium carbide is obtained. Mix the carbide with water and, as every farmer knows, acetylene bubbles up. From the acetylene, Father Nieuwland obtained an entirely new product, chloroprene, which clumps several hundred times more rapidly than isoprene. Du Pont chemists took up the work under Father Nieuwland's direction. From the chloroprene, a rubber-like compound was produced. Automobile tires have been fashioned from the Nieuwland-Du Pont compound and we have reason to look at them with awe. Once they were acetylene—a gas.

Du Pont has patented this synthetic rubber under a trade name, "DuPrene," and has already found many industrial uses for it—despite its cost, $1 a pound, as against natural rubber's 15 cents. A smooth inner tube of "DuPrene" in rubber hose resists the action of oils and solvents. It has been applied successfully to power transmission belting; to covered rolls for use in textile, paper and other industries; to oil well drilling accessories, such as packers, pistons, swab cups and sealing plugs; as jackets and sheaths on ignition cables, neon sign wires and other high voltage conductors.

At present "DuPrene" is in a "semi-works" state, as Du Pont terms a product which is hovering between the test tube and mass production.

Sometimes its purchases have lead Du Pont into activities remote from its natural fields. In 1933, learning that the Remington Arms Company, long divorced of its typewriter and cash register experiments, was turning its thought toward the manufacture of smokeless powder, Du Pont bought a controlling interest in Remington, and landed in the cutlery business. For Remington, in addition to its output of shotshells, metallic cartridges and arms, is the largest producer of steel knives in the United States. Under Du Pont, it is still making knives and several other grades of cutlery.

Du Pont loses no opportunity to emphasize the negligible peace-time returns from its military sales. It separates its military and commercial explosives by putting the former in the Smokeless Powder Division; the latter in its Explosives Division. Last year industrial explosives earned over $2,000,000, while smokeless powder, sporting as well as military, earned less than $200,000.

[281]

Du Pont, indeed, has found the uses of peace sweeter than those of war. Since 1918, it has piled up profits of perhaps $300,000,000, exclusive of its colossal General Motors income, from its chemical and allied lines. Today it is steadily clicking out a profit of $1,000,000 a week, or some $50,000,000 a year.

But, beneath the glittering surface of these peace-time products, still hides the face of Mars.

Part Six

THE FAMILY

Chapter One

DOMINATION OF DELAWARE

AT TWO o'clock in the morning of January 1, 1889, the public rooms of the Hotel Richardson in Dover, the tiny capital of Delaware, glowed with unaccustomed animation. This was not entirely due to the cheer and song of the New Year. Dover, at that moment, was the focal point of a political situation unprecedented in the history of Delaware. In uninterrupted succession for many years the State's representatives in the United States Senate had been Democrats. That long dominant party, however, had recently become split in factional rivalry. There seemed every prospect that Delaware would send its first Republican to the Senate. Several prominent Republicans were reaching eagerly for the plum. The Legislature, which convened on the morrow, would decide the issue. Meanwhile, the Hotel Richardson was a hive of excitement. Amid the New Year's revelers, politicians, camp followers and newspaper correspondents crowded along the noisy bar.

At the height of the hubbub, a stranger entered. His appearance was impressive. He wore a fur coat and a silk hat. In his Ascot tie gleamed a great pearl. Beneath a broad forehead and thick eyebrows, hazel eyes shot fire like those of a stallion. Apparently in his mid-forties, the great sweep of his cavalryman's moustache was as yet untouched with gray.

The stranger's name was John Edward O'Sullivan Addicks, better known in other parts of the United States as "Gas" Addicks.

No one at the bar, however, had heard of him or seen him before, which implied, considering his striking appearance, that Mr. Addicks had not been in Delaware long. He hadn't.

For a while the newcomer ordered his drinks, chatted casually with one or two chance neighbors. Then, without warning and apparently on the spur of the moment, he demanded the attention of newspapermen present and issued this statement:

"I have just returned from Europe and have learned that the Republicans have control of the Legislature. I understand that they may have some trouble in electing a United States Senator. If they cannot agree on a man they might elect me, and I will settle for it afterward."[1]

The newspaper men took Addicks's announcement as more or less of a joke and the people of Delaware took it pretty much the same way when it appeared in print. It was, but on them. "Gas" Addicks remained in Delaware seventeen years and made the State's politics just as hot as his nickname would imply. It finally took a Du Pont to get him out.

Son of the health officer of the Port of Philadelphia,

[1] In this period, direct election of U. S. Senators was hardly ever thought of; legislatures everywhere voted for the men with the most money and the most political influence.

John Edward O'Sullivan Addicks had begun life as a department store errand boy. Then he sold flour, dabbled in real estate and ward politics, speculated in wheat, and finally jumped into the infant industry of producing water gas for illuminating purposes. He built gas works in Boston, Brooklyn, Jersey City, Chicago and elsewhere. Obtaining franchises for the laying of pipes and construction of plants, he would sublet the contracts to himself, making tremendous profits on his original investments. In 1882, he was the prime mover in the Chicago Gas Trust. Two years later, he organized the Bay State Gas Company, of Massachusetts, reaping a fortune. Late in 1888, he went to Europe and cleaned up a million in the promotion of a Siberian railroad. It was upon his return, while lolling in a New York hotel, that he picked up a newspaper and read of a possible deadlock in Delaware over the impending choice of a Senator. A whimsical idea leaped into his agile mind. Why not go after the job himself? Summoning his Boston political agent, John Donohue, and two other artful politicians from Philadelphia, of whose sebaceous services he had often availed himself, Addicks departed for the Delaware capital, expecting to buy his way into the august United States Senate just as he had often bought lucrative gas franchises. He could qualify as a citizen of Delaware, for he owned a fine estate near Claymont, in the extreme northern portion of the State.

It was in this unconventional manner that J. Edward Addicks began his campaign to be elected United States Senator—a campaign that lasted until 1906 and in which he spent millions to obtain control of the Delaware Legislature.

He and his managers started out, the day after his statement to the press, to make the name of Addicks a rallying cry. Soon everybody was asking: "Who is Addicks?" Anthony Higgins, a Republican, however, won the election and for several years Addicks was a negligible quantity in Delaware politics. But the whim to go to the Senate became a ruling passion and Addicks was accustomed to getting what he went after.

Addicks soon realized that he could make but little headway in the political life of Delaware's northern county, New Castle.[1] Accordingly, he concentrated upon the remaining counties of Kent and Sussex. These two lower counties on the Delaware were the last stand of the eighteenth century in America, a land of proud, stubborn, self-perpetuating families, who, though the first to ratify the Constitution, had subsequently, in their isolation, quit bothering much about what happened to the rest of the nation. Here the old English law still prevailed more intact than anywhere else in the United States, together with the pillory and the whipping post, which still survives throughout the state. In general the people didn't have much money or education and didn't resent their lack. They had two trains a day which left on time and arrived late. Their farm produce frequently went to waste for lack of transportation. But the citizens of that low, flat, fertile section of the Delaware-Maryland Peninsula raised peaches, ate fried chicken, voted Democratic and felt independent. Southern in sympathy, these Delawareans discouraged the negro vote. The negroes, who numbered about one-fifth of the total population, further muddled the po-

---

[1] Of which Wilmington became the county seat in 1879.

litical situation by refusing to vote Democratic and only voting Republican when paid for their "time."

At that time an income of $300 a year in Sussex county was considerably above the average. More than that was apt to excite envy and admiration. But shortly after the appearance of Addicks, men who had no income at all joined the $300 class, and those who had been $300 a year men went higher, some joining the ranks of the plutocrats who revelled in incomes of $1,500 and more. Both Sussex and Kent blossomed with a wonderful prosperity. New houses were erected by local political leaders, new bank accounts opened, and large blocks of stock in the multitudinous gas companies controlled by Addicks began to appear at the banks as collateral for loans of considerable size.

In the campaign of 1892, Addicks spent $100,000 and demonstrated to his own satisfaction that the State of Delaware was for sale to the highest bidder. He gained almost complete control of Kent and Sussex. By 1895, when the Senatorial election again came before the Legislature, the gas magnate had become an overshadowing menace to the Democrats and the regular Republican organization. It was then that he coined and issued a celebrated pronunciamento: "Me or nobody!"

As happened, it was nobody.

Addicks had six of the nineteen Republican votes, not enough to elect himself but enough to keep the Legislature from electing anyone else. The fight went on, amid excitement, caucusing, wire-pulling, for more than four months. Most of Addicks's enmity seemed directed against Senator Anthony Higgins, who was a candidate for re-election. Finally, Higgins stepped aside and his friends offered the Addicks men a choice of eight or ten other Republicans as compromise possibilities. All were rejected by Addicks.

On May 8, 1895, the Higgins men pulled a new name out of the box, putting forward as an unexceptionable compromise candidate a wealthy and influential man who had never before held public office—Colonel Henry Algernon du Pont.

Colonel du Pont, eldest son of old General Henry, had resigned his army commission in 1874 to enter the family business, becoming a partner four years later. In addition to his duties with the company, he also became president of the Wilmington and Northern Railroad. He was the first Du Pont since the original Victor to enter politics.

Colonel Henry drove to Dover, pleased as a peacock at the prospect of leaving the prosaic precincts of the Brandywine for the national political arena. Next morning, on the early ballots, a slight fissure appeared in the Addicks ranks. Addicks lost one of his six supporters. To lose a second would be fatal. While his managers surrounded the Faithful Five, threatening, cajoling them to hold firm, Addicks himself engineered a coup.

During the balloting, Governor Marvel had died and been succeeded under the constitution by William T. Watson, Speaker of the State Senate, and a hold-over Democrat. Addicks went to the new Governor and persuaded him to return to the Senate and vote. With Watson's ballot in the joint session, sixteen votes were now required for a majority. On thirty-five ballots, Du Pont could muster but fifteen. Amid a wild outburst, with Addicks glaring at his bewildered opponent after the fashion of a villain in melodrama, Governor Watson, in his old rôle as Speaker of the State Senate, declared no election and adjourned the Legislature sine die. Not until then did the outraged Du Pont forces belatedly protest Watson's right to vote. They got the Speaker of the House, an opponent of Addicks, to rule out Watson's ballot, and issue a certificate of election to Du Pont.

It was a fiery baptism for a political neophyte but Colonel Henry's fighting blood was stirred. Armed with his certificate of election, he moved on Washington, and demanded that the Senate seat him. By the close vote of thirty-one to thirty, on May 15, 1896, the Senate denied his claim. The Colonel, being a McKinley man, was licked by a combination of Senate Democrats and free-silver Republicans.

The seat remained vacant and the battle was far from over. The issue of Du Pont vs. Addicks was permanently joined.

When the Republican State convention met in Dover to elect delegates to the 1896 national convention at St. Louis, Addicks had a majority of the delegates. He personally directed how every vote should be cast, ignoring old party rules. The delegates from New Castle bolted and held a convention of their own. Both sent delegations to St. Louis. With McKinley's manager, the incomparable Marcus Alonzo Hanna, pulling the strings, the New Castle bolters were seated after a bitter battle over credentials.

The Addicks delegates returned home to fight as they never had before. The Republican party split into the Regulars and the Union Republicans (Addicks). Addicks spent money more furiously than before, scattering it broadcast throughout the entire State. What had been a whim, then a passion, now became an obsession. For the next two years, Addicks continued to spend and to perfect his political machine. In 1898 he neared his goal.

The joint membership of the Legislature that year was fifty—twenty-nine Republicans and twenty-one Democrats. On the first ballot Addicks had fifteen votes, William S. Hilles two, and Henry A. du Pont eleven. The twenty-one Democrats, of course, voted solidly for the Democratic caucus nominee, whose chance was nil, since twenty-six votes were required for election.

Finally Addicks broke the ranks of his opponents. Three Republicans, who had been elected on a promise not to vote for the gas man, turned Judas, making the Addicks total eighteen.

Several days later—amid jeers from the crowded galleries—a Democrat voted for Addicks. Two days later, two more Democrats did the same, giving him altogether twenty-one votes, five less than he needed. For two months this deadlock held, and for the second time Delaware was without her proper representation in the United States Senate.

In 1901, when two Senators were to be elected, Addicks started off with sixteen votes to Colonel Henry du Pont's eight. His high-water mark was twenty-two, again only five short of election. And again, he carried his threat "Me or nobody!" down to the hour of adjournment. For the succeeding two years, Delaware had no representative whatever in the Senate of the United States.[1]

By 1903, the factional fight in Delaware had become a

[1] In spite of Addicks, Delaware had managed until 1901 to have one Senator in Washington though entitled, of course, to two.

national scandal. In the face of demands for Federal supervision of Delaware elections, Addicks weakened and consented to a compromise. The Legislature elected James Frank Allee, nominated by Addicks, and L. Heisler Ball, selected by the Regular Republicans, to serve out the remainder of the two Senatorial terms. Colonel du Pont was not at all pleased but thought it politic not to permit his name to be offered. Because of the long deadlock, Ball's term would expire March 4, 1905. Addicks growled that in 1905 he'd wipe his enemies "off the face of the earth." In 1905, when the regular election period came around, the battle was renewed. Again—"no election."

Then a special election was called for June 12, 1906. This time Colonel Henry du Pont entered the lists with a new campaign manager, none other than his cousin, Coleman.

The situation changed immediately.

As a promoter and manipulator, Addicks was still in the amateur'class compared to the meteoric, six feet four Du Pont trust-builder. Besides, Coleman could match Addicks dollars to dimes any old day, and raise the stakes if necessary. Soon Addicks's henchmen were leaving Coleman's office with bigger cigars and bulging pockets. Before me lies a yellowed newspaper cutting of June 13, 1906. It reads:

Dover, Del., June 12—The Delaware Legislature at noon today elected Col. Henry A. du Pont United States Senator for the term beginning March 4, 1905. The election was practically unanimous as the Democratic members voted blanks and only State Senator Thomas C. Moore, of Kent County, voted for Addicks. The election will be formally declared at the joint session tomorrow. J. Edward Addicks left Dover for New York on the 4 20 train this morning. A passenger on the same train was T. Coleman du Pont, cousin of Senator-elect du Pont and manager of his campaign, who from New York took passage for Europe. Addicks's friends say he will resume the fight next fall, when he will endeavor to defeat his former ally, J. Frank Allee. There is general jollification here. Senator Allee this afternoon received the following telegram: "Washington, D. C., June 12—Telegram received. I am much pleased with the good news you send and heartily congratulate you upon the result which you have been so instrumental in bringing about and I congratulate even more heartily the people of Delaware. (signed) Theodore Roosevelt."

Henry A. du Pont served out his first shortened term and, in 1911, was re-elected for a full term of six years, expiring March 4, 1917.

There was no come-back for J. Edward Addicks.

Addicks's fall was as spectacular and dramatic as his rise. Unmercifully drubbed by Thomas F. Lawson, in *Frenzied Finance*, heavy financial reverses overtook most of his gas companies. Out of them grew litigation that impoverished him and kept him dodging subpoena servers and attachment papers from one end of the country to the other. Marital troubles added to his woes. Within two years after Coleman had driven him out of politics, process servers located him in a mean Hoboken tenement where he was living under an assumed name. His gas and light, ironically enough, had been shut off for nonpayment of bills by a company he had formerly controlled. He fled through a window. Later, unable to raise bail, he was jailed in attachment proceedings. Now and then his name popped up in the papers, usually in connection with fraud charges. He died in New York, in obscurity, August 7, 1919. This was the end of a man who at one time boasted that he had paid $80,000 for control of a dozen votes in one session of the Legislature. His greatest mistake, Henry Seidel Canby observes wryly in his *The Age of Confidence*, seems to have been that he did not know how to buy votes like a gentleman.

During the Henry du Pont-Addicks tussles, Willard Saulsbury, Jr. had usually received most of the minority Democratic votes for United States Senator. Saulsbury was the young Wilmington lawyer who, in 1893, had married May Lammot du Pont, divorced cousin-wife of Colonel Henry's brother, William. In the brave days of Democratic power, three Saulsburys had gone to the Senate from Delaware. Willard Saulsbury's ambition to become the fourth was realized in 1912, when Theodore Roosevelt's Bull Moose party split the Republicans in State and nation.

Prior to his election Saulsbury had sought, unsuccessfully, through Senator Jim Reed of Missouri, to unseat Colonel Henry for alleged wholesale corruption in his last contest with Addicks. During the campaign, Saulsbury further asserted that, if he entered the Senate, his senior colleague "would go out by the back door." In other words, he showed little respect for his wife's cousin and former brother-in-law.

So marked was the bad feeling between the gentlemen from Delaware that Senator Henry refused to present Saulsbury to the Senate; when the latter took the oath of office Saulsbury ignored the breach of Senatorial courtesy and strolled down the aisle on the arm of a Maryland Senator, while Mrs. May Lammot du Pont Saulsbury proudly looked on from the gallery.

On more than one occasion the Saulsburys were enabled to return snub for snub for, as a member of Woodrow Wilson's campaign cabinet, Saulsbury was an influential figure in the Wilson administration. During part of his term he was President pro tem of the Senate.

Meanwhile, Coleman du Pont's appetite for politics had been whetted, and he was building up a machine of his own through a typical Colemanesque project.

"I am going to build a monument one hundred miles high and lay it down on the ground," boasted Coleman. Organizing the Coleman du Pont Road, Inc., for the purpose, he set about purchasing a strip, two hundred feet wide, to traverse the State. This met with strenuous opposition from the farmers, who feared increased taxes, and distrusted modern methods, and the overlords of the Brandywine on general principles. After much litigation and exorbitant payments for right-of-way, Coleman got his strip.

The purpose of a tract so wide was that Coleman had an innovation of his own in the matter of highways. The fifty-foot cemented roadway was to be flanked on either side by a seventy-five-foot stretch to be landscaped and leased to roadside commercial enterprises for the self-maintenance of the highway. "If this plan had been followed with Broadway in New York," asserted Coleman, "that city now would be drawing an income of $100,000,000 a year."

Coleman supervised the first work in person, camping out on the job. Then he turned the project over to the new State Highway Commission, with orders to finish the road and send him the bill. The bill was $5,000,000.

Ultimately, Coleman promised to deed this highway—which runs from Wilmington to the Maryland line—to the State. This purpose, substantially, has been carried out. It has been said that Coleman's deepest wish was to live and die a "road builder."

The road, as could no other element, brought the lower part of the State within the influence of Wilmington, and of the Du Ponts.

While building his highway, Coleman decided that he would like to be United States Senator long enough to reform the Senate into a working legislative body. "I'd leave the Senate in the hands of a salaried person competent to run it right," grinned Coleman, partly serious. He undoubtedly would have gone to the Senate earlier than he did if it had not been for that stormy petrel within the Du Pont family—Alfred I.

Alfred I. blocked him more effectually than had the farmers.

At that time Alfred's quarrel over Pierre's purchase of Coleman's powder company stock was at its height. With a recklessness no younger Du Pont ever before had shown, Alfred now jumped into politics. He demanded that the clan chieftain, Senator Colonel Henry, break with Coleman. The Colonel, of course, refused. Alfred then added a string of down-state weeklies to his Wilmington *Morning News*; and put an independent Republican into the field in 1916. Again the Republican party was split. Josiah O. Wolcott, a Democrat, won Colonel Henry's Senate seat.

The defeat soured the old Colonel. Retiring to his broad acres, Winterthur, he occupied himself raising blooded cattle and writing Huguenot and family history.

There, in 1926, he died, at the age of eighty-eight, a querulous, short-tempered old gentleman. After his death, a Washington woman sued his estate, claiming that he was the father of her son, born in 1913, when the Senator was seventy-six. The case never reached trial.

Meanwhile, one bright morning in the summer of 1921, Delaware woke up to learn that Josiah Wolcott, its Democratic Senator, had resigned to accept appointment to the State's highest judicial office, that of Chancellor. The political maneuver was engineered by Governor Denney, a Republican, who appointed T. Coleman du Pont to serve the remainder of Wolcott's term in the Senate.[1]

There was a terrible howl over "Delaware's Dirty Deal." Wolcott was denounced as a traitor, Denney as a tool, and Coleman as a corruptionist. Coleman appeared hurt, but not so deeply that he could not deliver himself of the following telegram to his benefactor, Governor Denney: "When called to duty by one's State or Country, there is but one thing to do, give the best there is in you . . . no one will work harder for the good of good old Delaware . . . ," etc.

The next year, however, "Good Old Delaware," showed little appreciation of Coleman's "best" when he ran for both the short and long Senatorial terms.

His opponent was Thomas Francis Bayard, Jr., a Democrat, who, though fifty-three, was invariably called "Young Tom" to distinguish him from his late father, Secretary of State and Ambassador to the Court of St.

[1] In 1913 an amendment to the Constitution of the United States provided for popular election of Senators. In many states, including Delaware, vacancies may be filled through temporary appointment by the Governor, pending a popular election.

James under Grover Cleveland. The Bayards, like the Saulsburys, had for generations represented Delaware in the United States Senate. "Young Tom," also, had married a Du Pont, Elizabeth, daughter of the Alexis du Pont-Bradford alliance. Her mother, you may recall, was the lady whom Alfred I. sued for allegedly slandering his fair cousin-wife, Alicia.

Amid the Du Pont internecine tangles, behold the curious spectacle of that 1922 campaign: two Du Pont in-laws, Thomas Bayard, Jr., and his supporter, Willard Saulsbury, both Democrats, demanding of the alarmed citizenry: "Shall Delaware belong to the Du Ponts? Are we a free people or shall we permit ourselves to be crushed under the weight of Du Pont wealth?"

Though Coleman and his political lieutenant, James Austin Ellison, spent money lavishly, they faced about the nearest thing to a popular uprising possible in Delaware. With due credit to Coleman's machine, the election was a narrow squeak. Bayard won the short term by a vote of 36,954 to 36,894, a margin of 60 votes; and the long term by 37,304 to 36,979, a majority of only 325, but enough.

Though Alfred I. had announced solemnly and without blinking that he would take no part in the 1922 campaign, his newspapers and his chief lieutenant, Edward M. Davis, were exceedingly active against Coleman.

In 1924, however, Alfred really lay low. His passive policy was not motivated by any sudden burst of friendliness. It was due entirely to certain epochal changes in Alfred's life and in his financial affairs.

In January, 1920, Alfred's cousin-wife, Alicia, died,

just as she and he were about to move into "White Eagle," a beautiful and costly estate at Roslyn, Long Island, for which agents had been scouring Europe for antiques and rare ancestral treasures. Alfred had wanted a home near New York, where he had recently organized a large company, Nemours Trading Corporation, to sell American goods to Europe; and purchased the Grand Central Palace for international trade expositions. "White Eagle" was never occupied. The beautiful furnishings, as well as the place itself, were later sold separately at public auction.

A year after Alicia's death, Alfred again married. His third wife was Miss Jessie D. Ball, a middle-aged woman of distinguished Virginia lineage. She had abetted Alfred's shattered hearing by teaching him the sign language. Soon after this marriage, Europe collapsed financially, and the Nemours Trading Corporation collapsed with it. Alfred lost millions and, temporarily, he was pressed for funds.

Pierre came to the rescue but, also, from no motives of friendliness. He arranged a loan for Alfred through J. P. Morgan & Co. One of the conditions, or consequences, of this loan was Alfred's surrender of the *Morning News* and other newspaper properties in Delaware. Already Pierre and his group owned the *Evening Journal*. To these they later added the only remaining daily paper in Wilmington, *Every Evening*, combining it with the *Journal*. Ever since, the newspapers have been operated like a department of the du Pont Company.[1]

Consequently, Coleman rode into the United States

---

[1] When Wilmingtonians wish to read about Du Pont scandals, they must buy the Philadelphia papers.

Senate in 1924 on the Coolidge landslide. He wrote Alfred a note from Capitol Hill—"Dear Alfred: I would like you to feel that, if there is anything I could do for you or for your interests in Washington, you will not hesitate to call on me."

Bluff and hearty, Coleman was popular in the Senate. But he seldom spoke and his appearances on the floor grew infrequent. The fifty and sixty cigarettes he smoked daily took relentless toll upon his vocal chords. A friend found him one day with a pad at his elbow, upon which he wrote, with a grimace: "Got to keep mum for a month. Doctors, damn 'em. Wart on the vocal chord." The trouble, however, was not a wart—it was a deadly cancer of the larynx. In October, 1927, Dr. John E. Mackenty, at Manhattan Eye, Ear and Throat Hospital, in New York, found it necessary to remove the larynx. In the middle of November violent attacks of hiccoughs reopened the wounds. A hypnotist was called in. He put Coleman in a trance, during which the hiccoughs ceased. But Coleman was doomed.

For the next three years the disease constantly progressed, and Coleman was able to speak only by means of an artificial larynx, connected by a tube, through a hole in the throat. This mechanical device was the invention of Dr. Harvey E. Lane, of the joint laboratories of the Western Electric Company and the American Telephone & Telegraph Company. Coleman hated it. "Can't talk, can't eat, hardly breathe—better dead," he rasped to his callers. But his sense of humor never left him. At his bedside were all sorts of mechanical and trick gadgets. He amused himself, too, collecting and fingering fine laces.

These days were passed on the old Alexander Hamilton estate in Irvington-on-Hudson, which he had purchased. In the winter of 1928 he was forced to retire from the Senate, and was too ill to be told that the Tea Pot Dome Oil Investigating Committee wanted him to answer charges that he had liquidated part of the Republican National Committee deficit of 1920 with $75,000 in the mysterious Continental Trading Company liberty bonds. The next year he was taken to Wilmington, where he died on Armistice Day, 1930.

Coleman's $17,000,000 estate was willed, in fairly equal division, to his widow, his son, and three married daughters. The son, Francis V. (Frank), was intrusted with management of the Equitable Building in New York, and bequeathed all stock in the Coleman du Pont Road, Inc., as we have mentioned. Coleman's political machine was largely inherited by C. Douglass Buck, second husband of his daughter, Alice, and once Chief Engineer of the State Highway Department. Buck is now serving a second successful term as Governor of Delaware.

Pierre, meanwhile, had become public spirited, too. Coleman had penetrated the State's wildernesses with his road, and Pierre decided to educate them. In 1918, he endowed an enterprise called the Service Citizens of Delaware, placing at its head a Presbyterian clergyman, Joseph Henry Odell. Dr. Odell and his staff, some of whom were experts of the Rockefeller General Education Board, uncovered appalling conditions in the rural schools.

While a new school code was being framed, and running a long and rocky course through the legislative mill at Dover, Pierre replaced, at his own expense, over a hundred ramshackle school buildings. He put out $500,000 alone on negro schools and even included the "Moors" on the coast of Sussex in his program. The children of this small racial group, probably of remote American Indian origin, but according to local tradition the descendants of Moorish shipwrecked folk, had been excluded from white schools, and their parents refused to send them to negro ones.

Pierre became tremendously enthusiastic over his "betterment" work. As a magazine reporter, I remember his eyes lighting up during an interview as he described his school crusade. Few, however, of the communities were grateful. When Pierre asked the local districts to pay half the cost of new buildings in order, he explained, not to cripple "local initiative and the instinct of self-help," the "wildernesses" openly grumbled. The new school code, providing compulsory attendance for longer periods each year, curbing local powers, and consolidating many country districts with those of neighboring villages, met bitter opposition. The Little Red School-house was hailed as the palladium of local liberty, Pierre's motives questioned, and his agents assailed. Finally, a code went through.

After he had spent some $4,000,000, Pierre found that new schools were not enough. Money was still needed for teachers' salaries and maintenance. The school fund came from tax collections. Pierre complained to Governor Robinson that taxes were not being collected. The Governor appointed him tax commissioner. Pierre set up his own staff, made a list of every one taxable in the State, and began pursuing them for back taxes. (All of this activity at a time when he was manipulating and building the Chemical Kingdom.) Those who failed to pay were haled into court. Since then the school fund has been ample and Pierre, now serving his third term, seems permanently slated for the tax-commissionership. Delaware, incidentally, has moved from thirty-second to tenth place in the U. S. literacy list and stands close to the top in secondary-educational facilities. In Delaware schools, the children chirp George Washington, Abraham Lincoln and Pierre du Pont in the same breath.

The school crusade stirred Pierre's interest in politics and in uplift generally. Omitting his ingrained conservatism, there is indication that he desires to emulate the distinguished ancestor for whom he is named, Pierre Samuel Du Pont de Nemours. Pierre's political activities are reflected in his charities. Among his philanthropies seldom mentioned are contributions to various Jewish causes. On one occasion, underwriting Wilmington's quota for distressed Polish and Russian Jews, he mentioned his own Semitic strain, which he rarely refers to, saying: "I am one-eighth Jewish. My grandfather was a Jew."

Pierre made a fuss for prohibition repeal when most important employers of labor were silent. His money kept the Association Against the Prohibition Amendment going in its struggling early days. For five years Pierre fought for repeal in Methodist-ridden Delaware. He circulated pamphlets, talked in his low, almost inarticulate tones over the radio and at public gatherings, and his wife also made repeal a social cause.[1]

[1] Upon repeal of the Eighteenth Amendment, Pierre du Pont helped to frame Delaware's liquor control law, and became the single control commissioner.

So ardent a wet was Pierre that in 1928, John Raskob got him on the Al Smith bandwagon. Raskob, who had long since passed his du Pont Company treasurership over to Walter Samuel Carpenter, Jr., and gone into General Motors exclusively, had been a rabid admirer of Al Smith for years. In the presidential campaign of 1928, Smith's manager was Raskob. The latter raised a rich fund from Pierre and others and, if Smith had won, Raskob would most likely have become Secretary of the Treasury. Unfortunately for Smith (perhaps fortunately, as it turned out), Raskob did not bring him the same luck as he had the Du Ponts.

Although individual Du Ponts have occasionally gone Democratic over issues such as the wet-dry fight, the family generally operates through the Republican machine in Delaware. The machine is run by a group—the Better Government League, with Pierre's brother-in-law, R. R. M. (Ruly) Carpenter in general supervision. "Ruly" is the family's political manipulator, collecting and distributing campaign funds and seeing that Coleman's former henchman, Ellison, and other machine politicians obey orders.

Sometimes, Du Ponts are to be found on both sides of the fence. For instance, in 1930, Pierre and his brother, Irénée, supported the Democratic wet, their in-law, Tom Bayard, for re-election as Senator. Bayard was defeated by Daniel O. Hastings, dry Republican. Their remaining brother, Lammot, and many other Du Ponts supported Hastings. Both sides used Du Pont cash liberally. In Bayard's pre-nomination campaign, more money per capita was spent than in the notorious Ruth

Hanna McCormick contest in Illinois or in the Vare-Pinchot-Pepper battle in Pennsylvania in 1927.

For a number of years, Delaware has been the "floating" home and pet roosting place for a large number of corporations outside of the Du Pont and General Motors group. This is due to the fact that Delaware laws are kinder to the corporations, and much more flexible, than those of other states. Delaware advantages include: lower cost of incorporation; stockholders and directors meetings may be held outside the State; Delaware law has never been changed suddenly; a corporation may have as many classes of stock as required, with no restriction on par value or preferred stock; law suits may be brought or defended by corporations doing business outside the State, either in a Federal Court anywhere or in Delaware courts (most corporations prefer the latter). The holding company, now under general attack on social grounds, came to its choicest flowering and widest employment in Delaware under Du Pont rule.

The bulk of the laws which have proven such a magnet to corporations were enacted in 1899, the year Du Pont changed from a partnership to a corporation. The Du Ponts had little, if anything, to do with their origination. However, they have enhanced and protected such legislation in the years that followed, to their own advantage. Their control of Delaware has obviously guaranteed their fellow capitalists against "sudden change" in the statutes dealing with corporations and the almost limitless powers of holding companies. Incidentally, even some lesser Du Ponts have a personal holding company or two tucked away somewhere.

In 1931, the Du Ponts were suspected of fathering a mysterious bill in the Delaware Legislature—repealing the old common law principle whereby an estate remains intact only during the lifetime of living heirs or for twenty-one years thereafter. This bill would have enabled the Du Ponts to keep their fortunes together ad infinitum—for countless generations of unborn Du Ponts. However, it never reached the floor, and its sponsor remains unknown.

On the whole the Du Ponts haven't gloated over their harvests much—they are still, in spite of their great power, sewing crops.

They are not so crude in their practices today as Coleman was, and once in charge, as in all their undertakings, they govern efficiently.

Impartial Delawareans have long since given up hope of honest elections. Privately, prominent Democrats in the State admit the Republicans (Du Pont) will probably rule Delaware for a great many years to come, though they say if the Australian system of secret balloting were installed, there would be a change.

Meanwhile, Delaware sighs and votes "Du Pont."

Chapter Two

THREE BROTHERS

IN 1919, Pierre du Pont, still retaining tight hold of the financial strings, passed the presidency of the du Pont Company over to his brother, Irénée, six years his junior.

Of all the du Ponts, Irénée is perhaps the most provocative personality. Bristling, aggressive, self-assured, he is the typical Big Business go-getter, with most of the virtues and many of the irritating faults of that much-praised, much-abused species.

Let's take a look at him in the spacious, roomy mansion, Granogue, near Wilmington, where he lives with his wife, Irene Sophie, a second cousin, their remaining two unmarried daughters, and a minor son, Irénée Jr. Ring the bell and Irénée may bounce to the door himself, in shirt sleeves, a ubiquitous pipe of curved briar suspended from rather loose, generous lips. If you are an old friend, he will usher you, with bubbling enthusiasm, into his private museum, perhaps to display some new "find" among the long rows of cabinets containing one of the most notable collections of minerals in the world. Approaching sixty, the master of Granogue is a powerful man of medium height, deep of chest and broad of shoulder, with the flesh of middle age and good living liberally larding his paunch and creeping up into a rapidly doubling chin. Above that chin is a fairly strong jaw, with the Du Pont dimple set squarely in the center; a big, sharp, prominent nose; keen, blue eyes, rather small and close together, rimmed in gold spectacles; and a forehead sloping back into a long head plentifully covered with tough, grizzled hair.

For years, Irénée has been the Du Ponts' public man and their best lobbyist. He has none of the shyness of Pierre nor the sober reticence of their younger brother, Lammot. He is a good mixer and loves a fight. Late in 1934, when the Nye Committee called the Du Ponts to Washington to tell about their munitions business and activities during the World War, Irénée gleefully grabbed the limelight. Brushing aside the buzzing swarm of lawyers, secretaries and assistants in the white marble caucus room of the United Senate Office Building, Irénée blew smoke rings from his pipe and irritated his inquisitors vastly with the volubility of his explanations and the didactic certainty of his manner. He was positive that Du Pont powder prevented the United States from becoming a German province; that the agitation for the nationalization of the munitions business was the work of Russian Reds. The proved peace-time practice of Du Pont and other American munitions makers in selling the latest war devices to potential enemies did not disturb him at all. In fact, such transactions he regarded as a patriotic duty, enabling Du Pont to keep its war machine oiled up and intact for future emergencies. Certainly, Du Pont lobbyists had worked in Washington for favorable tariff and other legislation. And why shouldn't Du Pont have a working agreement with its old friend, the great British Imperial Chemical Industries Ltd., to divide territories and profits?

Irénée's bland assertions robbed the hearings of a great deal of sting, with the result that those who came to hear the cannon roar had, for the most part, to content themselves with a volley of cap pistols. It was Irénée, rather than the costly attorneys, who enabled the Du Ponts to leave the Senate Committee sessions, after sixteen days, with their suave assurance unruffled.

Irénée, like Pierre and Lammot, is a graduate of the Massachusetts Institute of Technology, where he took a B. S. in 1897 and an M. S. in 1898. Before joining the du Pont Company in 1903, he worked in machine shops to get first-hand experience and was for a time in the contracting business. With Du Pont, he quickly found his forte in safety engineering. He distinguished himself by reducing industrial fatalities, dynamite becoming about as safe as bricks to handle; and tuberculosis mortality among employes dropping from thirty-three to fifteen per cent of those afflicted. The company of course benefited accordingly in reduced insurance rates and pension allowances.

Irénée's interests are varied and widespread. It was he, as Chairman of the Finance Committee, who led Du Pont into the purchase in 1926 of 114,000 shares of U. S. Steel common stock for $14,000,000—thus foreshadowing a formidable community of interests among Du Pont, General Motors and the great Morgan steel combination. What this purchase would have led to no one knows. The Federal Trade Commission stepped in and Du Pont hastily divested itself of its Steel holdings.

It was Irénée who got his brothers so interested in U. S. Rubber that by December, 1928, the family held 200,000 shares out of total outstanding 1,400,000, a fourteen per cent interest. Since then, Irénée and other Du Ponts have bought large additional blocks. Francis Breese Davis Jr., a Du Pont executive, was installed as President and Chairman of U. S. Rubber. There was an immediate and conspicuous increase in profits. Davis draws a salary of $125,000 a year, much better pay than that enjoyed by any Du Pont employe.

Irénée backed the attempts of Edward R. Armstrong, another Du Pont man, to build airship landing stations at sea, and financed the Frenchman, Georges Claude, in his experiments to get power from sea water off Cuba. The Du Pont fixed nitrogen plant at Belle, West Virginia, operates under Claude patents. This Du Pont is also interested in cancer research and, as a director of Cousin Coleman's former Equitable Life Assurance Society, helped to organize an inter-company crusade for public health and life extension. Incidentally, he carries almost as much life insurance as his brother, Pierre, who is said to be the largest policyholder in the United States ($7,000,000).

With a fertile mind and a deep interest in science, Irénée occasionally appears in the public prints with some new technical idea. He once suggested that chemists might be able to find "an antidote for sleep" and thus increase the working capacity of the human race—a typical Du Pont suggestion. He also thought that some new chemical compound might be discovered so stimulating to the mind that all of us might become supermen or geniuses.

Irénée often appears in his office at eight in the morning and is capable of tremendous bursts of industry. He plays with equal ardor—golfs, hikes, rides horseback. Often he bounds away for cruises in southern waters aboard his yacht, *Icacos*, stopping perhaps at his summer home in Atlantic City or his big plantation facing the ocean in Cuba. In Cuba, he built his own water supply system, laying miles of pipes. He is a generous and exuberant host. He often surprises women guests and relatives by slipping over their wrists gold bracelets which he calls, with a laugh and a shout, his "slave bracelets." He has given large sums to political causes, mostly Republican.

His wife, Irene Sophie du Pont, is a sister of A. Felix, of the Alexis line. She is quiet, serious, conscientious and spends much time with her books and in church work. Friends say she is a perfect mate for Irénée. They have had eight daughters, and two sons, one of whom, David, died in 1908. One girl, Doris Elise, died in 1930. Five daughters are married. Two of the sons-in-law are with the du Pont Company: Ernest N. May (Development Department) and Crawford H. Greenewalt, a director of the Experimental Station. A very liberal "dot" has been attached to each daughter. One son-in-law, Colgate W. Darden, Jr., who married Constance, is said to have spurned the marriage settlement, taking his wife back to his home town, Norfolk, Virginia, from where he has since been elected to Congress.

Irénée, like most Du Ponts, has the infallible money sense. Several years ago he established a number of trust funds, the income of which was to be used to pay the premiums on life insurance policies. The U. S. Govern-

ment contended that this was a device to avoid income
and inheritance taxes. As a test, the case was taken to
the United States Supreme Court, which upheld the
Government contention in a six to three decision,
handed down May 29, 1933.

Irénée went through but one rocky period during the
seven years of his Du Pont presidency. This was in 1921
when America got the backwash of the European col-
lapse. The General Motors income diminished and
Du Pont itself was consolidating many partly owned
companies and clearing out some of its accumulated
deadwood. However, Pierre stood by, and things were
soon righted.

In 1926, Irénée stepped out of the presidency to make
way for a third and still younger brother, Lammot.

In temperament and characteristics, Lammot du Pont
differs from Irénée as distinctively as a Great Dane does
from a fighting bulldog. One look at Lammot and immediately the adjectives "solid," "calm," "deliberate"
come into mind. He is tall, dark, soberly garbed, pon-
tifical in manner and speech. At fifty-five, his hair is
still sleek and brown. His face is long and dark, its
principal feature a wide nose, with a decided hook.
That hook, together with his rimless spectacles, gives
him the appearance of a studious, thoughtful Jew.
Though he chops wood and plays some golf and tennis,
Lammot's real hobby is business, and more business.
He dotes upon mathematics, economics and management. Practically all of his reading is along these lines.

Unlike Pierre and Irénée, Lammot is not a chemist.
He took a degree of mechanical engineer at M. I. T. in

1901 and, after a brief period as a draftsman with the U. S. Steel Corporation, entered the du Pont Company in March, 1902. His progress was slow but sure. He became a director in 1915 and a vice president the following year. As head of the Miscellaneous Manufacturing Department, he helped lead the company into pyralin and plastics, dyestuffs, lacquers, paints and chemicals. He watched explosives dwindle in importance while rayon, cellophane and the other variegated products became the backbone of the business. As a result, he is far more familiar with the detailed processes of the modern company than either Pierre or Irénée. That is one reason why Lammot will probably remain Du Pont's active boss for a great many years to come. Others are that, besides being exceedingly capable, he is in excellent health and works harder than any man ever at the helm. Then, too, though there is no dearth of children in the direct Pierre-Irénée-Lammot line, there *is* a disquieting dearth of eligible successors. Pierre is childless, Irénée's only son, and namesake, too young to be considered.

Lammot has five daughters and four sons. Of the sons, one is an infant. Another, Reynolds, is a schoolboy. Lammot's older boys, thus far, have shown little exceptional ability. Lammot, Jr., twenty-six, has a job in the family bank, the Wilmington Trust Company, while his brother, "Pete," twenty-four, is employed in the Experimental Station. Pete bears the honored name of Pierre Samuel du Pont III. He is a bright lad, but Wilmington looks elsewhere for the next boss of Du Pont.

President Lammot is a wizard on cost reduction and economical management. Overhead and general managerial expenses melt before his close calculations like ice in an August sun. During the depression, he cut the payroll brutally, firing 7,000 enlisted men, a good many officers, and hundreds upon hundreds of chemists and engineers. Accordingly, even during, the low year of the economic drought, 1932, Du Pont showed a profit of $26,000,000, and dividends were paid as regularly as clockwork. The performance pleased Pierre immensely. Ever since, he has given Lammot a free rein.

Unlike Pierre and Irénée, Lammot never wanders from the Republican [fold, and is a stalwart member of the Union League Club of Philadelphia. Nor is he as lavish with his charity-checkbook as the others. Though his home, St. Amour, on the Kennett Pike, outside of Wilmington, has been remodeled into something of a show place by Alfred's young architect son, Alfred Victor, Lammot does not indulge in any of the ostentatious diversions of the very rich.

As fate would have it, this staid, sober-minded individual has had as many marital adventures as a giddy movie star. He has had four wives. His first wife, Natalie Driver Wilson, bore him three sons and five daughters and died in 1918. Two of the daughters, Natalie and Mary Belin, went in for banking and nursing, respectively, but soon graduated into marriage. Lammot has no son-in-law working for the du Pont Company. His second wife, Bertha Taylor, died in 1928. In the fall of 1930, he married Mrs. Caroline Hynson Stollenwerck, a young widow and niece of his first wife. Lammot, Jr. was his dad's best man. The marriage was a failure. In March, 1933, Mrs. du Pont got a Reno divorce and, according to report, a financial settlement that ran nicely into seven figures. The following November

Lammot married Margaret A. Flett, sister-in-law of a Du Pont vice president, William F. Harrington. They have one child, David Flett du Pont, born in August, 1934.

In considering Du Pont with all its far-flung interests, one invariably returns to Pierre.

At sixty-six, Pierre is still the Godhead of the family. He controls both company and clan. His hobby is Longwood, now a veritable principality, with several hundred employes. His horticultural experiments have grown into a mammoth winter garden, covering six acres under glass, housing orchids, azaleas, acacias, rare plants from all quarters of the globe. Great rooms are filled with tropical fruits. Melons, grapes and peaches are enjoyed by Pierre's friends when January blizzards sweep the nearby hills. The winter garden's crowning feature is a huge organ with 3,650 stops, built for Pierre's wife who, though grown almost totally deaf, is still able to hear this type of percussive music with the aid of an Acousticon. Nearby are acres of fabulous outdoor gardens and a theater, seating twelve hundred, set in a natural amphitheater, its curtain a sheet of water. There are lakes and forests. At night, lights, controlled by a keyboard similar to an organ, play upon the flowers and trees and water, producing indescribably beautiful color harmonies. The public is admitted to the gardens daily and to the greenhouses on stated days. Pierre still lives in the original brick mansion, which is scarcely more pretentious than a dozen houses he has built for his engineers and superintendents. Each Tuesday, he and his wife slip over to New York City for an evening of theater or opera. They have an apartment in New York.

Pierre has enriched all Du Ponts close to him, and all his in-laws. In 1916, he began to distribute some of his wealth, without the embarrassment of the inheritance tax, through a personal holding company, Delaware Realty & Investment. Of its 10,000 shares, he is said to have given 1,000 shares each to his two brothers and four sisters and to two nephews of brothers long since dead—Henry Belin du Pont, son of Henry Belin du Pont Sr., who died in 1902; and Samuel Hallock du Pont, son of William Kemble du Pont, who died in 1907. Young Hallock raises dogs at his place, Henry Clay, near Wilmington. He used to take pot shots at cats and practice knife-throwing at another place, appropriately called Squirrel Run. After a first marriage that misfired and a period of wildness, Hallock has recently married again and apparently settled down. He does not work for the company.

Young Henry Belin du Pont, on the other hand, has for some years been active with Du Pont businesses and is a favorite with Pierre. His record at Yale, however, was not remarkable. Upon graduation in 1920, young Belin first went into General Motors, then to the head offices in Wilmington. Later he did a good job managing General Motors aviation subsidiaries. He has yearly grown in greater favor with his uncles, and is often spoken of as a future du Pont Company president. He is thirty-seven.

Pierre's four sisters married, respectively, Charles Copeland, long secretary of the du Pont Company, Rodney Sharp, R. R. M. Carpenter, and the late William

Winter Laird. Only "Luly" Copeland (Louisa d'Andelot du Pont) is dead. Messrs. Copeland, Sharp and Carpenter are directors of Delaware Realty & Investment, as are brothers, Irénée and Lammot, and nephews, Belin and Hallock.

However, Delaware Investment holds only $16,000,000 in Du Pont stock.

Preëminent power over the whole works is vested in a super-holding company, the Christiana Securities Company, named for a tributary of the Delaware River. Christiana Securities holds 3,049,000 shares of Du Pont common stock, constituting 27.56 per cent of the 11,000,000 odd shares outstanding. On July 1, 1935, the Christiana holdings had a value on the New York Stock Exchange of $307,949,000. Individual holdings of the Du Ponts, relatives and close associates would, of course, at least double this total. It is certain that fewer than twenty individuals, most of them Du Ponts and in-laws, own today more Du Pont stock than do all the rest of the 51,865 stockholders.

Christiana is the Du Pont's private Big Eagle.

The three brothers, Pierre, Irénée and Lammot, own more than two-thirds of Christiana. Pierre is president, Irénée treasurer, Lammot vice president. Nephew Belin du Point is secretary and there are but three other directors: A. Felix du Pont, R. R. M. Carpenter and John J. Raskob.

Christiana grew out of the du Pont Securities Company, formed in 1915 by Pierre to take over Coleman's stock; and the percentage of control in Christiana is almost identical with what it was in du Pont Securities. The same close-knit group selected by Pierre as associates when he seized the company in 1915, have remained within his small Inner Circle.

Christiana's guiding genius, however, does not appear on the list of officers and directors. He is Robert H. Richards, a lawyer, who has been called, with little exaggeration, "the most powerful man in Delaware." Tall, redheaded, thin to the point of emaciation, he was once dubbed by a newspaper wit "the spider man of Delaware." Richards graduated from Dickinson College in Pennsylvania forty years ago. He made a name as Deputy Attorney General of Delaware and then went into the practice of corporation law. A good corporation lawyer in Delaware naturally attracts wide attention.

Coleman du Pont's talent-seeking eyes lighted on Richards twenty-five years ago. Whereupon he became Coleman's closest legal adviser, always keeping that bold individual on the right side of the law. Then he was drafted into the service of Pierre. Subtle, brilliant, close-mouthed, he has never been defeated in a case of importance. New York and Philadelphia law firms have often tempted him with lucrative partnership offers. He prefers to remain the power behind Pierre's throne and to operate, like the Du Ponts, from his home base.

In Christiana, also, is vested control of the Du Pont bank, the Wilmington Trust, largest in the State, and the Wilmington newspapers.

The du Pont Company is a model, yet somewhat of a mystery to many observers of corporate management. The mystery is partially dispelled if one bears in mind that the shrewd, capable brothers Du Pont have never, for one moment, relaxed their grip on the helm. Pierre

[319]

is board chairman, Irénée vice chairman, Lammot president. They have rotated in similar capacities in General Motors.

The brothers run Du Pont through two all-powerful committees: the Finance Committee and the Executive Committee.

The Finance Committee has nine members. Four are Du Ponts: the three brothers and Colonel Henry du Pont's only son and heir, Henry Francis (Harry) du Pont. While no amateur as a financier, Harry's interest in business is chiefly academic. He collects antiques and rare manuscripts, cruises on his yachts, and entertains with austere formality in a new $2,000,000 mansion on his estate, Winterthur, and at homes in New York and Florida. However, his inherited stock interest in the company is too extensive to be ignored. Hence his place on the Finance Committee.

The chairman of the Finance Committee is Walter Samuel Carpenter, Jr., husband of Irénée's former governess, brother of Ruly Carpenter. Walter Carpenter succeeded Raskob as treasurer and was promoted to his present position in 1930 when Irénée found the job too burdensome. Walter has gone forward with sure, quiet, swift strides. Save for the misfortune of not having been born a Du Pont, he would perhaps be the unanimous choice for the future presidency. Raskob, though fatigued and now yearning, he says, only to become a Maryland farmer, is also a finance committeeman. Other committee members are Harry G. Haskell, a Du Pont veteran; Angus Blakey Echols, son of a University of Virginia mathematics professor, who shifted to finance from the Du Pont chemical department; and

Donaldson Brown, who married Greta du Pont Barksdale, daughter of the late Ethel du Pont Barksdale, of
the original Victor line. As chairman, also, of the
General Motors Finance Committee, Mr. Brown is a
sort of financial liaison man between General Motors
and Du Pont.

Du Pont's active, detailed, day-by-day management
is in the hands of eight men comprising the Executive
Committee.

Here, though Lammot du Pont is chairman, family
influence is not so apparent. Messrs. Carpenter (Walter)
and Echols, of the Finance Committee, are also members
of the Executive Committee. Its other members are
John Thompson Brown, J. E. Crane, W. F. Harrington,
F. W. Pickard, and C. M. A. Stine.

J. Thompson Brown is a brother of Finance Committeeman Donaldson Brown. He has been with Du Pont
since 1903, as draftsman, superintendent of various dynamite plants, and manager of the Explosives Department.

J. E. Crane was an executive of the Arlington Company when it was purchased by Du Pont in 1917. During
the war he was in charge of military-material researches.
Afterwards, from headquarters in London, he conducted
highly important European negotiations with Chemical
Industries Ltd., and other chemical combinations forming in Europe for manufacture of new post-war products.
Lammot du Pont has great respect for his judgment.

William F. (Buck) Harrington is a native of Wilmington, who graduated from Massachusetts Tech in 1905
and at once got a job with Du Pont. He is a sort of left-
handed Du Pont brother-in-law inasmuch as his wife is
a sister of Lammot's fourth (present) wife.

F. W. Pickard came to Du Pont in 1903 when Coleman snapped up the Oriental Powder Company of Cincinnati, with which he was connected. Before that he had been managing editor of the Portland, Maine, *Transcript*. He managed Du Pont's dye department for some time. Now, as head of the Foreign Relations Committee, he keeps in touch with the salesmen and agents maintained by Du Pont all over the world. Some of the missions he directs are exceedingly delicate, concerning as they do the intricacies of foreign politics and governments. Needless to remark, he is a very able and discreet individual.

Dr. Stine is the chemical contact man. He succeeded his preceptor, Dr. C. L. Reese, as chemical director. It is Dr. Stine's business to keep the Executive Committee informed of the work of the great research laboratories, to submit scientific reports, and to assign knotty problems, as they arise, to research men.

The Executive Committee is subject to call at a moment's notice. It keeps in daily touch with the operations of every department, of every important plant. It is run very much like G. H. Q. behind a line of battle. Each operating company is expected to equal or exceed a certain ratio of return upon the amount of capital invested. These ratios appear on "vital statistics" charts, worked out with the well known Du Pont devotion to percentages. When a department or an operating company falls below expectation, its executive head is brought up with a jerk. Operating men often complain that, in their worship of mathematics, the big boys in Wilmington make little allowance for fluctuating conditions on the firing line.

Below the top committees are the captains, lieutenants and privates of an army of some 40,000 salesmen, superintendents, chemists, foremen and laborers. A few of the operating heads are rough and ready, two-fisted survivors of the old dog-eat-dog days in the powder trade. Others are highly educated specialists in technical or other lines, who have gone into Du Pont's new and developing businesses to carve permanent careers.

Du Pont likes to enlist its men for life; likes, too, to impress upon them the institutional aura of family as well as company. Du Pont pays low salaries, which are augmented with bonuses based upon earnings, and awards for "special services." In 1934, fifty-one officers and employes received compensation totaling $2,236,850, or an average of about $43,860 each, including bonuses. In its registration statement to the Securities and Exchange Commission, Du Pont filed information on its bonuses confidentially, as well as the amounts paid to its three highest officers and to directors.

Du Pont has had remarkable success in attracting good management men. And it has learned the art of salesmanship and showmanship. It believes thoroughly in reciprocity. It is almost an axiom in commercial circles that "you can't sell anything to Du Pont unless you buy something from it." Since Du Pont has something to sell to everybody, this would not seem difficult. The company, also, encourages anonymity. The men who make its products and sell its goods are practically unknown save in their immediate fields.

Du Pont has the usual group insurance plans and provisions for attractive investment in its stock for certain classes of employes, through instalment payments. It pays about $60,000,000 a year in salaries and wages. Its labor policy differs little from the policy of most old-line corporations. It has a strong company union—the Works Councils—which dickers with the management on such matters as wages, working conditions, etc. Originally the Works Councils were composed of equal number of employe-selected and management-appointed representatives. In 1934 there was some restlessness over famed Section 7-A of the Industrial Recovery Act. At about two-thirds of the company's plants, the men voted to have the Works Councils composed exclusively of representatives elected by themselves. The company did not oppose this modification with any particular vigor.

In point of net income earnings, Du Pont ranks third among the leading American corporations. It is led only by American Telephone & Telegraph and by its own General Motors. It is a richer gold mine than Standard Oil of New Jersey, American Tobacco, Consolidated Gas, General Electric or the Pennsylvania Railroad. Combined with General Motors, it comfortably outranks the nation's leading money-maker, American Tel. & Tel. The net income figures reported by these companies for 1934 follow: American Telephone, $125,-351,786; General Motors, $94,769,131; Du Pont, $46,701,465.

"The Du Pont group," wrote John Jacob Raskob in March, 1934, "controls a larger share of industry, through common stock holdings, than any other group in the United States. There is no group, including the Rockefellers, the Morgans, the Mellons, or anyone else that begins to control and be responsible for as much industrially, as does the du Pont Company."

In 1932, Pierre and Irénée du Pont, in their interest in prohibition repeal, again went Democratic and voted for Franklin D. Roosevelt. This they consider their greatest mistake.

Raskob, though disappointed at the failure of his friend, Al Smith, to obtain the nomination, also voted Democratic. Raskob early sensed the pitfalls of a coming trend in the Roosevelt administration. By the spring of 1934, he became alarmed. He wrote Ruly Carpenter, the Du Pont political manager, urging the formation of an organization to combat the radical elements in the nation. People, he said, should be encouraged to work and get rich and communistic fallacies exposed.

Four months later, the American Liberty League was formed, with heavy Du Pont backing, to "uphold and defend" the Constitution of the United States, with particular emphasis upon property rights. Since, the League has rallied to the defense of liberties it considers endangered by the Roosevelt program. A dozen Du Ponts and Du Pont in-laws have contributed to it. So far as known at the present writing, Pierre has contributed only $500 through his wife. Irénée and Lammot, however, have made large donations and given expression to Old Guard sentiments that smack of the Penrose era. Irénée has taken to hobnobbing with W. R. Hearst in California and has enthusiastically joined Hearst's violent anti-Red crusade. In an interview for the Hearst papers, Irénée exhumed all the Coolidge-Hoover maxims except the ones about the chicken in every pot and the two cars in every garage, adding that even Americans on the dole were living better than skilled and employed European mechanics.

Lammot du Pont attacked President Roosevelt's assertion that withdrawal of governmental supervision over business would mean that the "old law of tooth and claw would reign once more." In a letter to one of the Du Pont newspapers, Lammot advocated that all supervision of business by government should be abolished, explaining:

I mean that all government regulation of business, as such, and as distinguished from any other forms of activity, should be abolished. I mean that business should not be prohibited by government, or compelled by government, to do things which private individuals are not prohibited or compelled to do.

If I have a hole in my back yard, as some residents of Western Pennsylvania do, and employed a man to dig coal out of it for my own use, I see no reason why I should be allowed to treat him any better or any worse, or pay him any better or any less, than a coal company employing 10,000 men to do the same thing.

Business is merely an aggregation of individuals to do something which a single individual can do, but far less efficiently and successfully. Business should be treated as an individual is treated—no better, no worse.

Here in a nutshell, is the business philosophy of the Du Ponts.

Under the law of "tooth and claw," the Du Ponts are confident they can take care of themselves. They are not so certain of the future under the New Deal, or under a newer deal more radical perhaps than the present experiments of Franklin Roosevelt. Hence, as acknowledged leaders of the nation's industrialists, they are girding, with their Liberty League, for America's political battle of the century in 1936. There is little doubt that the

PIERRE SAMUEL DU PONT DE NEMOURS

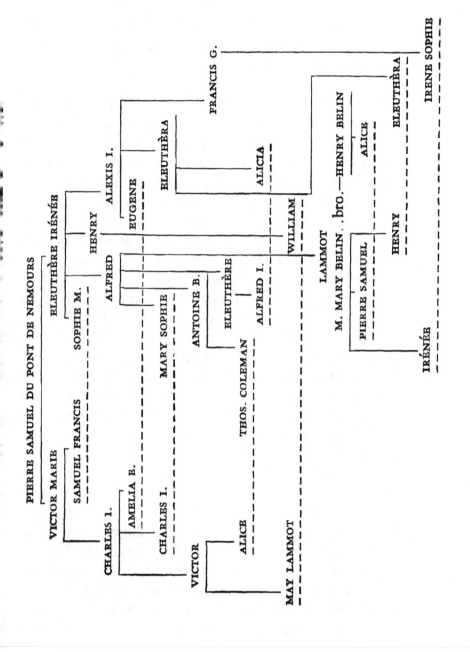

Du Ponts, aided perhaps by Mr. Hearst, certainly by other powerful allies, will vigorously oppose President Roosevelt for re-election.

The Du Ponts are a great, sprawling family. Yet the several hundred individuals making up the clan have held surprisingly close to the manners, customs and traditions of their French bourgeois origin. They have sunk their transplanted roots in one section and one soil, cultivating the same acres and inhabiting the same houses generation after generation. There are twenty or more Du Pont estates within an hour's ride of Wilmington. Four of them are vast. For a century, these people lived so much within themselves that, considering the largeness of their family, consanguine marriages were the natural result. Professor Crew, of Edinburgh, the eminent biologist, wrote in 1927: "Inbreeding is only disastrous if the ingredients of disaster are in the stock. Inbreeding will purify a stock, but the process may be most expensive." Inbreeding among the Du Ponts has brought out both recessive and dominant traits, as the biologists term them. There have been erratic, abnormal, insane individuals among the Du Ponts, though the percentage has not been higher, perhaps, than the statistical average. Colonel Henry du Pont, as *pater familias*, years ago forbade further cousin marriages. Pierre in turn has tried to enforce the dictum, though he himself married a first cousin. The younger Du Ponts of today have shown no tendency in this direction. Divorces and scandals have been, of course, numerous, often attracting attention because of the family's prominence. No doubt they too jibe with the statistical average.

The family elders are chiefly concerned with the demoralizing effects of great wealth upon the younger Du Ponts. They feel that their youth of today does not take the same interest or apply themselves in company matters as the generation that made this wealth possible. There is no doubt but that these boys and girls have become accustomed to extreme luxuries. On many Du Pont estates, airplanes are "stabled" as so many horses or automobiles might be, and used with the same casual indifference. Du Ponts yacht, sail, motor, shoot, ride to hounds, most of them being outdoor enthusiasts.

The du Pont Airport is on Henry Belin du Pont's land. Belin detests social activities, so when the family decided a clubhouse should be built at the airport, A. Felix du Pont put up the money. Felix has more millions than he knows what to do with anyway. He stuck with Pierre during the feud with Alfred when he and his sister, Irénée's wife, were the only members of his large family to do so, and in consequence has been rewarded handsomely. Felix runs the Smokeless Powder Department. He is very religious, and shy. He deals with U. S. Army and Navy customers through a maternal cousin, Colonel Aiken Simons, of South Carolina. Felix is also an honorary member of the Wilmington Police Band, plays the baritone horn, and often dons a uniform and marches, "incognito," in parades. His children, Felix, Jr., Richard and Alice, are all licensed pilots. Richard, who is always getting lost (and found) in some remote spot, is a champion glider, as is his young wife, the former Helena Allaire Crozier, of Philadelphia. Felix, Jr. married Eleanor Hoyt, also a licensed pilot, whose vivid little scarlet monoplane used to be a familiar sight over Long Island. The Felix Seniors have a pretentious summer seat on Cape Cod, which they reach by air or in the family's big, sea-going steam yacht.

The tall, ruddy, youthful-looking Felix takes life very seriously. Once his superiors thought little of him. Alfred I. used to tell this story: "Coleman du Pont said to me one day: 'Alfred, I think we will have to raise Felix's salary.' I naturally inquired: 'Why?' 'Well,' Coleman answered, 'this morning he made a bright remark.' It afterward turned out that the remark was not original, so his salary was not raised." A year ago, this anecdote was published by the magazine *Fortune*. Felix went around for days with a stricken look, which we hope will not revive with this repetition.

The oldest living Du Pont is Miss Evelina, Colonel Henry's surviving sister, who lives in a rambling old mansion called Lyndham, a few miles from Wilmington. She is ninety-six. Miss Evelina runs her own household, entertains old friends and describes fascinatingly and without sadness the days that are past.

And what of Alfred I.?

In 1926, when Pierre, as commissioner, began to tighten the tax regulations, Alfred transferred his citizenship from Delaware to Florida. He established a vast, semi-tropical winter estate, Epping Forest, on the St. John's River, near Jacksonville. He cruised much on his Diesel yacht, *Nenemoosha*, successor to the *Alicia*, and helped to rehabilitate the Florida banking system, which had collapsed with the real estate boom. He also invested in Colorado radium mines and spent large sums producing and testing radium for use in the treatment of cancer. But he hung on to every share of his stock in the du Pont Company, some five per cent of the whole.

Alfred's third wife (Jessie Ball) brought about a reconciliation with his children and gradually got Alfred on speaking terms with most of his relatives, with the exception of Pierre. His son, Alfred Victor, after breaking away from the du Pont Company, had become a successful architect and gone into partnership in Wilmington with young Gabriel Massena, who had designed the staircases of Frank Gould's Palais de la Méditerranée at Nice. Massena & Du Pont had as their first commission the designing of elaborate sunken gardens, fashioned after those at Versailles, at Alfred I.'s *Nemours*, near Wilmington. In 1933 they also designed the comfortable State Welfare Home for the aged and indigent at Smyrna, north of Dover, Delaware—Alfred I.'s pet project. Here, largely through Alfred's efforts, old people are provided not only with beds but with apartments and gardens, recreation facilities, medical care and amusement. The Welfare Home is one of the most delightful places in Delaware.

Alfred and his third wife adopted a lovely little girl, Denise. The daughter of Alfred's second wife, little Alicia of the playhouse "Wren's Nest," was now grown. In June, 1922, she married Harold Glendenning, whose father was a Norwalk, Connecticut, rural letter carrier. Glendenning had worked his way through Dartmouth College and won a Rhodes scholarship. The marriage ended in divorce and Alicia 2nd took as her second (and present) husband Victor Llewellyn, an Englishman.

Alfred I.'s hectic career ended with a heart attack at his Florida estate on April 29, 1935, as he was preparing for his usual spring migration to Delaware. Three days later, his children, distinguished national leaders, friends and many Du Ponts (but not Pierre or Alfred's first wife,

[331]

Bessie Gardner), gathered in the great hall of *Nemours* while the Bishop of the Episcopal Diocese of Delaware read the burial service, and the famous choir from the Cathedral of St. John the Divine, in New York, sang.

The will, drawn the day before the bank holiday of 1933, disposed of an estate valued in Florida probate proceedings at $32,736,000. Alfred's wealth had once been estimated as high as $200,000,000. Vast amounts had been distributed, and lost. After providing liberally for his widow, children and other members of his family, the bulk of the fortune, together with the *Nemours* estate, went to establish "Nemours Foundation" for the "care and treatment of crippled children, or old men and women, particularly old couples, first consideration being given to the residents of Delaware."

Alfred's final resting place is a crypt at the base of a thirty-one-bell carillon erected at *Nemours* in memory of his parents. Nearby is buried a one-eyed Airedale mongrel, named Yip, who survived his master only a few days. Yip, picked up on a golf course, was Alfred's constant companion in the last years of his life.

There is a legend in Queenstown, Ireland, of how a tall handsome American millionaire set out to see the town, while the large liner on which he was traveling docked there for a few hours. He hadn't gotten very far when he stopped to refresh himself at a pub. Then he got no further, for behind the bar was a comely, rosy-cheeked young Irish lass, with whom the millionaire at once became enrapt. So entranced, in fact, that he forgot all about his boat and refused to leave Queenstown until the fair maiden had promised to become his wife and live happily ever after with him in Paris.

THREE BROTHERS

This was Maurice du Pont, Alfred I.'s younger brother, who, forty-odd years ago, married a bar maid and has lived like a gentleman ever since, far away from Wilmington.

Index

INDEX

[335]

INDEX

INDEX

228; business expansion during World War, 231; dividends, 232; employes, 232, 236, 315, 323; Executive Comm., 235, accidents, 236; products, 236, 264; sabotage, 237; foreign patent alliances, 240; secret processes withheld from U. S. Government, 240; assists building of Old Hickory, 243; Wilmington Trust Co., 247, 319; invests in General Motors, 254, 256; control of General Motors, 260; chemical products, 264–282; buys Arlington Co., 266; Viscoloid Co., 266; Duplate Corp., 266; Film Manufacturing Co., 267; Rayon (Fibersilk Co.), 267; Cellophane, 268; Duco, 273; Fabrikoid, 273; Pontop, 273; Ethyl Gasoline Corp., 275; Experimental Station, 277; buys Grasselli Chemical Co., 278; Roessler & Hasslacher Co., 279; fixed nitrogen plant, 279; refrigerants, 280; Kinetic Chemicals, Inc., 280; Du Prene, 280, 281; buys Remington Arms Co., 281; Smokeless Powder Division, 281; Explosives Division, 281; profits since 1918, 282; in Del. politics, 285; control of Del. newspapers, 300, 319; Raskob leaves Co. for General Motors, 305; Irénée made president in 1919, 308; Nye Comm. investigation, 244, 309; invests in U. S. Steel Corp., 310; in U. S. Rubber Co., 311; financial difficulties in 1921, 313; Lammot made president in 1926, 313; during depression, 315; payroll and employes cut, 315; profits in 1932, 315; Delaware Realty Co. formed, 318; Christiana Securities (holding Co.), 318; Wilmington newspapers, 319; Finance Comm., 320; Executive Comm., 320; management, 322; salaries, 323; labor policy, 324; Works Councils, 324; earnings in 1934, 324; holdings, 324; business policy, 326

Du Pont de Nemours Père, Fils & Cie, 42, 47, 58, 71

Du Pont de Nemours, Pierre Samuel, 8, 46, 327; education, 9; becomes watchmaker, 12; studies medicine, 13; secretary to Quesnay, 19; employed by government, 20; marriage to Marie Le Dée, 20; edits *Ephemerides*, 21; in Poland, 22; Turgot's assistant, 22; made Inspector General of Commerce, 24; raised to nobility, 25; wife's death, 26; member of States-General, 32; changes name to Dupont de Nemours, 34; establishes printing business, 35; hides from Revolutionists, 36; arrest, 38; release, 37; marriage to Madame Poivre, 39; publishes *L'Historien*, 40, changes name to Du Pont de Nemours, 42; sons adopt du Pont for name, 42, organizes *Du Pont de Nemours Père, Fils & Cie*, 42; sails for America, 44; home in Bergen Point, N. J., 47; writes treatise on education, 50; returns to France, 58; seeks aid for Victor's company, 64; liquidates company, 71; returns to America, 82; death, 86

du Pont de Nemours, V. & Co., 56, 58, 64

du Pont, Denise, 331

du Pont, Dorcas Van Dyke (Mrs. Charles I.), 93

du Pont, Eleanor Hoyt (Mrs. A. Felix, Jr.), 329

du Pont, Eleuthéra, 83

du Pont, Eleuthéra, 327

du Pont, Eleuthéra Paulina, 178

du Pont, Eleuthère Irénée, 21, 26; studies with Lavoisier, 30; enters printing business, 36; marriage to Sophie Dalmas, 36; sails for America, 44; genealogy, 46, 138, 154, 327; visits France to finance powder plant, 51; establishes Eleutherian Mills, 56; building of plant, 60; dissension with Bauduy, 61, E. I. du Pont de Nemours & Co., 62; woolen mills, 60; sued by Bauduy, 83; wife's death, 94; death, 98

du Pont, Eleuthère Irénée, 2nd, 106; invents metallic keg, 107; junior partner, 117; wife's death, 124; death, 124; genealogy, 138, 154

du Pont, Elizabeth, *see* Bayard, Elizabeth du Pont (Mrs. Thomas Francis, Jr.)

du Pont Engineering Corp., 244

du Pont, Ernest Archibald, 221

du Pont, Ethel, *see* Barksdale, Ethel du Pont (Mrs. Hamilton)

du Pont, Eugene, 113; junior partner, 117; genealogy, 118, 138, 154, 327; manager of Co., 137; marriage to Amelie du Pont, 137; president of Corp., 148; death, 148

du Pont, Eugene E., 213, 220

du Pont, Evelina, *see* Bidermann, Evelina du Pont (Mrs. Antoine)

du Pont, Evelina, 330

du Pont, Felix, *see* du Pont, A. Felix

du Pont Film Manufacturing Corp., 267

du Pont, Francis G., 118, 125, 133, 137; genealogy, 138, 327; experiments on

[337]

INDEX

smokeless powder, 140, 141; vice president of Corp., 148
du Pont, Francis I., 141, 182, 213, 221, 222
du Pont, Francis V., 302
Du Pont, Francois Poivre (Mrs. Pierre Samuel de Nemours), 40, 43, 46
du Pont, Gabrielle, 74, 83
du Pont, Helena A. Crozier (Mrs. Richard), 329
du Pont, Henry, 83; partner of Co., 102; manager from 1850 to 1889, 106, 117; genealogy, 118, 327; death, 136
du Pont, Col. Henry Algernon, 179, 213, 222; Civil War service, 115, genealogy, 118, 138, 154; enters Co., 125; president of Wilmington and Northern R. R., 126, 290; vice president of Corp., 148; enters Republican politics in Del., 165, 290; defeated for Senate, 291; elected, 293; Winterthur, 297; death, 298; estate sued, 298
du Pont, Henry Belin, 263, 317; secretary of Christiana Securities Co., 318
du Pont, Henry Francis (Harry), 213, 220, 320
du Pont International Powder Co., 164
du Pont, Irene Sophie, 327
du Pont, Irénée, see du Pont, Eleuthère Irénée
du Pont, Irénée, 2nd, see du Pont, Eleuthère Irénée, 2nd
du Pont, Irénée. 210, 214; on Executive Comm., 235; made president of Co., 308; Granogue, 308; testifies at Nye Comm., 309; expands business, 310; interest in cancer research, 311; director of Equitable Life Assurance Co., 311; life insurance policy, 311; interest in politics, 312; U. S. Gov't opposes trust funds, 313; resigns presidency in 1926, 313; treasurer of Christiana Securities Co., 318, vice chairman of Du Pont, 320; votes for Roosevelt, 325; supports American Liberty League, 325; joins Hearst's anti-Red crusade, 325; genealogy, 327
du Pont, Irénée, Jr., 308
du Pont, Jessie Ball (Mrs. Alfred I.), 300, 331
du Pont, Josephine de Pelleport (Mrs. Victor Marie), 46
du Pont, Julia, see Shubrick, Julia du Pont (Mrs. Irvine)
du Pont, Lammot, 108; makes soda powder, 109; Mammoth powder, 110; goes

to London for Civil War supplies, 112; ill with typhoid, 113; junior partner, 117; genealogy, 118, 138, 154; marriage to Mary Belin, 120; president of Repauno Chemical Co., 130; killed in explosion, 132
du Pont, Lammot, 210, 235, 327; president of Co. in 1926, 313; management during depression, 315; St. Amour, 315; marriage to Natalie Wilson, 315, to Bertha Taylor, 315; to Mrs. Caroline Stollenwerck, 315; to Margaret A. Flett, 316; vice president of Christiana Securities Co., 318; supports American Liberty League, 325
du Pont, Lammot, Jr., 314
du Pont, Louis, 125, 134
du Pont, Louisa, see Copeland, Louisa du Pont (Mrs. Charles)
du Pont, Madeline, 181
Dupont, Marie Le Dée (Mrs. Du Pont de Nemours, Pierre Samuel), 14, 20, 26
du Pont, Mary Belin (Mrs. Lammot), 120, 239, 315, 327
du Pont, Mary Foster (Mrs. Henry Algernon), 126
du Pont, Mary Sophie, 327
du Pont, Maurice, 125, 333
du Pont, May Lammot (Mrs. William), 139; divorced, 139; marriage to Willard Saulsbury, 139; genealogy, 327
du Pont, Natalie. 315
du Pont, Paul, 221
du Pont, Philip Francis, 213, 221
Dupont, Pierre Samuel (1st), see Du Pont de Nemours, Pierre Samuel
du Pont, Pierre Samuel, 155; experiments on smokeless powder, 133; works for Johnson Co., 138, 158; treasurer of du Pont Co., 150, 159; genealogy, 154, 327; executive vice president, 175; quarrel with Alfred I., 183; shares of Co. stock, 184; letters to Coleman, 187-209; buys Coleman's stock, 209; opposed by Alfred, 210; offers stock to Co., 215; sued by Alfred, 221; buys *Wilmington Journal*, 227; gets control of Co., 228; 234; Longwood estate, 238, 316; Pierre's Park, 238; horticulture hobby, 238, 316, adopts Lewes Mason, 239; marriage to Alice Belin, 239; director of General Motors, 261; gets Alfred's newspapers, 300; interest in Delaware schools, 302; endows Service Citizens of Del., 302; made tax commissioner, 303, 330; philanthropies, 304; works

INDEX

INDEX

INDEX

CPSIA information can be obtained
at www.ICGtesting.com
Printed in the USA
LVHW060732290419
615902LV00030BA/453/P